MARK CRILLEY

VOLUME SIX

Issues 32 ~ 34
"Stranded in Komura"

Issues 35 ~ 38
"Moonshopping"

SIRIUS ENTERTAINMENT   UNADILLA, N. Y.

This book is dedicated to my "Roomie"
Ian Jackson
and his wife, Francesca, and sons,
Thomas and George

SIRIUS

AKIKO TRADE PAPERBACK VOL. 6. JUNE, 2003.
FIRST PRINTING. PUBLISHED BY SIRIUS ENTERTAINMENT, INC.
LAWRENCE SALAMONE, PRESIDENT. ROBB HORAN, PUBLISHER.
KEITH DAVIDSEN, EDITOR. CORRESPONDENCE: P.O. BOX X, UNADILLA, NY 13849.

Introduction

The Akiko comic book series has always been characterized by a very restless approach to style. My methods of illustration and storytelling are constantly shifting as I charge first down one path, then another. It all stems from a need to keep the work as fresh as possible: to avoid at all costs the trap of being so familiar with my own creative processes that I already know exactly what I'm going to do even before I've done it.

The two story arcs contained in this volume represent two very different experiments. **Stranded in Komura** was my first earthbound tale. True to form, I chose a somewhat exotic place-- rural Japan--for the location. It is the only Akiko story ever narrated by a character other than Akiko, Spuckler, Gax, or Mr. Beeba. The extensive use of subtitled word balloons and the attempt to imitate certain manga illustration techniques also represented unfamiliar territory for me. The story was a great pleasure to work on, not least because I was able to involve my wife, Miki, in the storytelling: Her translations are what made it possible for me to include Japanese language in the story.

Moonshopping was, for me, a way of doing something new and old at the same time. It started as an effort to revisit the dream-like, whimsical storytelling style I'd used at the very beginning of the series, where one event rolled on to the next in a spontaneous, playful way, with little regard for logic. The artistic technique was the result of removing one of my most cherished tools--the gray tones--as a challenge to myself. The story moves through three different 'Farflux' environments: The first is a sort of generalized homage to classic children's book illustrations, the second and third are tributes to two comic book writer/illustrators whose work I greatly admire: Linda Medley and Jeff Smith. (My clumsy attempts to emulate their styles only deepened my respect for what they do!)

I sincerely hope you enjoy these two stories. As always I welcome your questions and comments. Just go on over to **www.markcrilley.com,** where you'll find--among many other things--a link from which to send me e-mail.

Stranded in Komura

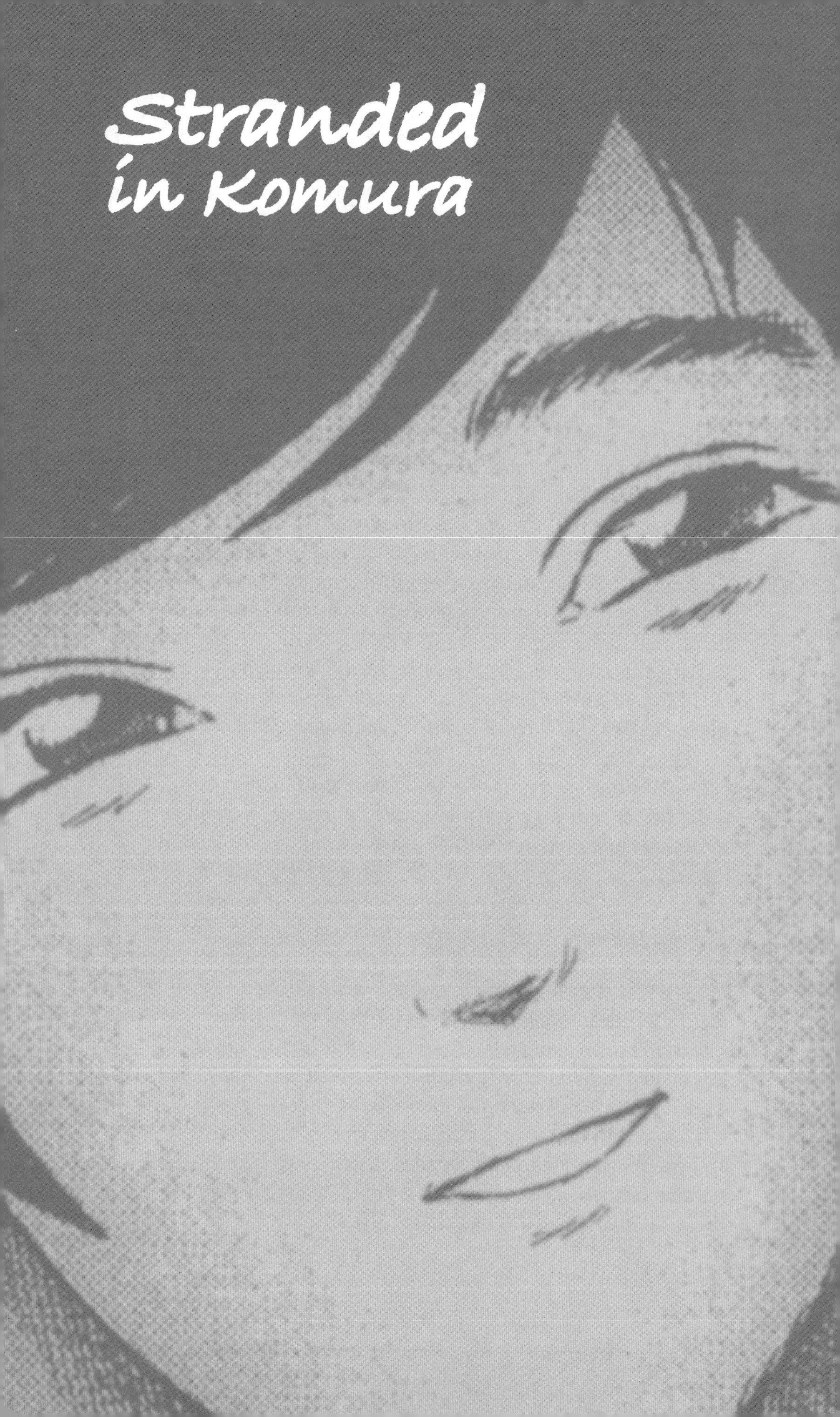

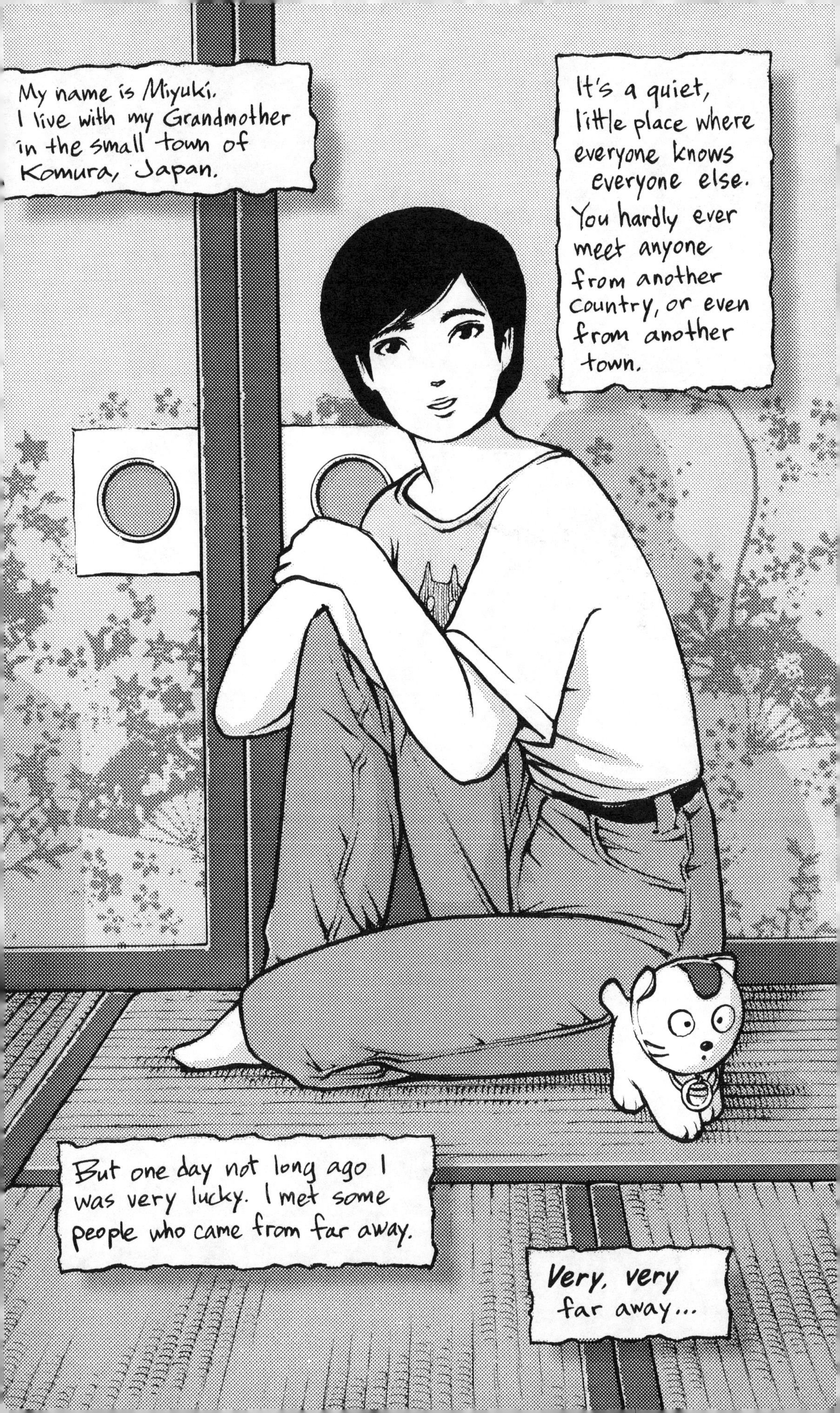
My name is Miyuki. I live with my Grandmother in the small town of Komura, Japan.
It's a quiet, little place where everyone knows everyone else. You hardly ever meet anyone from another country, or even from another town.
But one day not long ago I was very lucky. I met some people who came from far away.
Very, very far away...

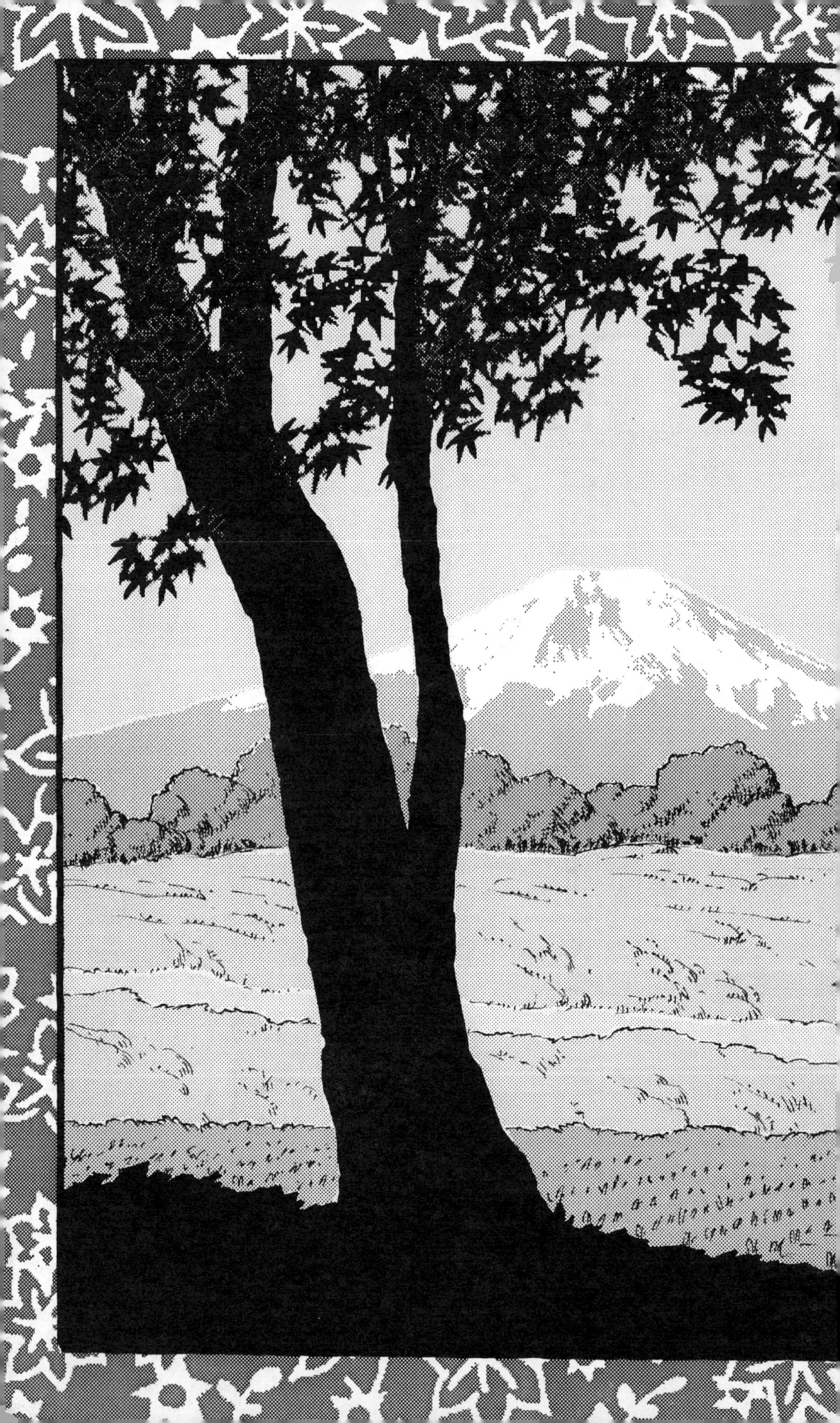

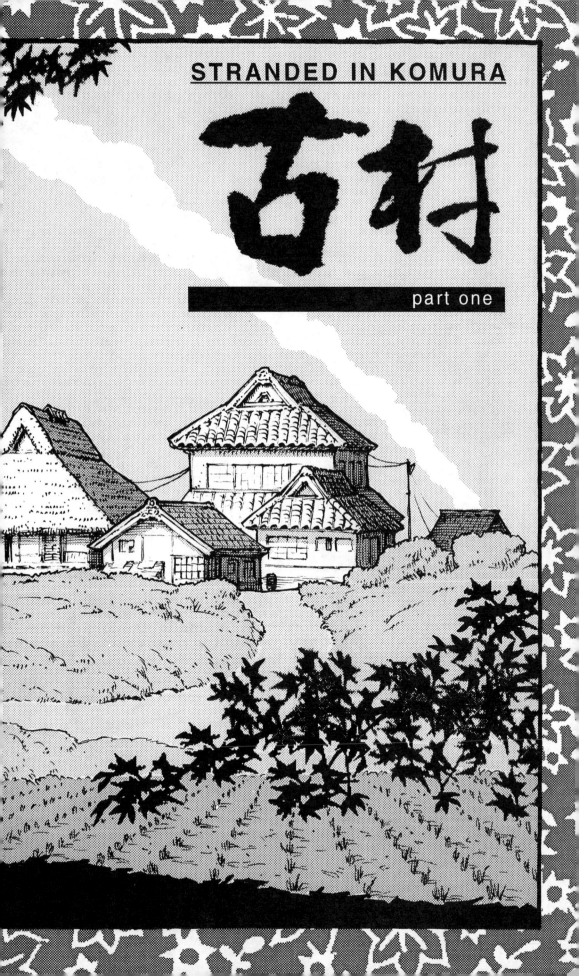

STRANDED IN KOMURA

古村

part one

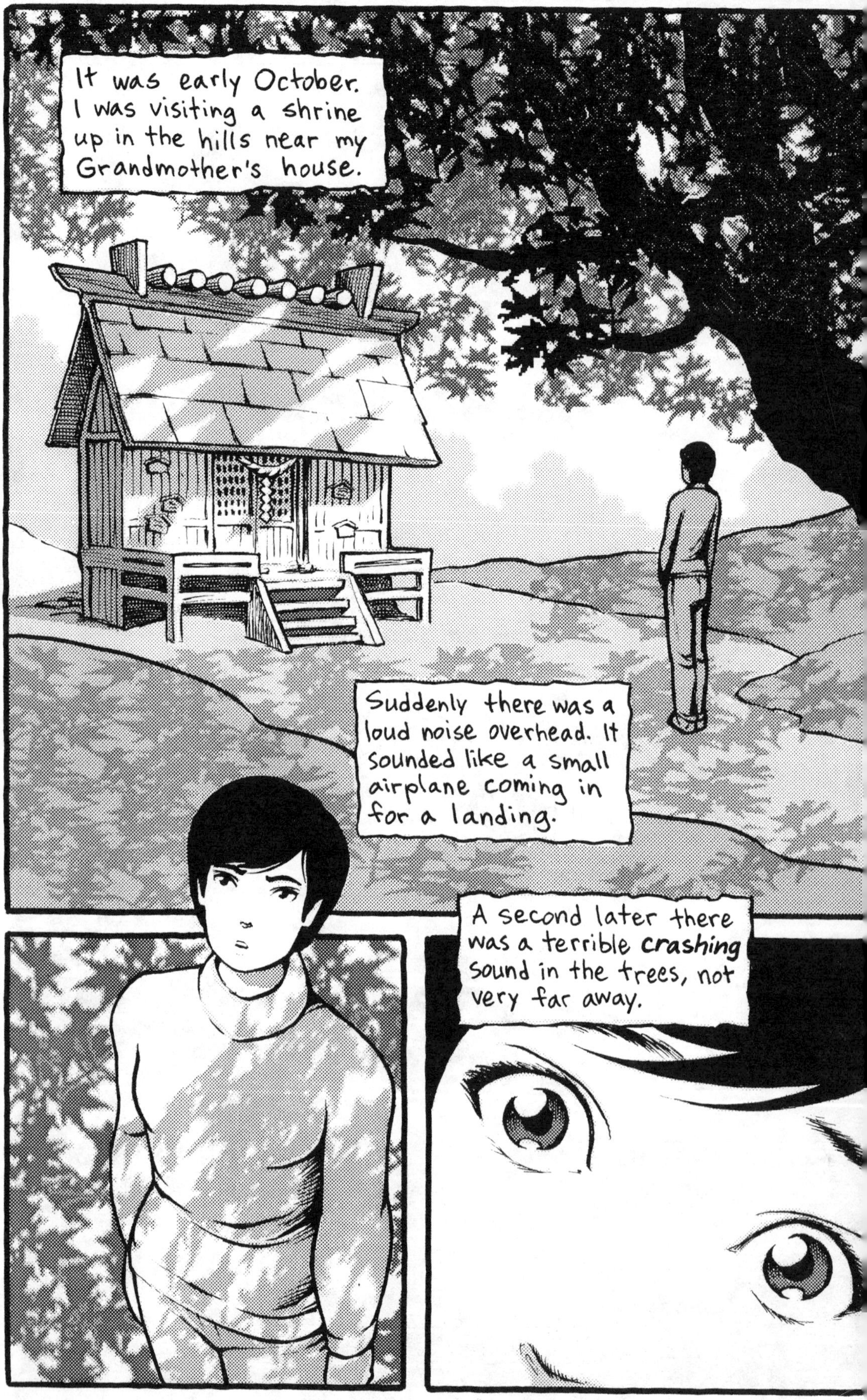
It was early October. I was visiting a shrine up in the hills near my Grandmother's house.
Suddenly there was a loud noise overhead. It sounded like a small airplane coming in for a landing.
A second later there was a terrible **crashing** sound in the trees, not very far away.

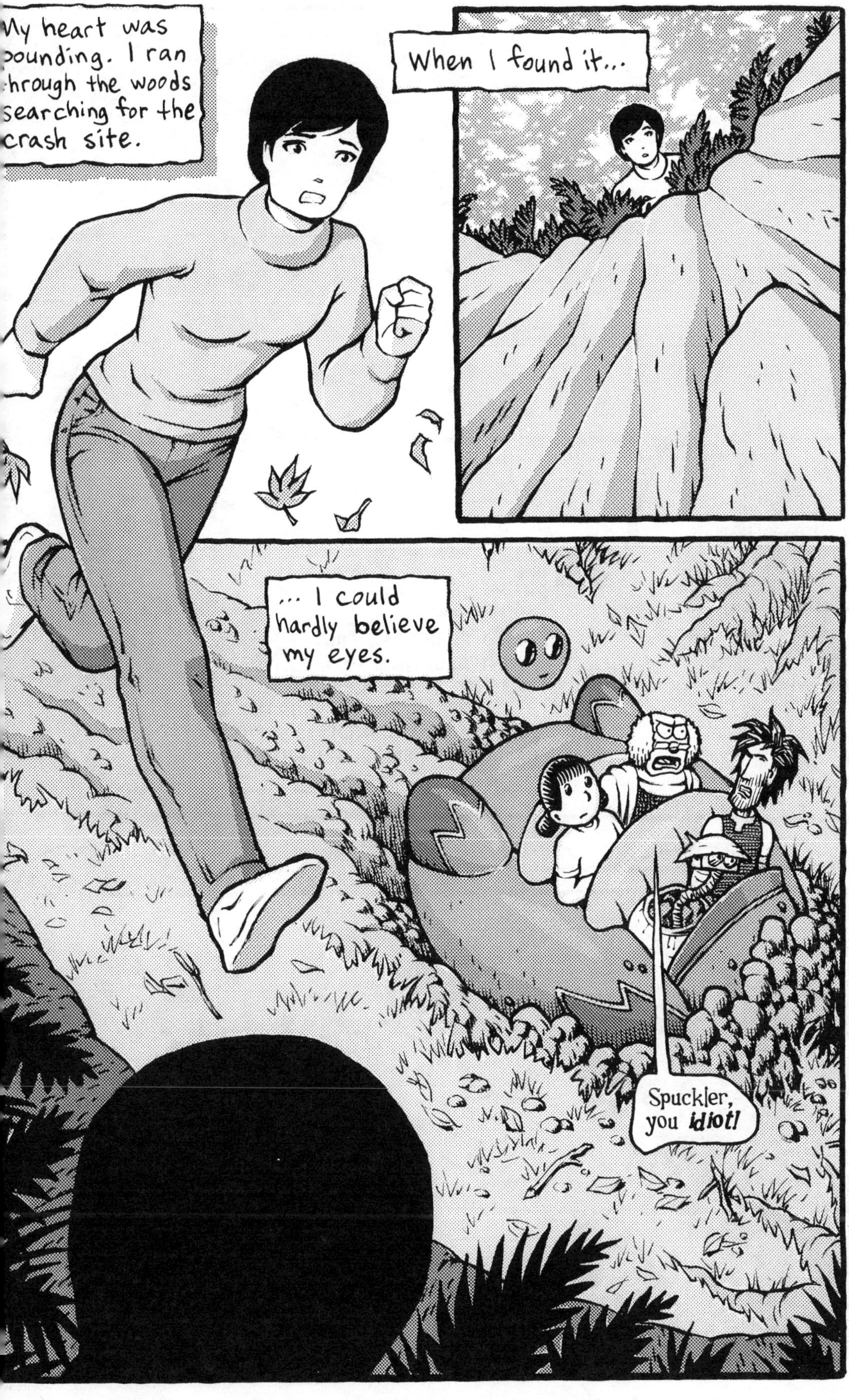
My heart was pounding. I ran through the woods searching for the crash site.
When I found it...
... I could hardly believe my eyes.
Spuckler, you idiot!

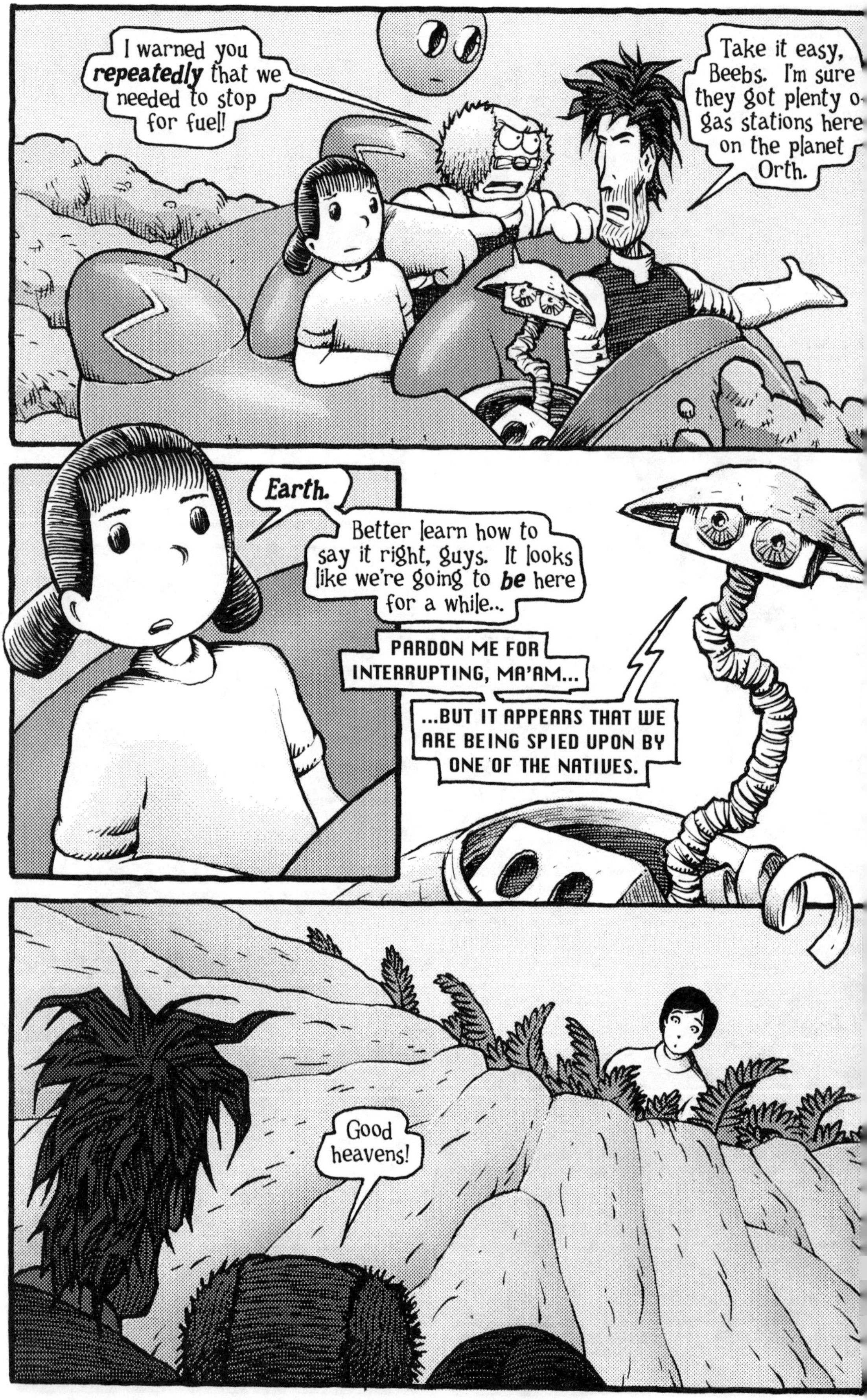
I warned you *repeatedly* that we needed to stop for fuel!
Take it easy, Beebs. I'm sure they got plenty o- gas stations here on the planet Orth.
Earth.
Better learn how to say it right, guys. It looks like we're going to *be* here for a while...
PARDON ME FOR INTERRUPTING, MA'AM...
...BUT IT APPEARS THAT WE ARE BEING SPIED UPON BY ONE OF THE NATIVES.
Good heavens!

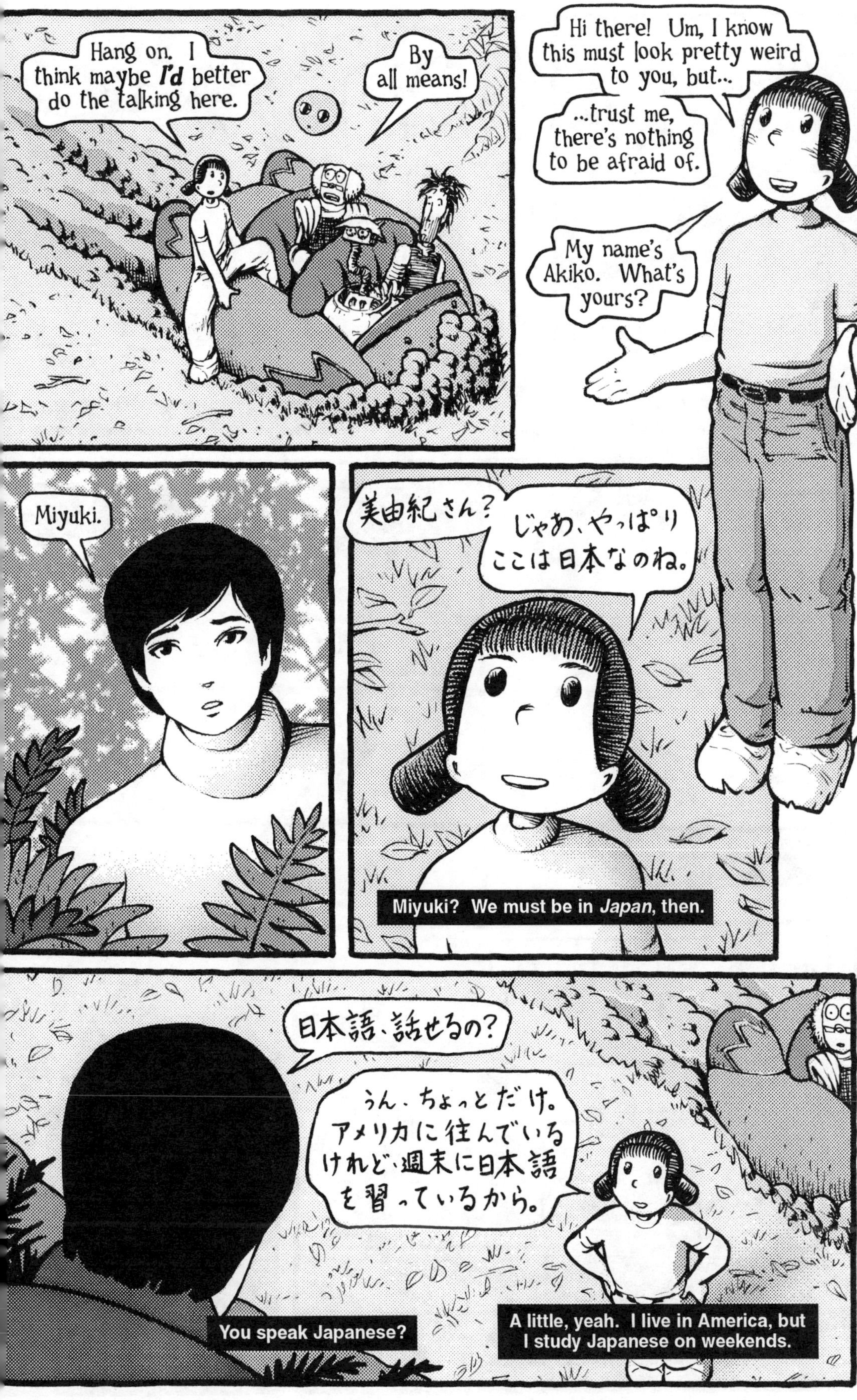
Hang on. I think maybe ***I'd*** better do the talking here.
By all means!
Hi there! Um, I know this must look pretty weird to you, but...
...trust me, there's nothing to be afraid of.
My name's Akiko. What's yours?
Miyuki.
美由紀さん？
じゃあ、やっぱりここは日本なのね。
Miyuki? We must be in *Japan*, then.
日本語、話せるの？
You speak Japanese?
うん、ちょっとだけ。アメリカに住んでいるけれど、週末に日本語を習っているから。
A little, yeah. I live in America, but I study Japanese on weekends.

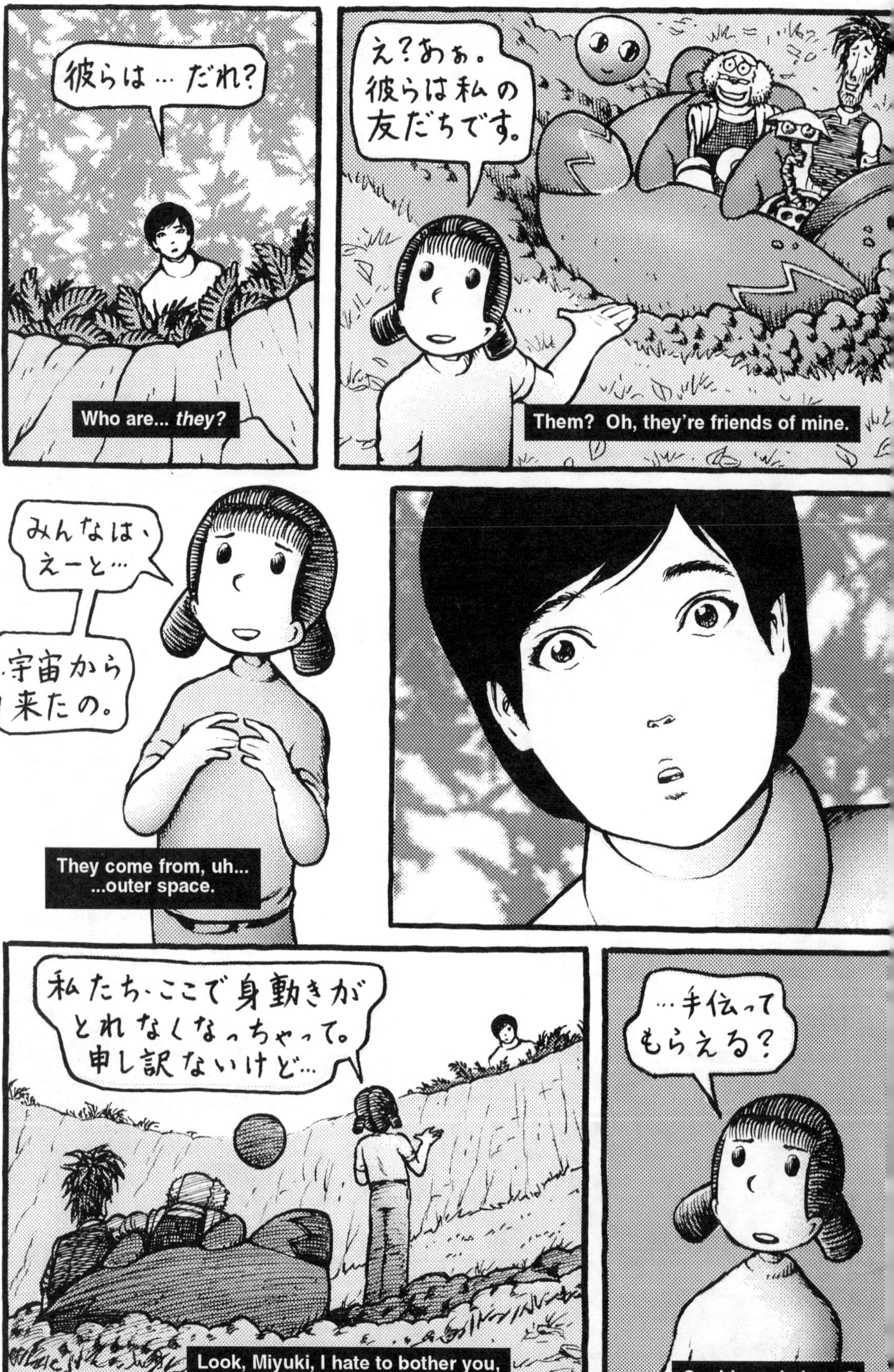
彼らは… だれ?
Who are... *they*?
え?あぁ。彼らは私の友だちです。
Them? Oh, they're friends of mine.
みんなは、えーと…
…宇宙から来たの。
They come from, uh... ...outer space.
私たち、ここで身動きがとれなくなっちゃって。申し訳ないけど…
Look, Miyuki, I hate to bother you, but we're kind of *stuck* here.
…手伝ってもらえる?
Could you help us?

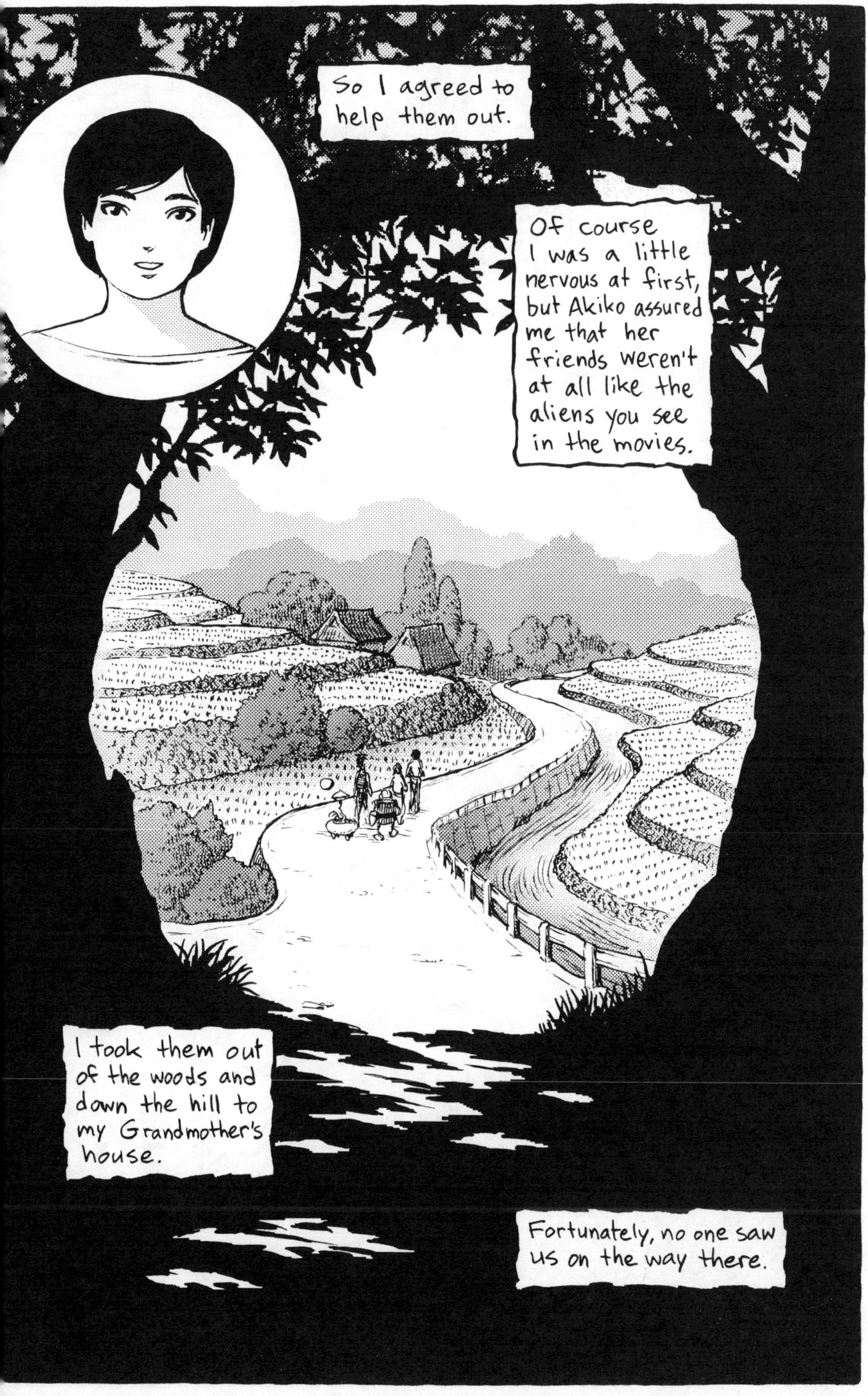
So I agreed to help them out.
Of course I was a little nervous at first, but Akiko assured me that her friends weren't at all like the aliens you see in the movies.
I took them out of the woods and down the hill to my Grandmother's house.
Fortunately, no one saw us on the way there.

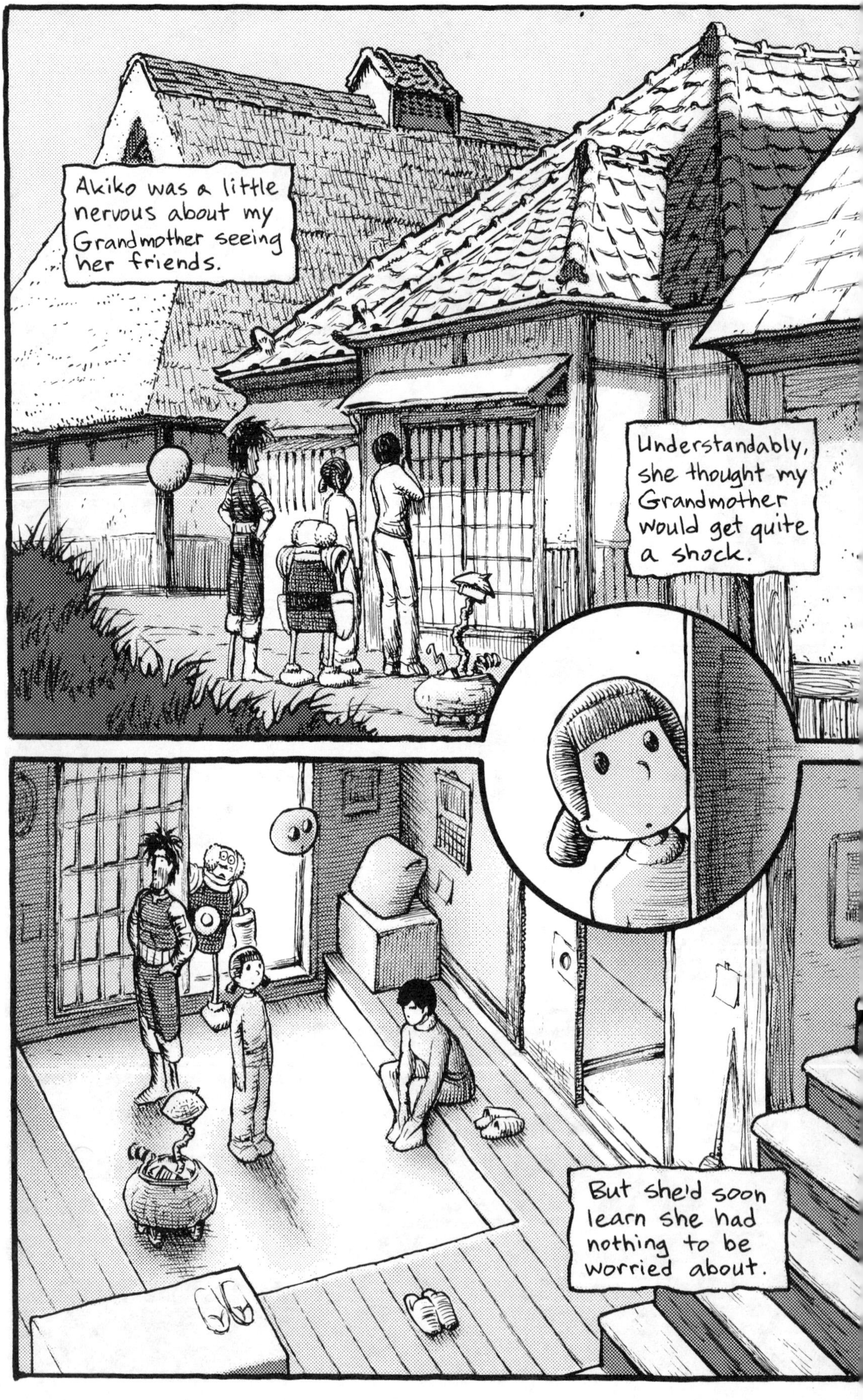
Akiko was a little nervous about my Grandmother seeing her friends.
Understandably, she thought my Grandmother would get quite a shock.
But she'd soon learn she had nothing to be worried about.

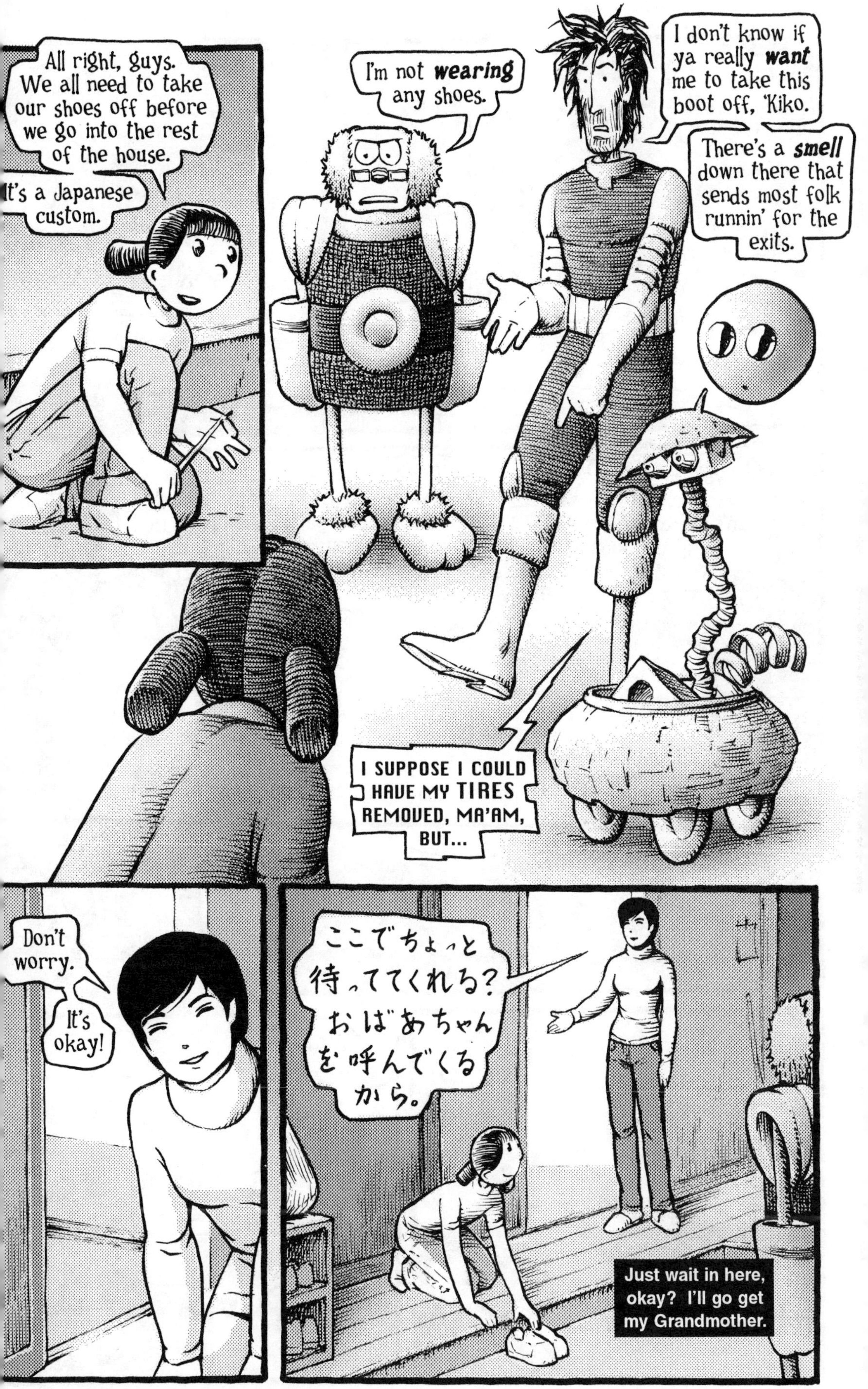
All right, guys. We all need to take our shoes off before we go into the rest of the house.
It's a Japanese custom.
I'm not **wearing** any shoes.
I don't know if ya really **want** me to take this boot off, 'Kiko.
There's a **smell** down there that sends most folk runnin' for the exits.
I SUPPOSE I COULD HAVE MY TIRES REMOVED, MA'AM, BUT...
Don't worry.
It's okay!
ここでちょっと待っててくれる?おばあちゃんを呼んでくるから。
Just wait in here, okay? I'll go get my Grandmother.

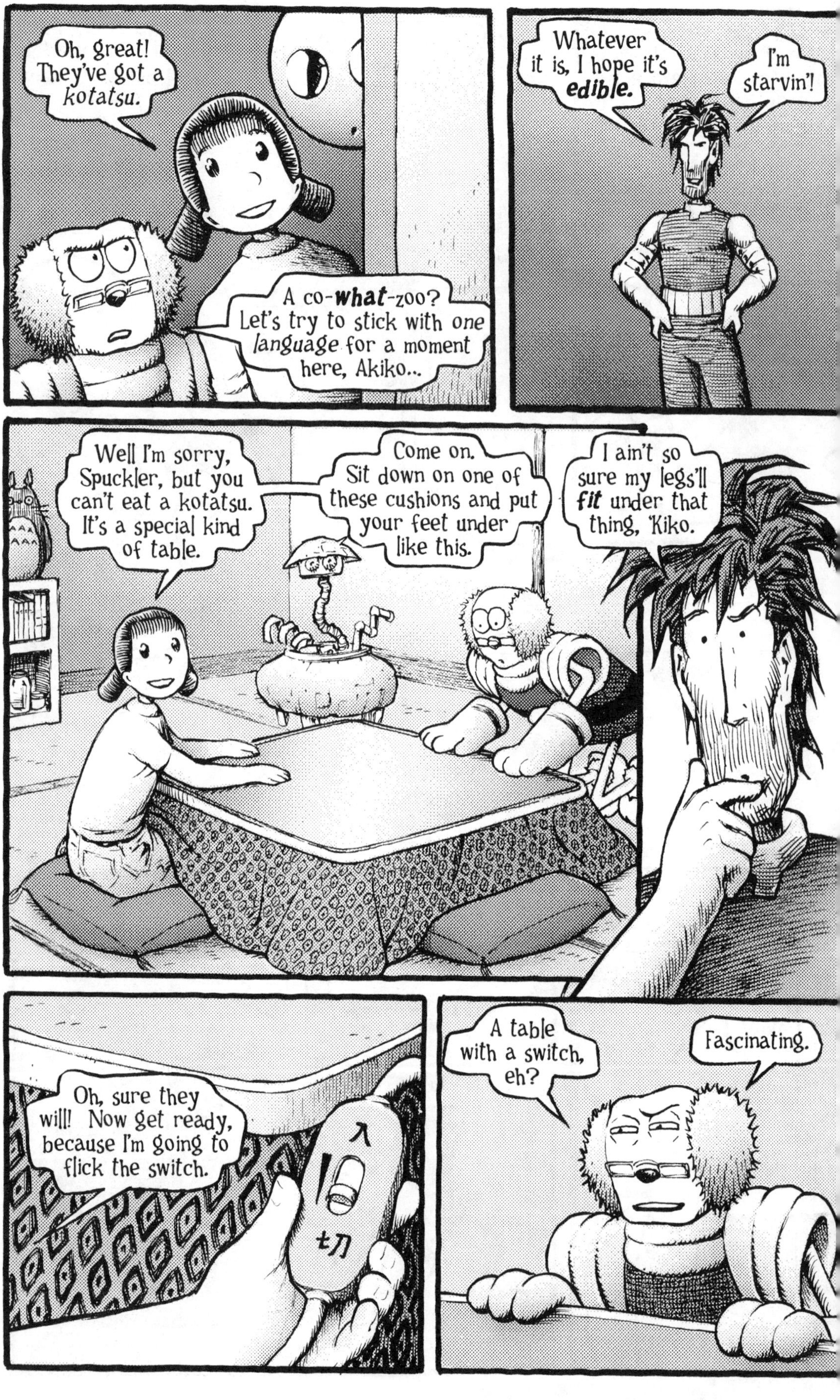

Oh, great! They've got a *kotatsu.*
A co-**what**-zoo? Let's try to stick with *one language* for a moment here, Akiko...
Whatever it is, I hope it's ***edible.***
I'm starvin'!
Well I'm sorry, Spuckler, but you can't eat a kotatsu. It's a special kind of table.
Come on. Sit down on one of these cushions and put your feet under like this.
I ain't so sure my legs'll ***fit*** under that thing, 'Kiko.
Oh, sure they will! Now get ready, because I'm going to flick the switch.
入
切
A table with a switch, eh?
Fascinating.

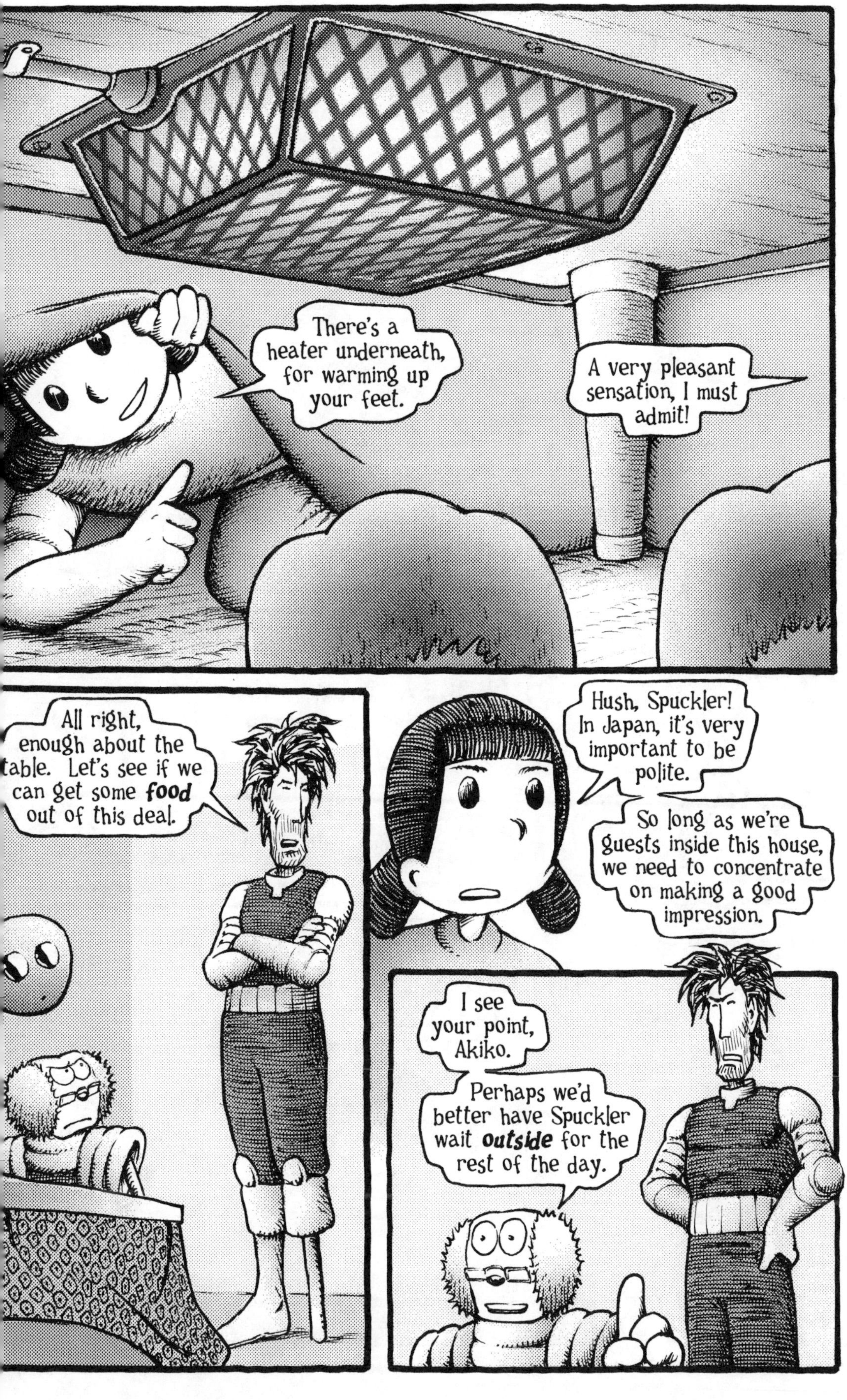
There's a heater underneath, for warming up your feet.
A very pleasant sensation, I must admit!
All right, enough about the table. Let's see if we can get some **food** out of this deal.
Hush, Spuckler! In Japan, it's very important to be polite.
So long as we're guests inside this house, we need to concentrate on making a good impression.
I see your point, Akiko.
Perhaps we'd better have Spuckler wait **outside** for the rest of the day.

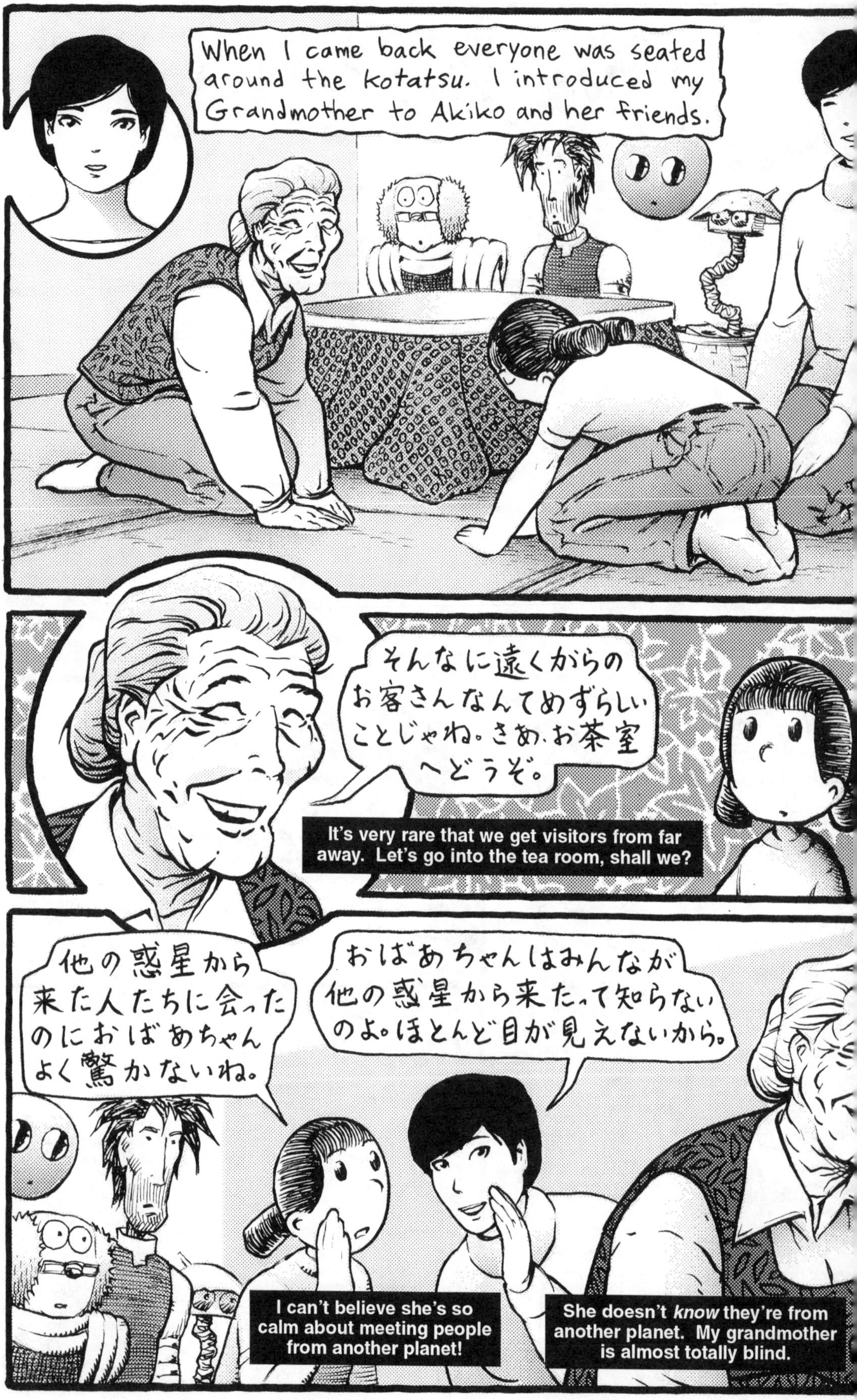
When I came back everyone was seated around the kotatsu. I introduced my Grandmother to Akiko and her friends.
そんなに遠くからのお客さんなんてめずらしいことじゃね。さあ、お茶室へどうぞ。
It's very rare that we get visitors from far away. Let's go into the tea room, shall we?
他の惑星から来た人たちに会ったのにおばあちゃんよく驚かないね。
おばあちゃんはみんなが他の惑星から来たって知らないのよ。ほとんど目が見えないから。
I can't believe she's so calm about meeting people from another planet!
She doesn't *know* they're from another planet. My grandmother is almost totally blind.

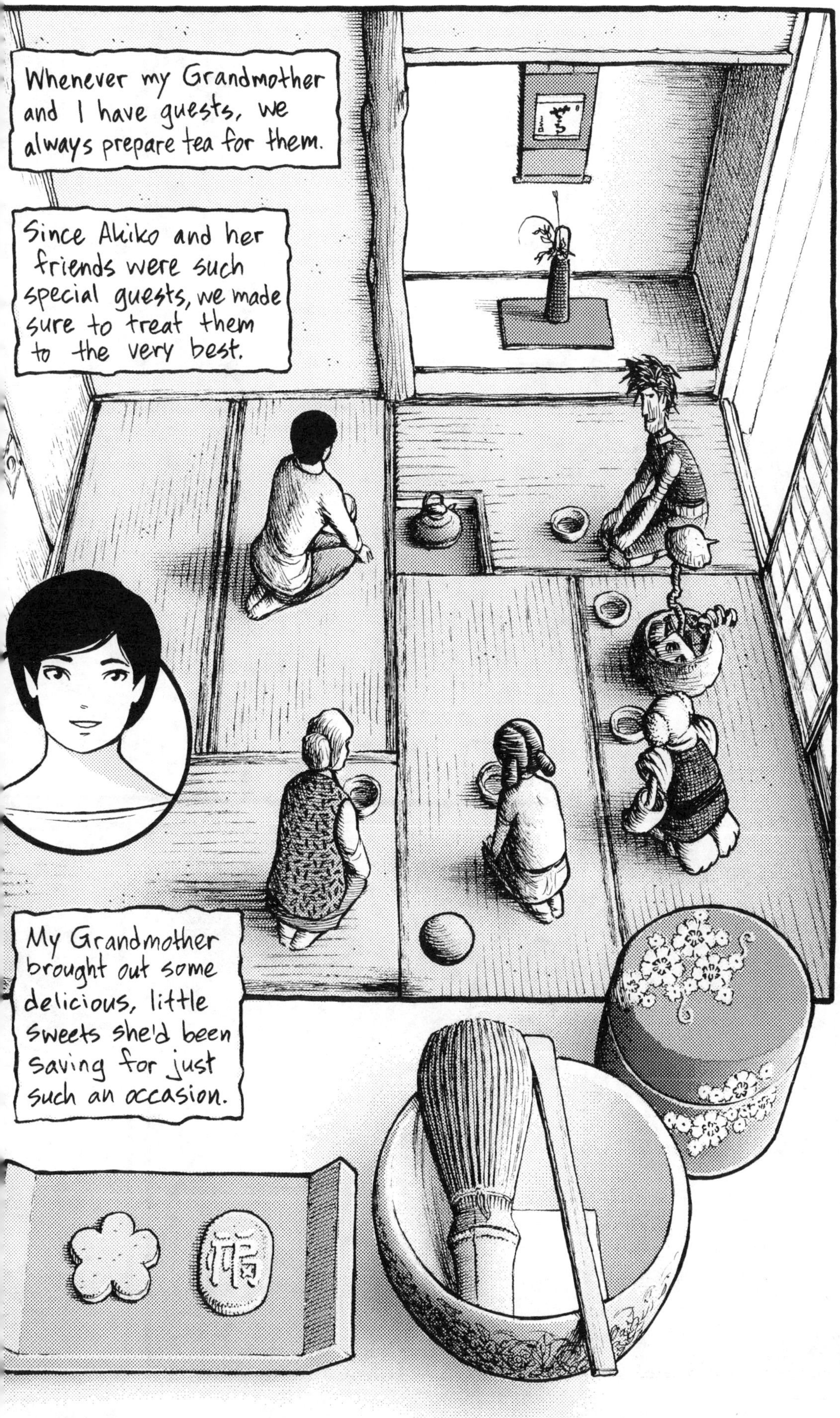
Whenever my Grandmother and I have guests, we always prepare tea for them.
Since Akiko and her friends were such special guests, we made sure to treat them to the very best.
My Grandmother brought out some delicious, little sweets she'd been saving for just such an occasion.

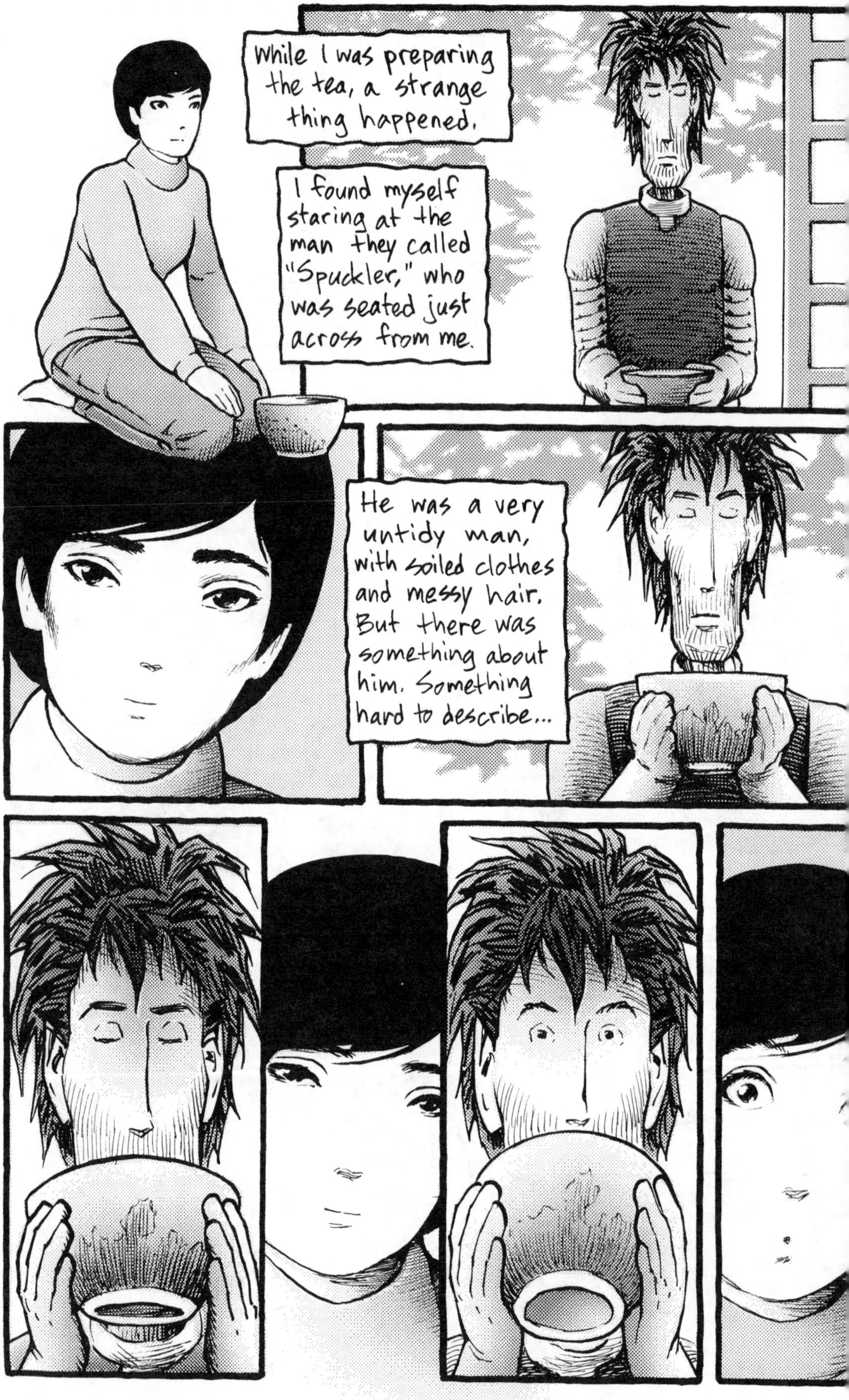
While I was preparing the tea, a strange thing happened.
I found myself staring at the man they called "Spuckler," who was seated just across from me.
He was a very untidy man, with soiled clothes and messy hair. But there was something about him. Something hard to describe...

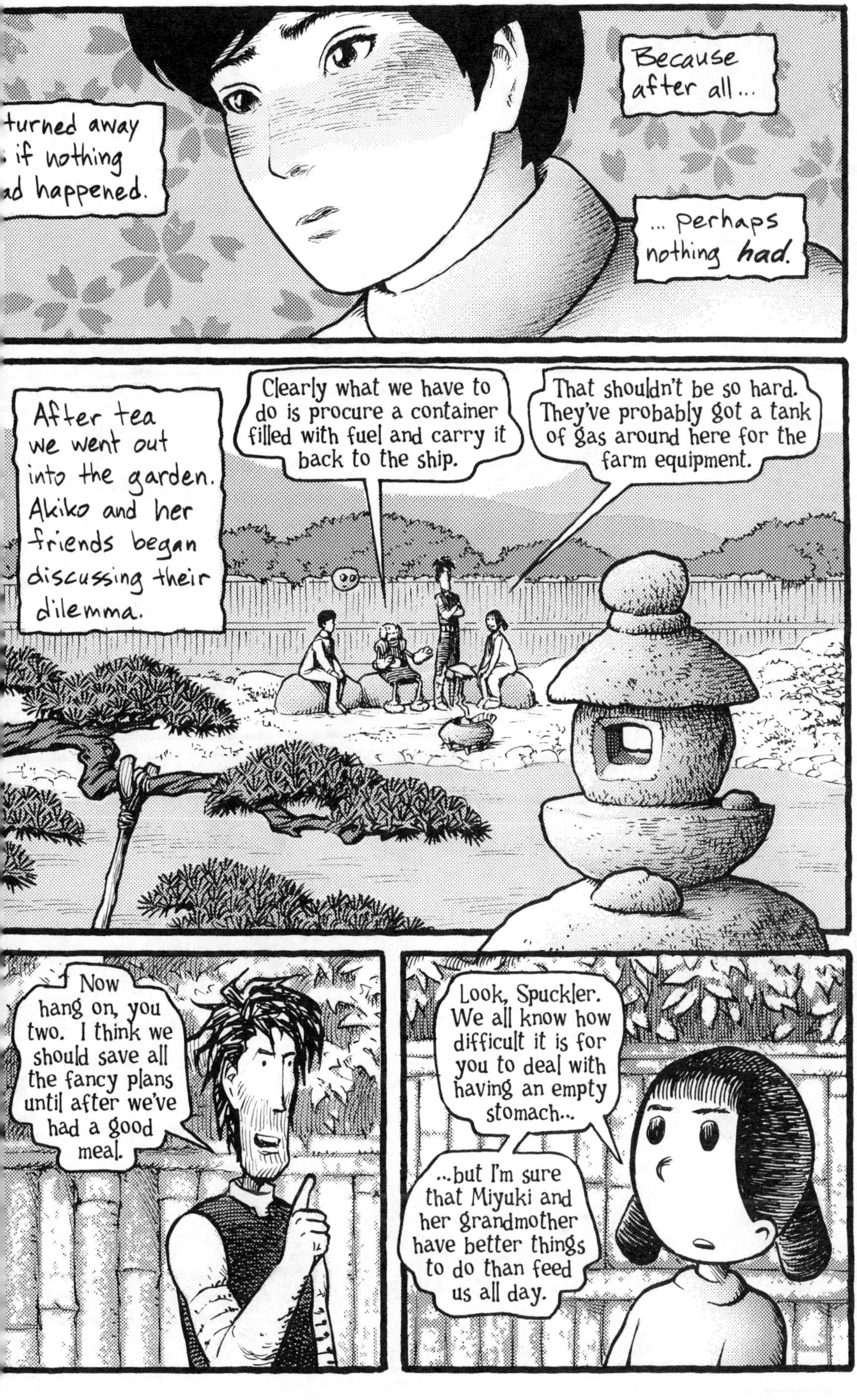

turned away
if nothing
ad happened.
Because after all...
... perhaps nothing had.
After tea we went out into the garden. Akiko and her friends began discussing their dilemma.
Clearly what we have to do is procure a container filled with fuel and carry it back to the ship.
That shouldn't be so hard. They've probably got a tank of gas around here for the farm equipment.
Now hang on, you two. I think we should save all the fancy plans until after we've had a good meal.
Look, Spuckler. We all know how difficult it is for you to deal with having an empty stomach...
...but I'm sure that Miyuki and her grandmother have better things to do than feed us all day.

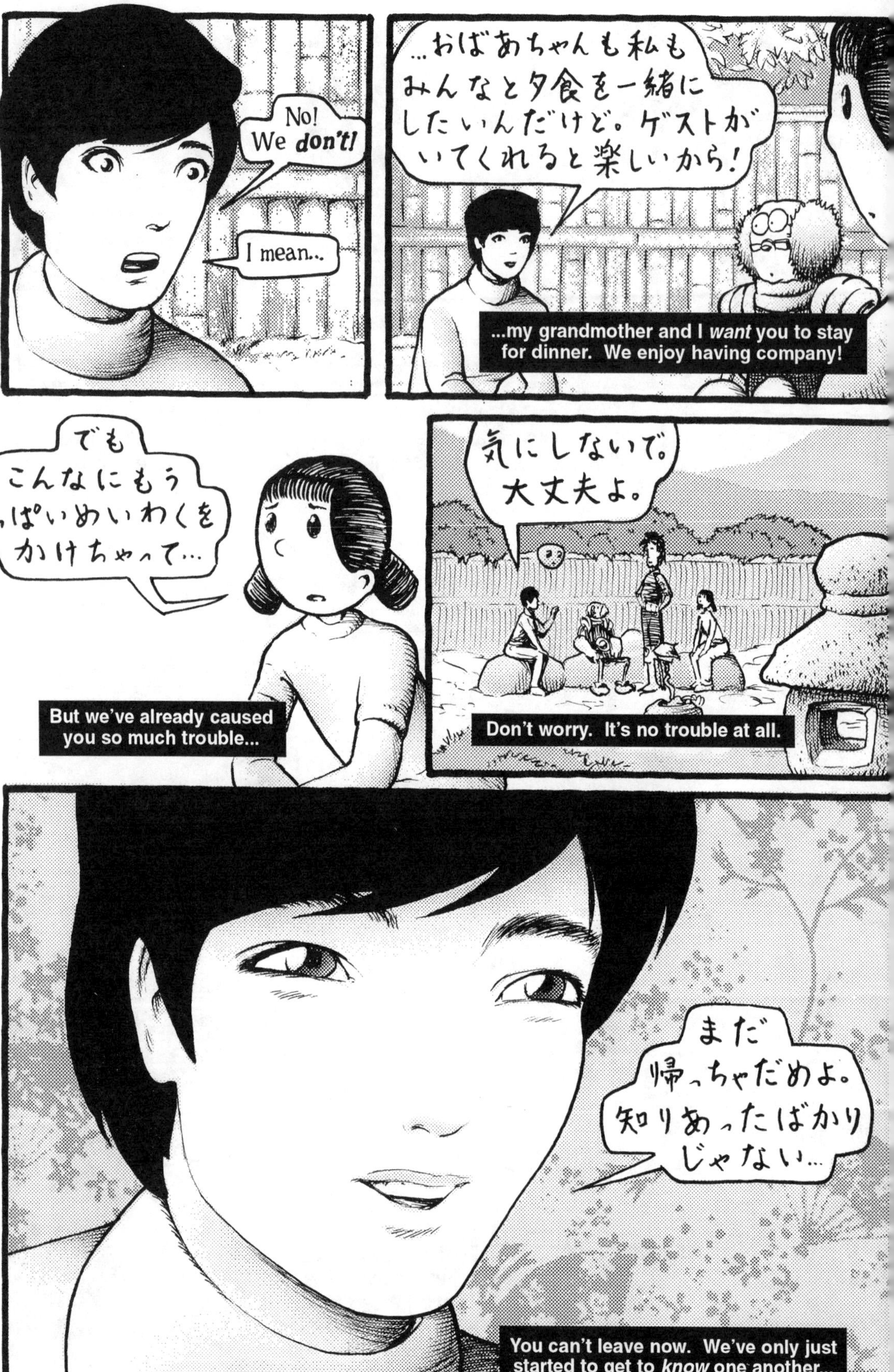
No! We don't!
I mean...
...おばあちゃんも私もみんなと夕食を一緒にしたいんだけど。ゲストがいてくれると楽しいから!
...my grandmother and I want you to stay for dinner. We enjoy having company!
でもこんなにもういっぱいめいわくをかけちゃって...
But we've already caused you so much trouble...
気にしないで。大丈夫よ。
Don't worry. It's no trouble at all.
まだ帰っちゃだめよ。知りあったばかりじゃない...
You can't leave now. We've only just started to get to know one another...

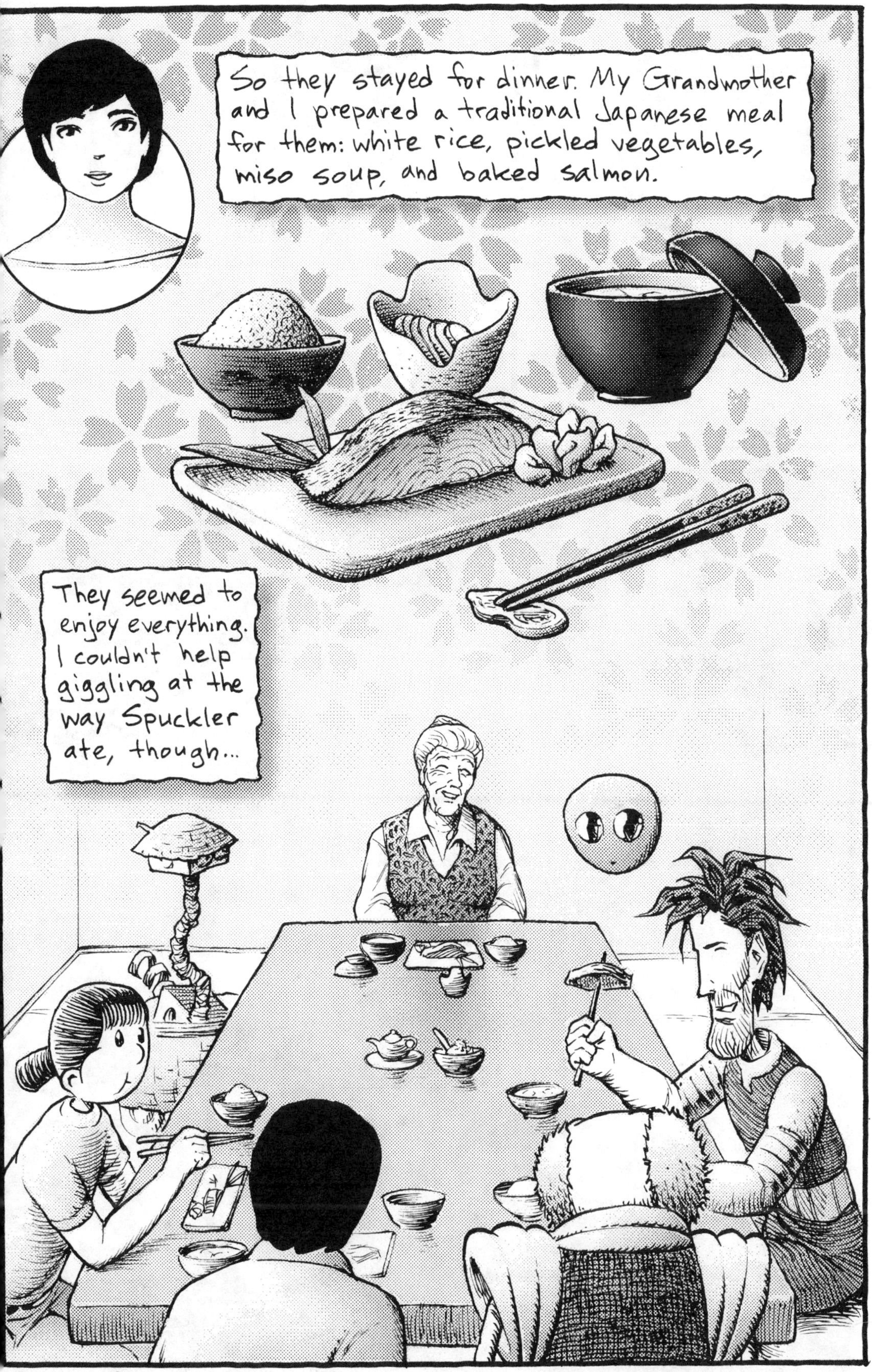
So they stayed for dinner. My Grandmother and I prepared a traditional Japanese meal for them: white rice, pickled vegetables, miso soup, and baked salmon.
They seemed to enjoy everything. I couldn't help giggling at the way Spuckler ate, though...

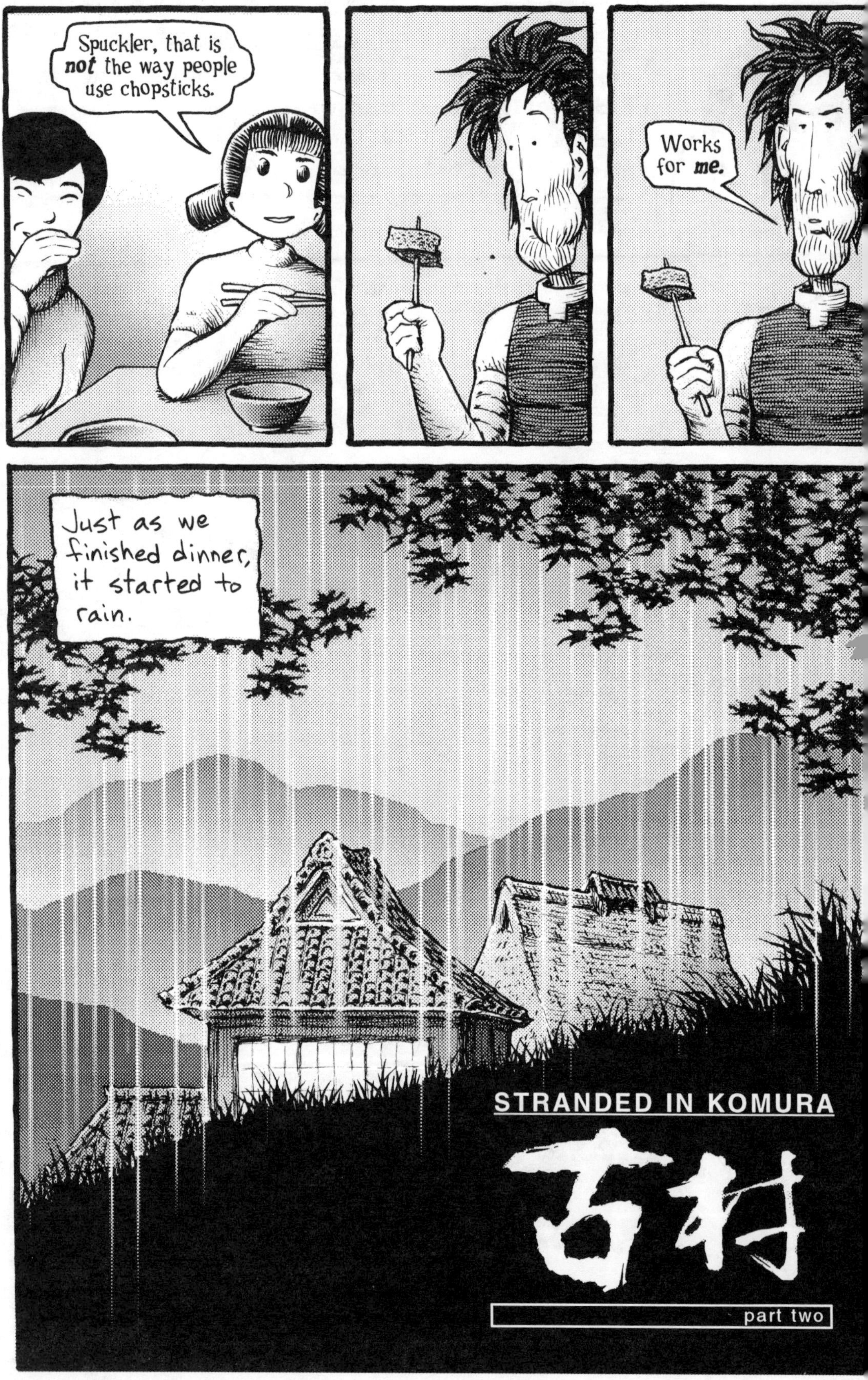
Spuckler, that is *not* the way people use chopsticks.
Works for *me.*
Just as we finished dinner, it started to rain.
STRANDED IN KOMURA
古村
part two

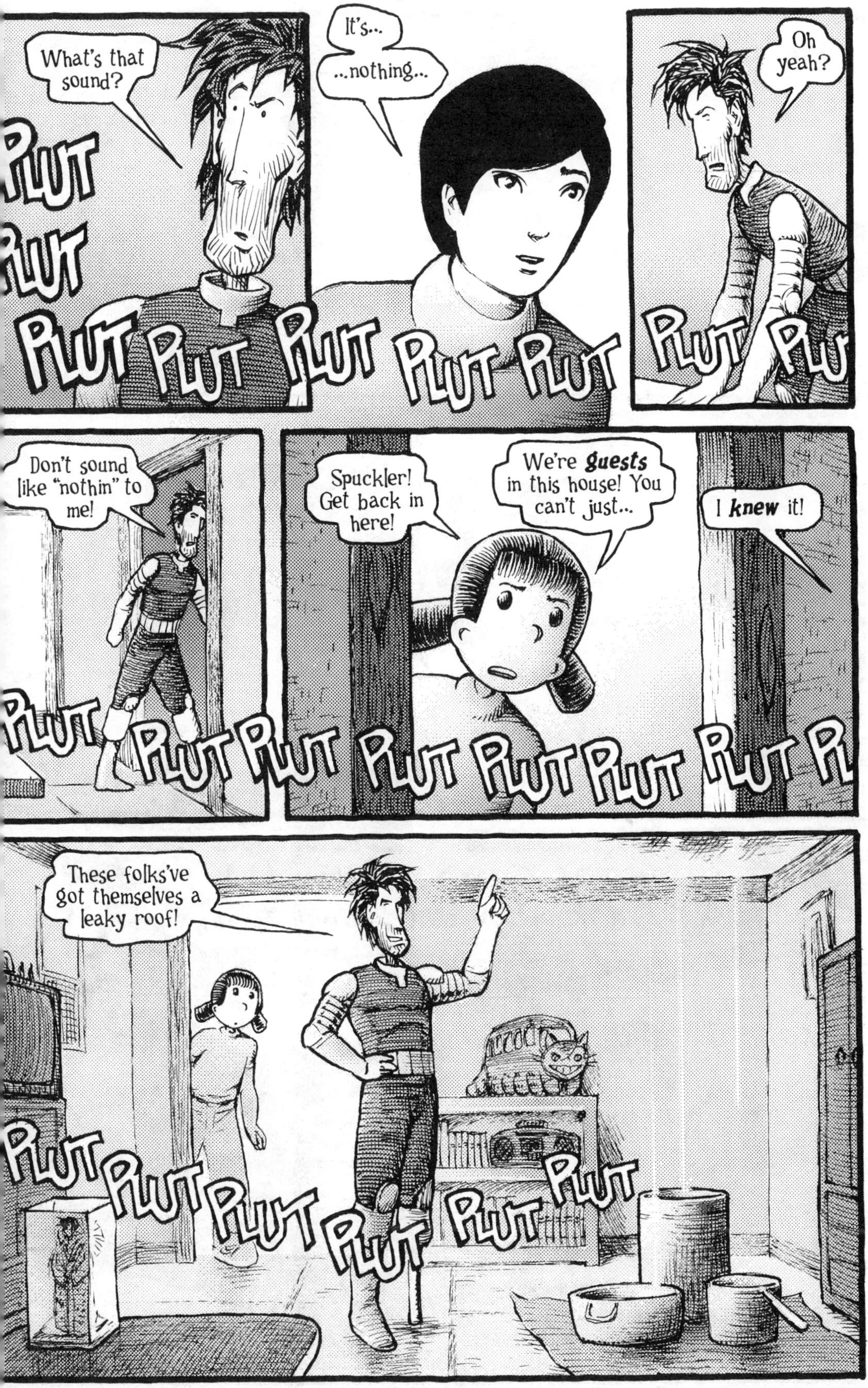
What's that sound?
PLUT PLUT PLUT PLUT PLUT
It's... ...nothing...
PLUT PLUT
Oh yeah?
PLUT PLU
Don't sound like "nothin" to me!
PLUT PLUT PLUT
Spuckler! Get back in here!
We're *guests* in this house! You can't just...
PLUT PLUT PLUT
I ***knew*** it!
PLUT PL
These folks've got themselves a leaky roof!
PLUT PLUT PLUT PLUT PLUT PLUT

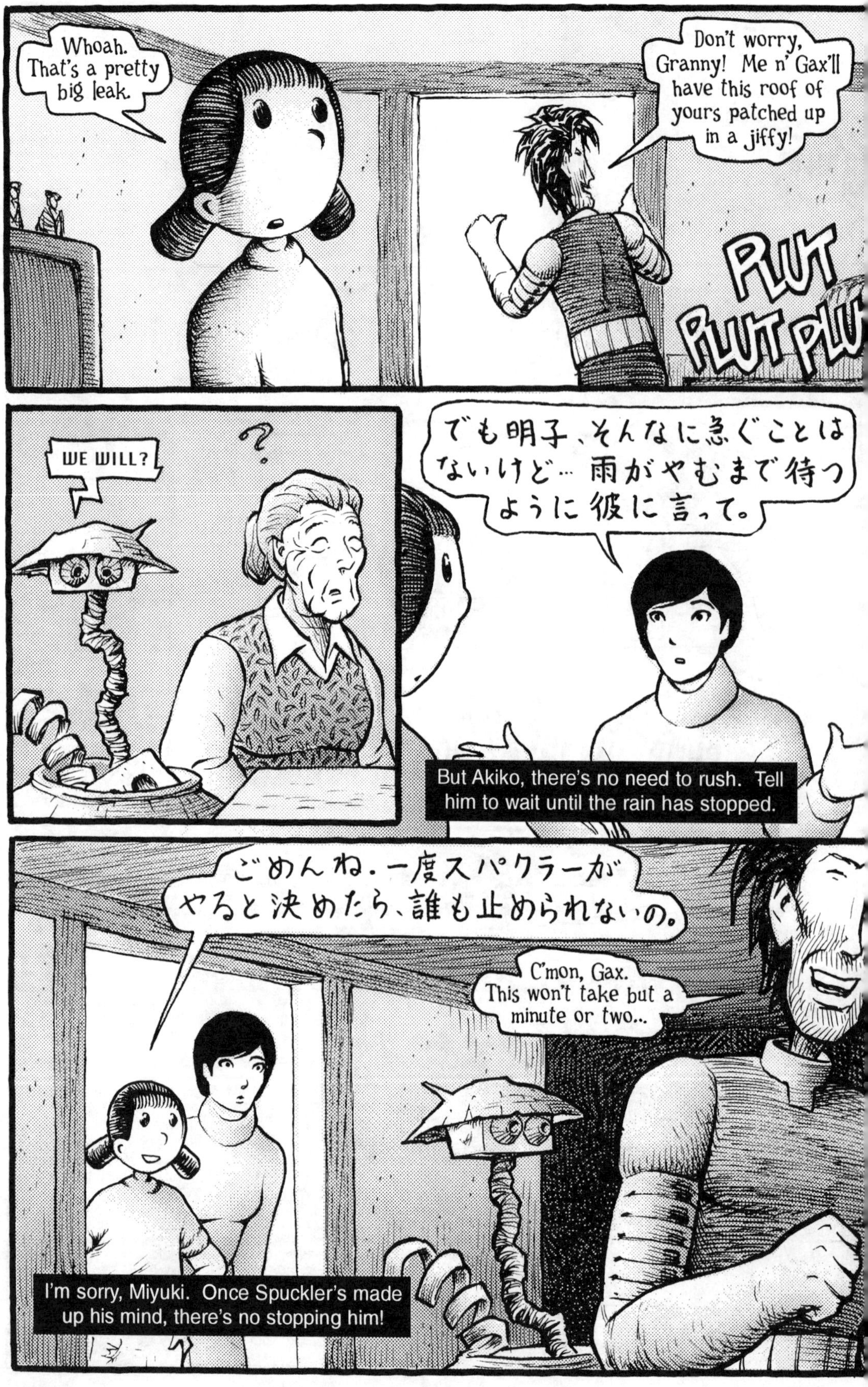
Whoah. That's a pretty big leak.
Don't worry, Granny! Me n' Gax'll have this roof of yours patched up in a jiffy!
PLUT PLUT PLU
WE WILL?
でも明子、そんなに急ぐことはないけど… 雨がやむまで待つように彼に言って。
But Akiko, there's no need to rush. Tell him to wait until the rain has stopped.
ごめんね。一度スパクラーがやると決めたら、誰も止められないの。
C'mon, Gax. This won't take but a minute or two...
I'm sorry, Miyuki. Once Spuckler's made up his mind, there's no stopping him!

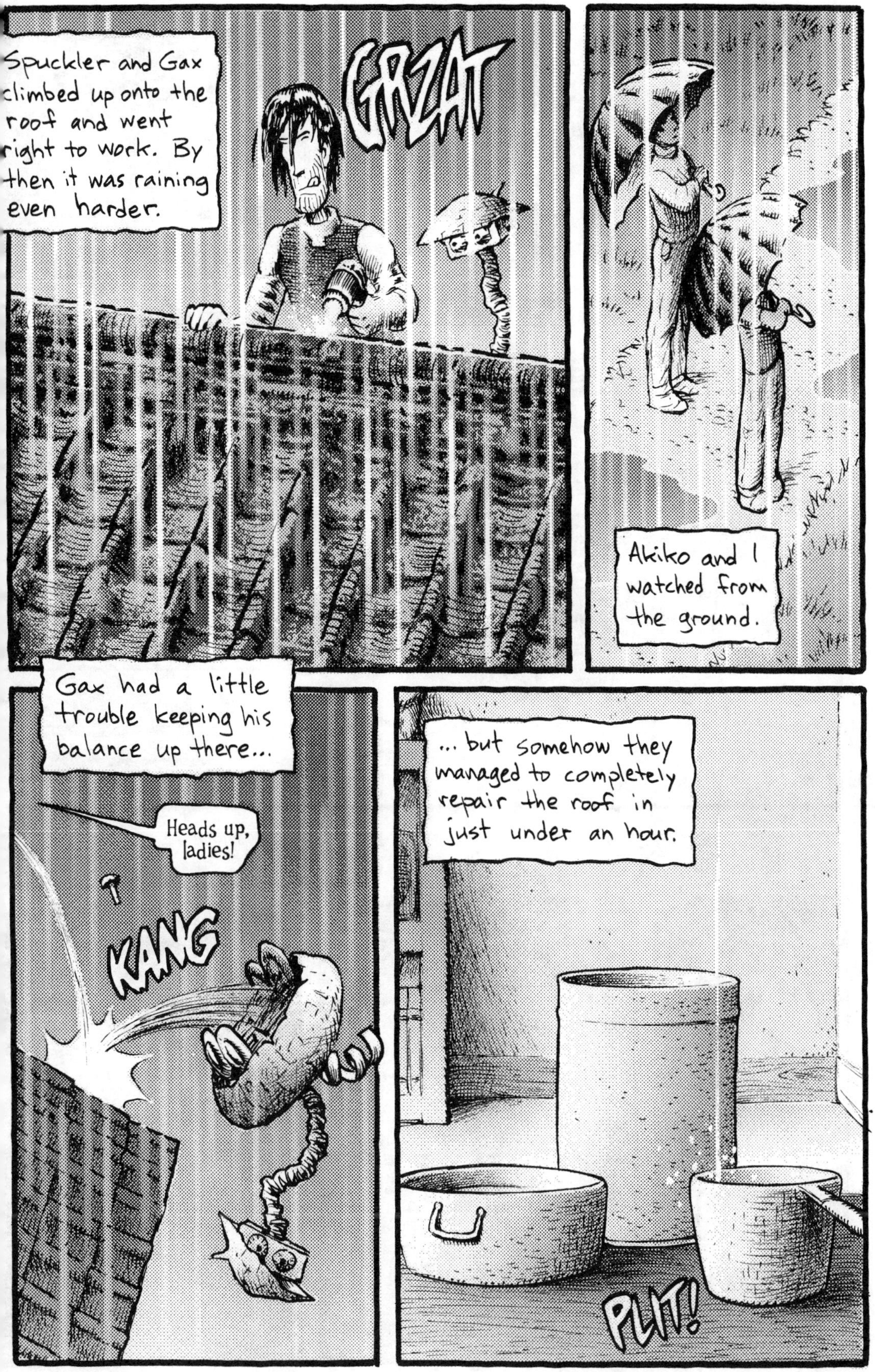

Spuckler and Gax climbed up onto the roof and went right to work. By then it was raining even harder.
GRZAT
Akiko and I watched from the ground.
Gax had a little trouble keeping his balance up there...
Heads up, ladies!
KANG
... but somehow they managed to completely repair the roof in just under an hour.
PLIT!

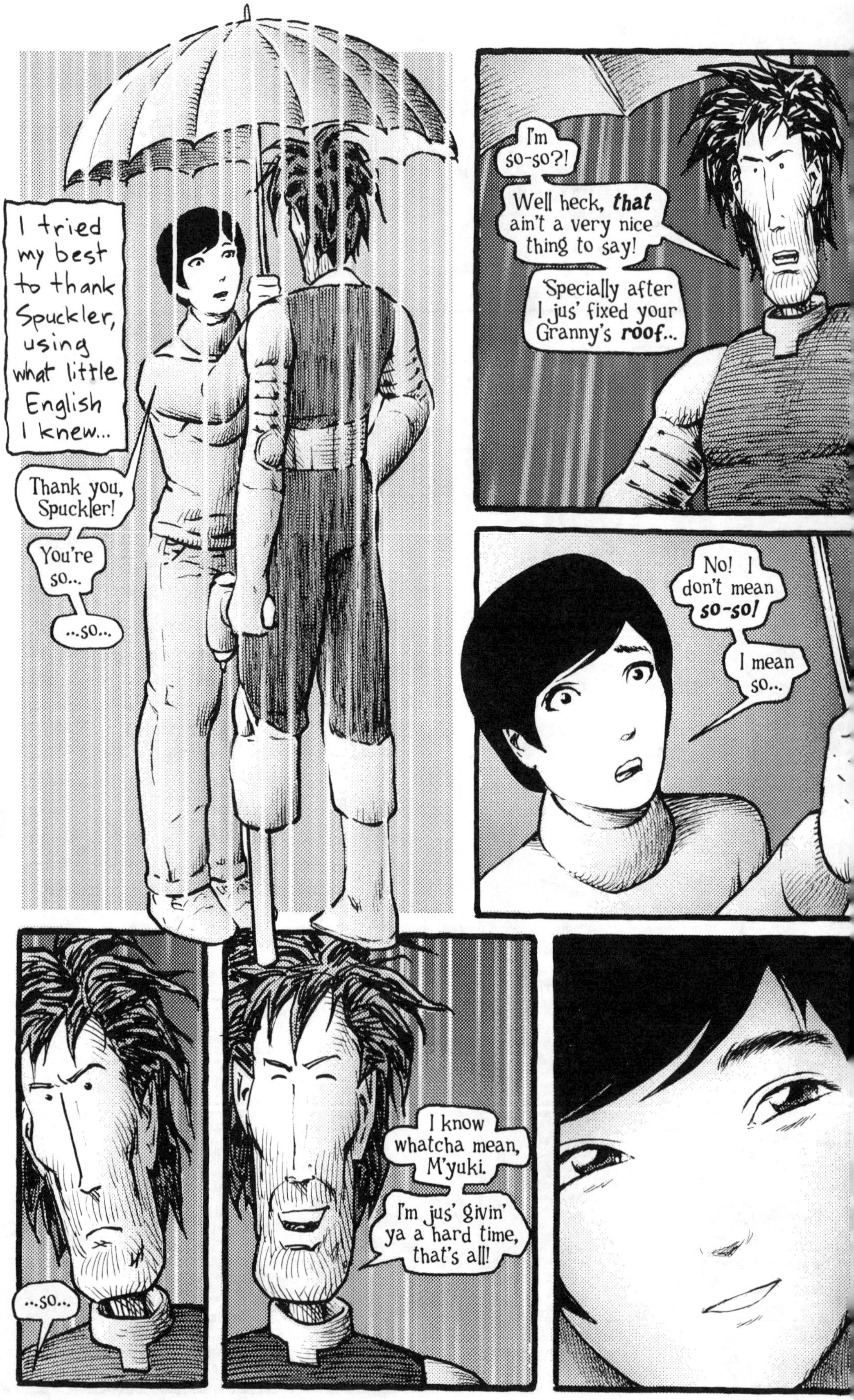
I tried my best to thank Spuckler, using what little English I knew...
Thank you, Spuckler!
You're so...
...so...
I'm so-so?!
Well heck, **that** ain't a very nice thing to say!
'Specially after I jus' fixed your Granny's **roof**...
No! I don't mean **so-so!**
I mean so...
...so...
I know whatcha mean, M'yuki.
I'm jus' givin' ya a hard time, that's all!

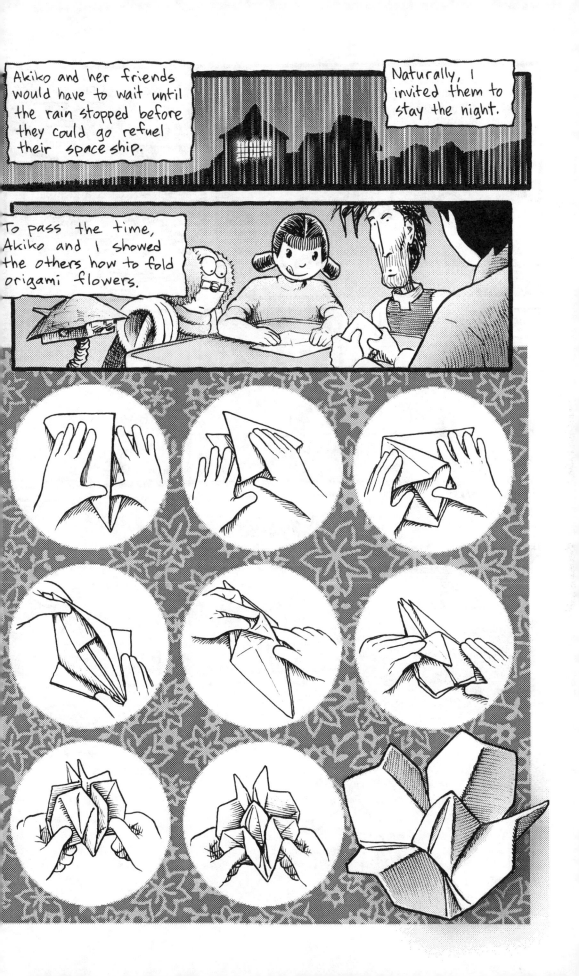

Akiko and her friends would have to wait until the rain stopped before they could go refuel their space ship.

Naturally, I invited them to stay the night.

To pass the time, Akiko and I showed the others how to fold origami flowers.

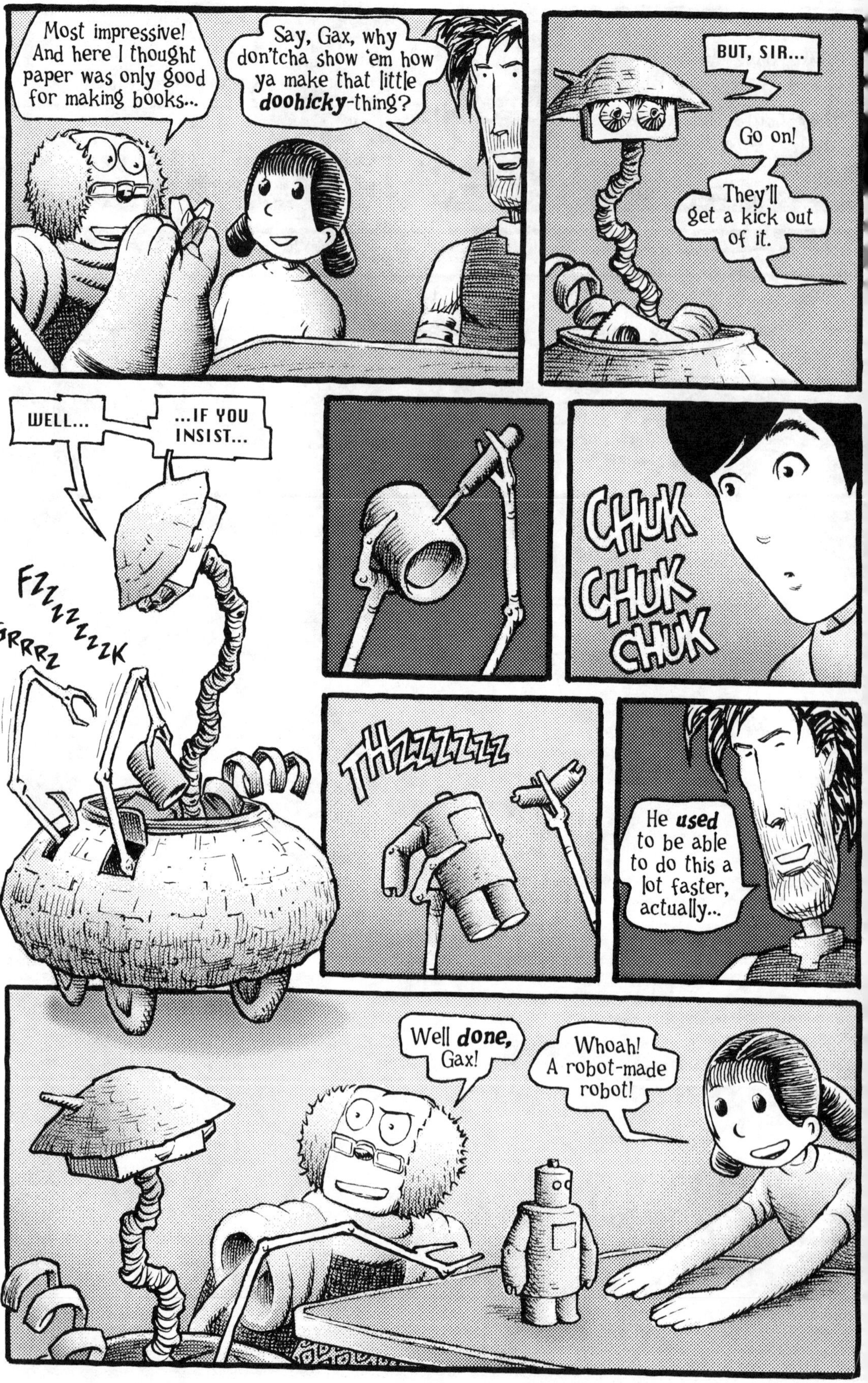
Most impressive! And here I thought paper was only good for making books...
Say, Gax, why don'tcha show 'em how ya make that little **doohicky**-thing?
BUT, SIR...
Go on!
They'll get a kick out of it.
WELL...
...IF YOU INSIST...
FZZZZZZZK
GRRRZ
CHUK CHUK CHUK
THZZZZZZZ
He **used** to be able to do this a lot faster, actually...
Well **done,** Gax!
Whoah! A robot-made robot!

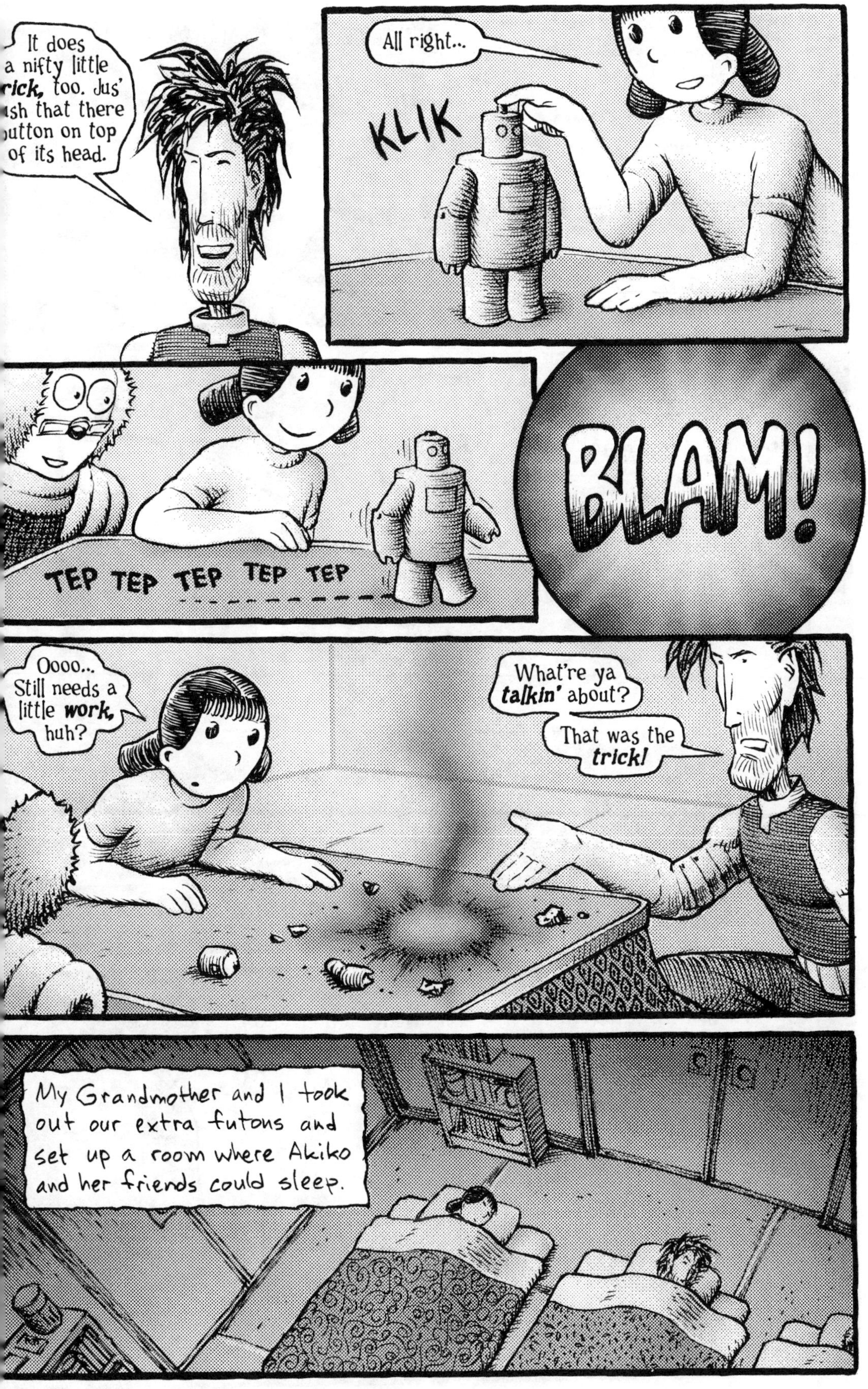
It does a nifty little trick, too. Jus' push that there button on top of its head.
All right...
KLIK
TEP TEP TEP TEP TEP
BLAM!
Oooo... Still needs a little work, huh?
What're ya talkin' about?
That was the trick!
My Grandmother and I took out our extra futons and set up a room where Akiko and her friends could sleep.

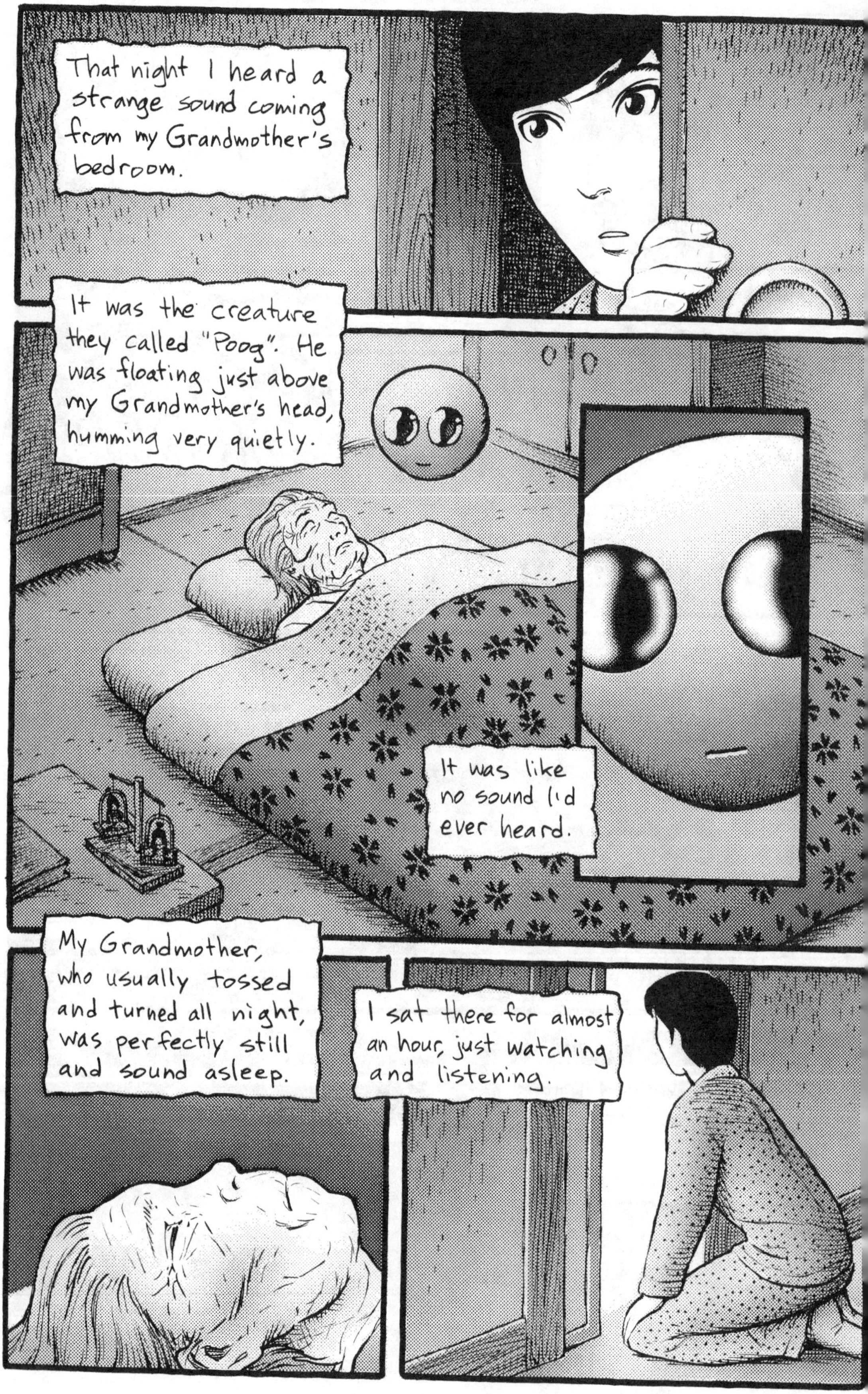
That night I heard a strange sound coming from my Grandmother's bedroom.
It was the creature they called "Poog". He was floating just above my Grandmother's head, humming very quietly.
It was like no sound I'd ever heard.
My Grandmother, who usually tossed and turned all night, was perfectly still and sound asleep.
I sat there for almost an hour, just watching and listening.

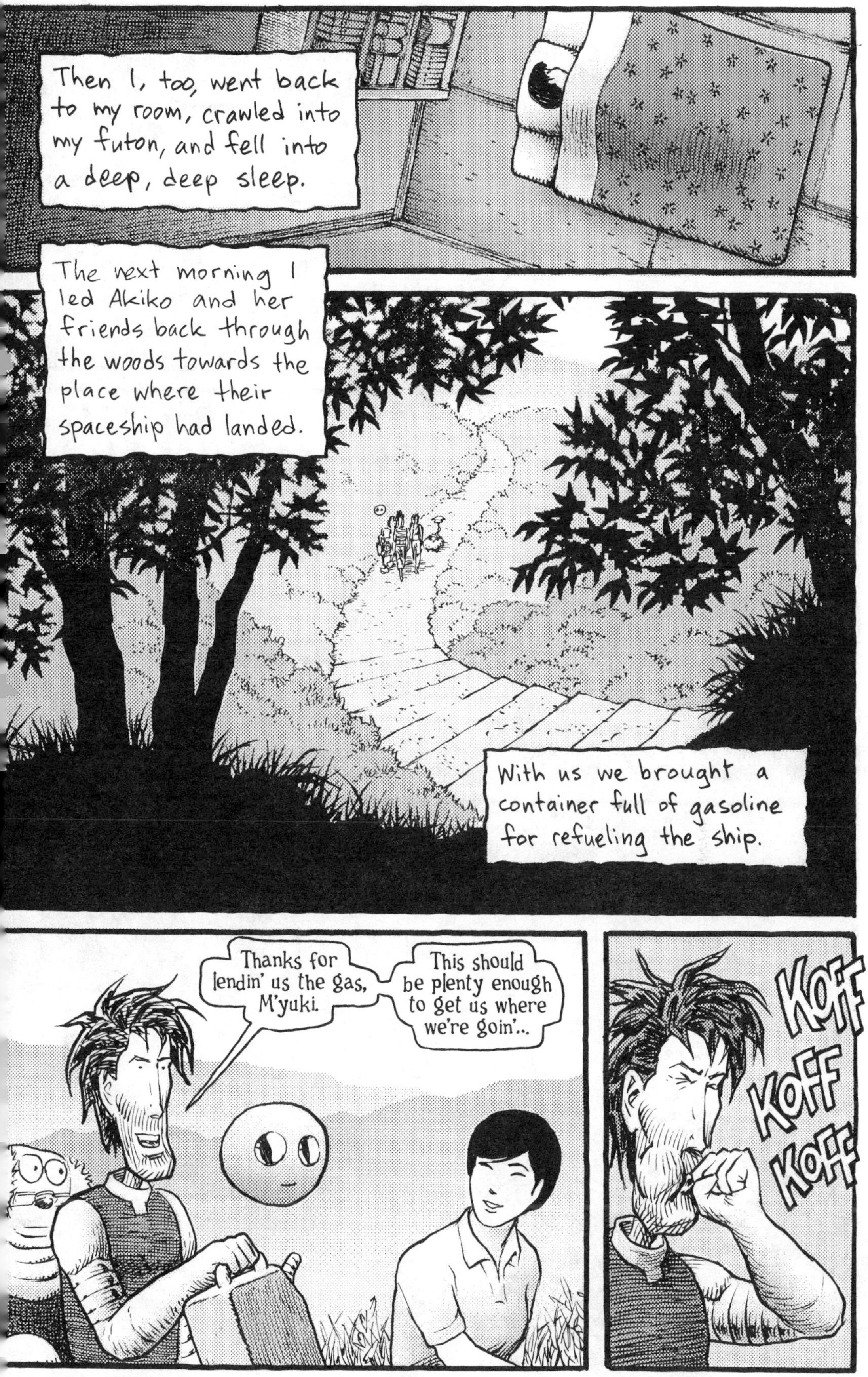
Then I, too, went back to my room, crawled into my futon, and fell into a deep, deep sleep.
The next morning I led Akiko and her friends back through the woods towards the place where their spaceship had landed.
With us we brought a container full of gasoline for refueling the ship.
Thanks for lendin' us the gas, M'yuki.
This should be plenty enough to get us where we're goin'...
KOFF
KOFF
KOFF

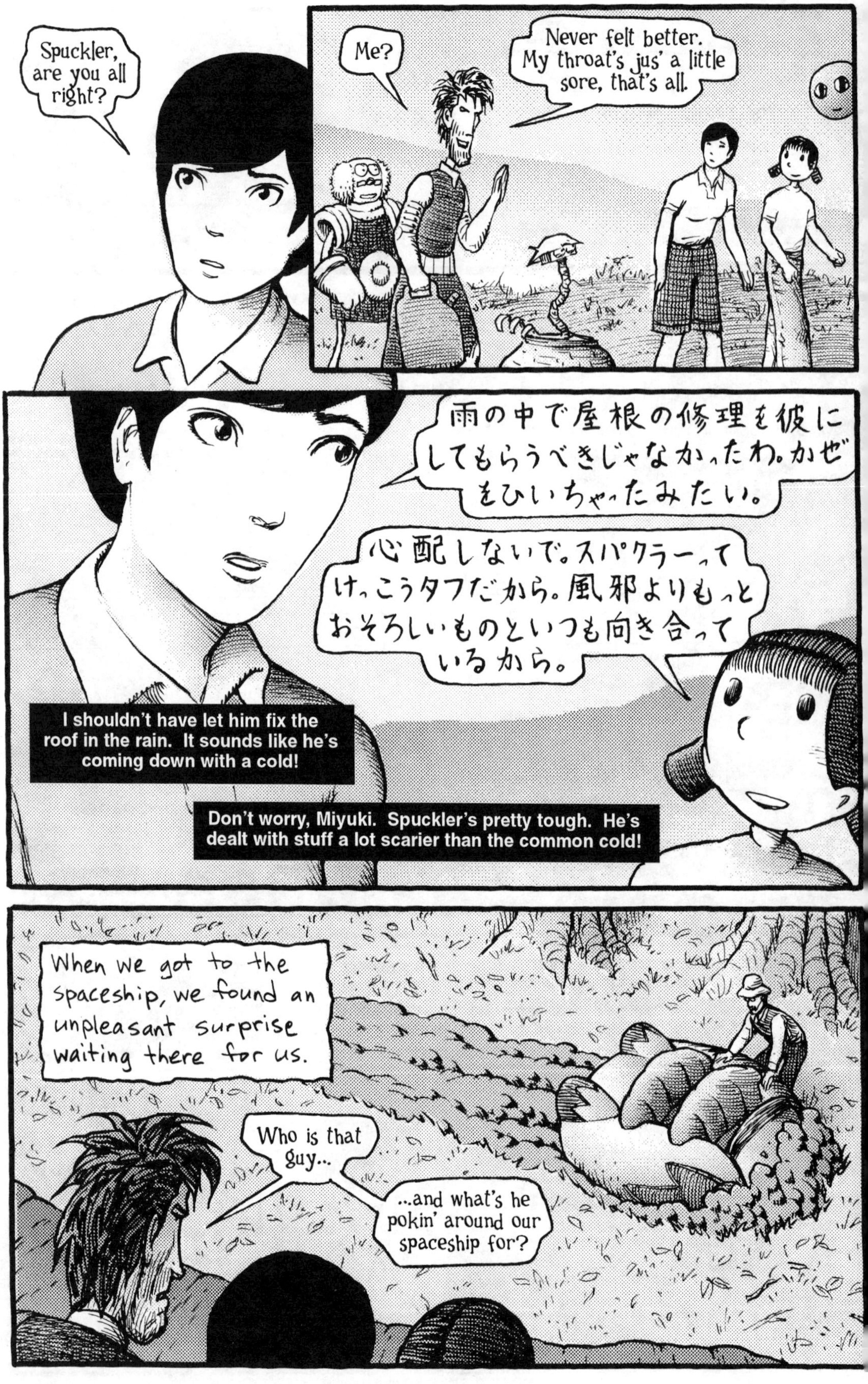
Spuckler, are you all right?
Me?
Never felt better. My throat's jus' a little sore, that's all.
雨の中で屋根の修理を彼にしてもらうべきじゃなかったわ。かぜをひいちゃったみたい。
心配しないで。スパクラーってけっこうタフだから。風邪よりもっとおそろしいものといつも向き合っているから。
I shouldn't have let him fix the roof in the rain. It sounds like he's coming down with a cold!
Don't worry, Miyuki. Spuckler's pretty tough. He's dealt with stuff a lot scarier than the common cold!
When we got to the spaceship, we found an unpleasant surprise waiting there for us.
Who is that guy...
...and what's he pokin' around our spaceship for?

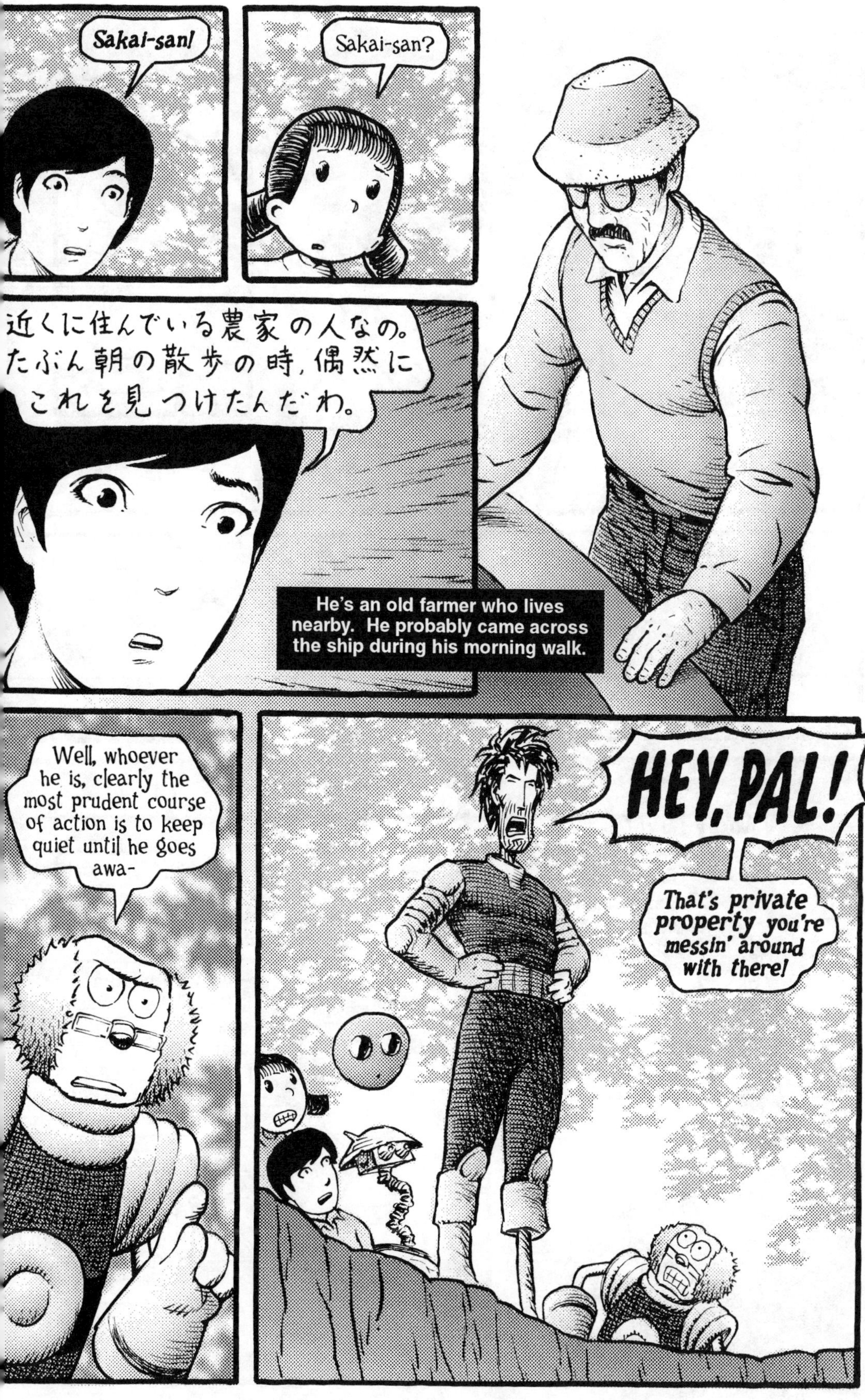
Sakai-san!
Sakai-san?
近くに住んでいる農家の人なの。たぶん朝の散歩の時，偶然にこれを見つけたんだわ。
He's an old farmer who lives nearby. He probably came across the ship during his morning walk.
Well, whoever he is, clearly the most prudent course of action is to keep quiet until he goes awa-
HEY, PAL!
That's private property you're messin' around with there!

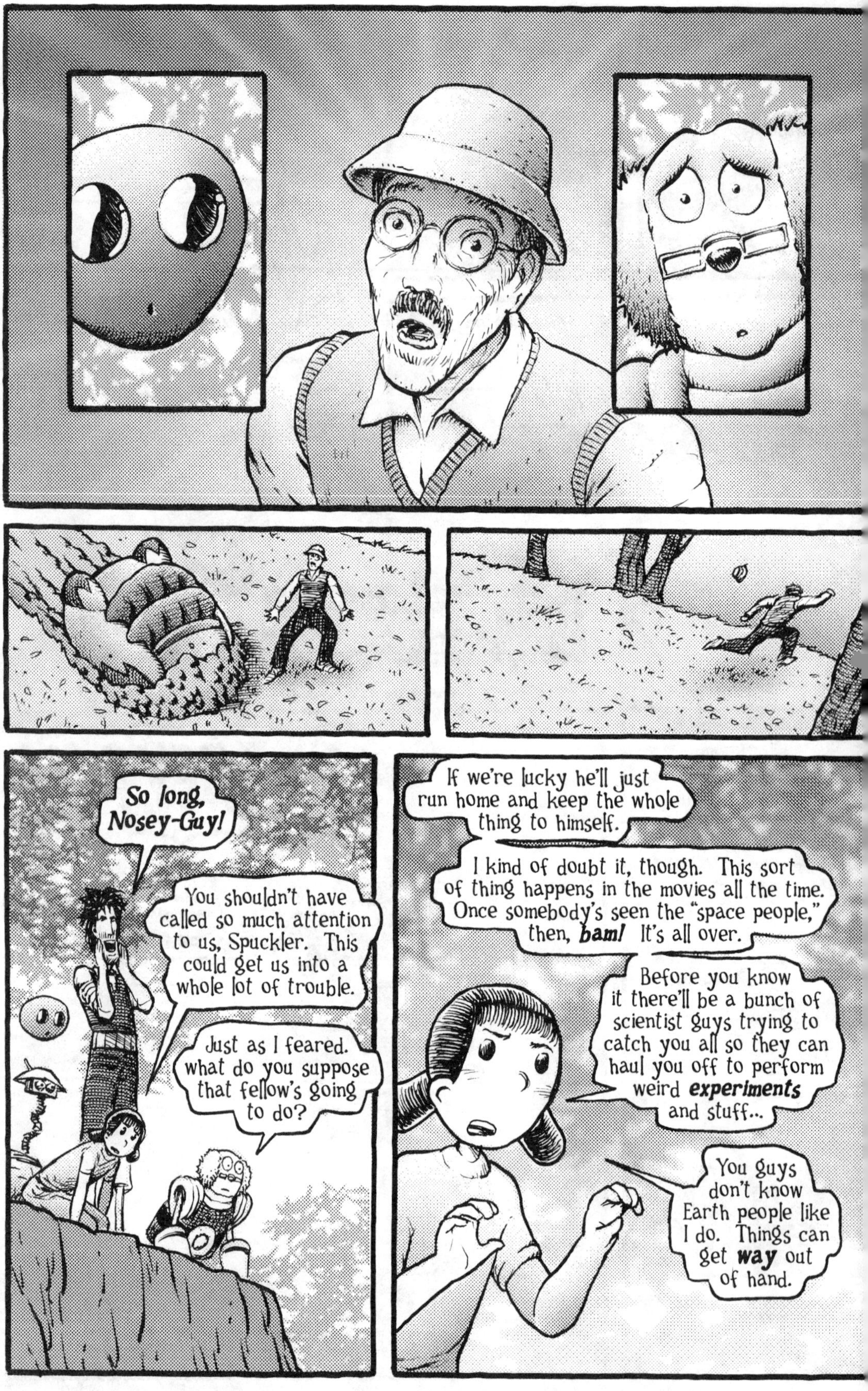
So long, Nosey-Guy!
You shouldn't have called so much attention to us, Spuckler. This could get us into a whole lot of trouble.
Just as I feared. what do you suppose that fellow's going to do?
If we're lucky he'll just run home and keep the whole thing to himself.
I kind of doubt it, though. This sort of thing happens in the movies all the time. Once somebody's seen the "space people," then, **bam!** It's all over.
Before you know it there'll be a bunch of scientist guys trying to catch you all so they can haul you off to perform weird ***experiments*** and stuff...
You guys don't know Earth people like I do. Things can get **way** out of hand.

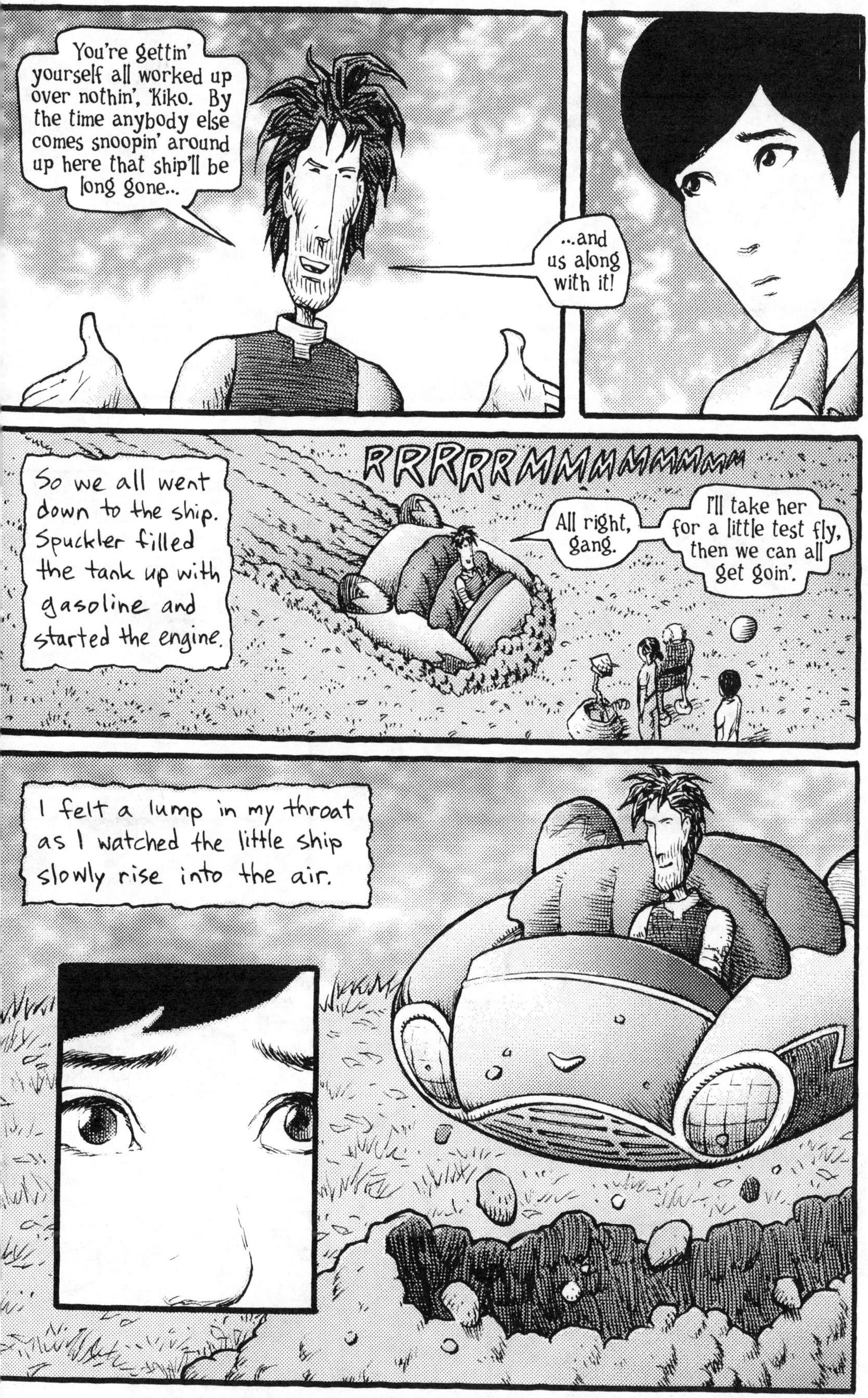
You're gettin' yourself all worked up over nothin', 'Kiko. By the time anybody else comes snoopin' around up here that ship'll be long gone...
...and us along with it!
So we all went down to the ship. Spuckler filled the tank up with gasoline and started the engine.
RRRRRMMMMMMM
All right, gang.
I'll take her for a little test fly, then we can all get goin'.
I felt a lump in my throat as I watched the little ship slowly rise into the air.

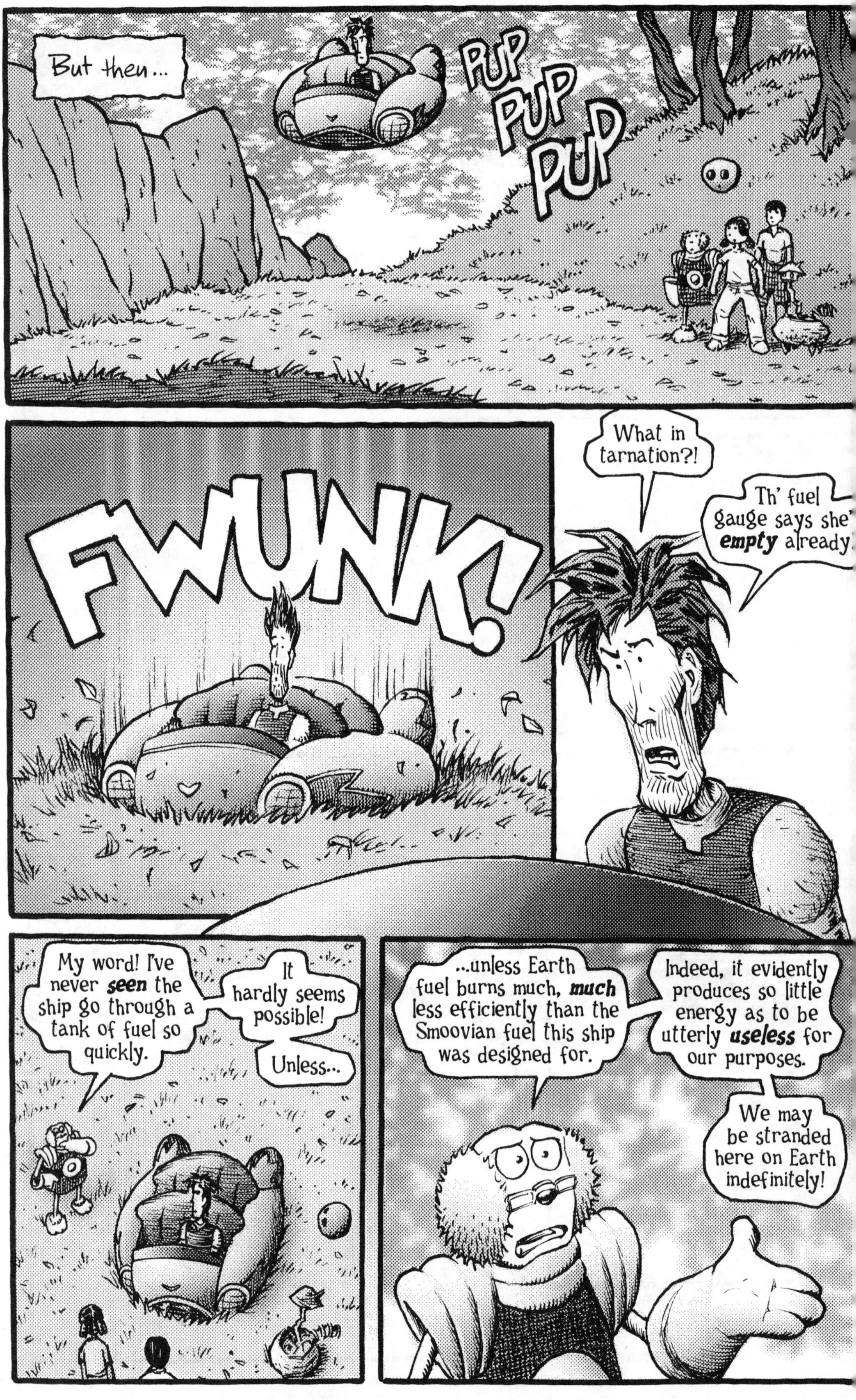

But then...
PUP PUP PUP
FWUNK!
What in tarnation?!
Th' fuel gauge says she' empty already.
My word! I've never seen the ship go through a tank of fuel so quickly.
It hardly seems possible!
Unless...
...unless Earth fuel burns much, much less efficiently than the Smoovian fuel this ship was designed for.
Indeed, it evidently produces so little energy as to be utterly useless for our purposes.
We may be stranded here on Earth indefinitely!

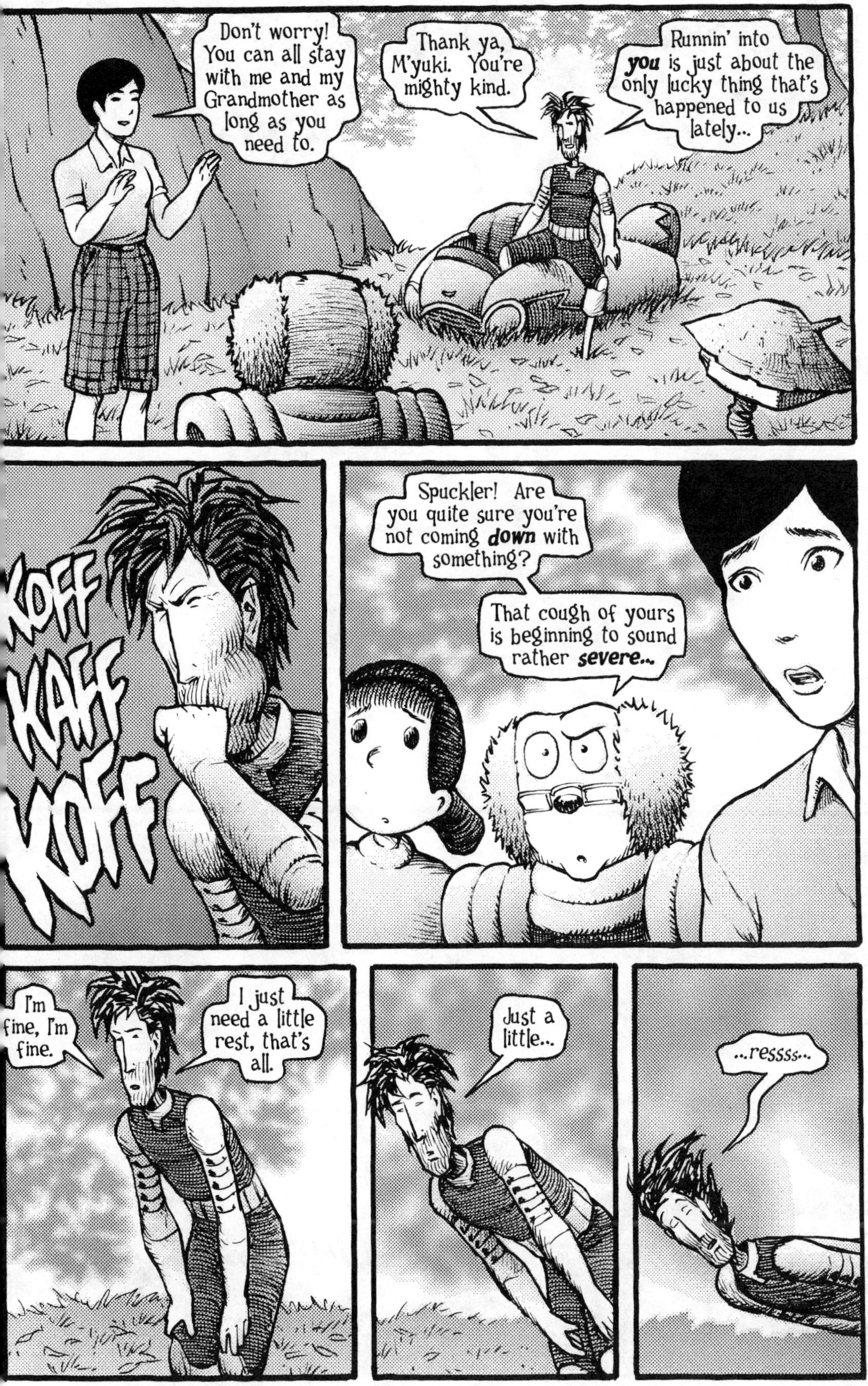
Don't worry! You can all stay with me and my Grandmother as long as you need to.
Thank ya, M'yuki. You're mighty kind.
Runnin' into **you** is just about the only lucky thing that's happened to us lately...
KOFF KAFF KOFF
Spuckler! Are you quite sure you're not coming **down** with something?
That cough of yours is beginning to sound rather **severe...**
I'm fine, I'm fine.
I just need a little rest, that's all.
Just a little...
...ressss...

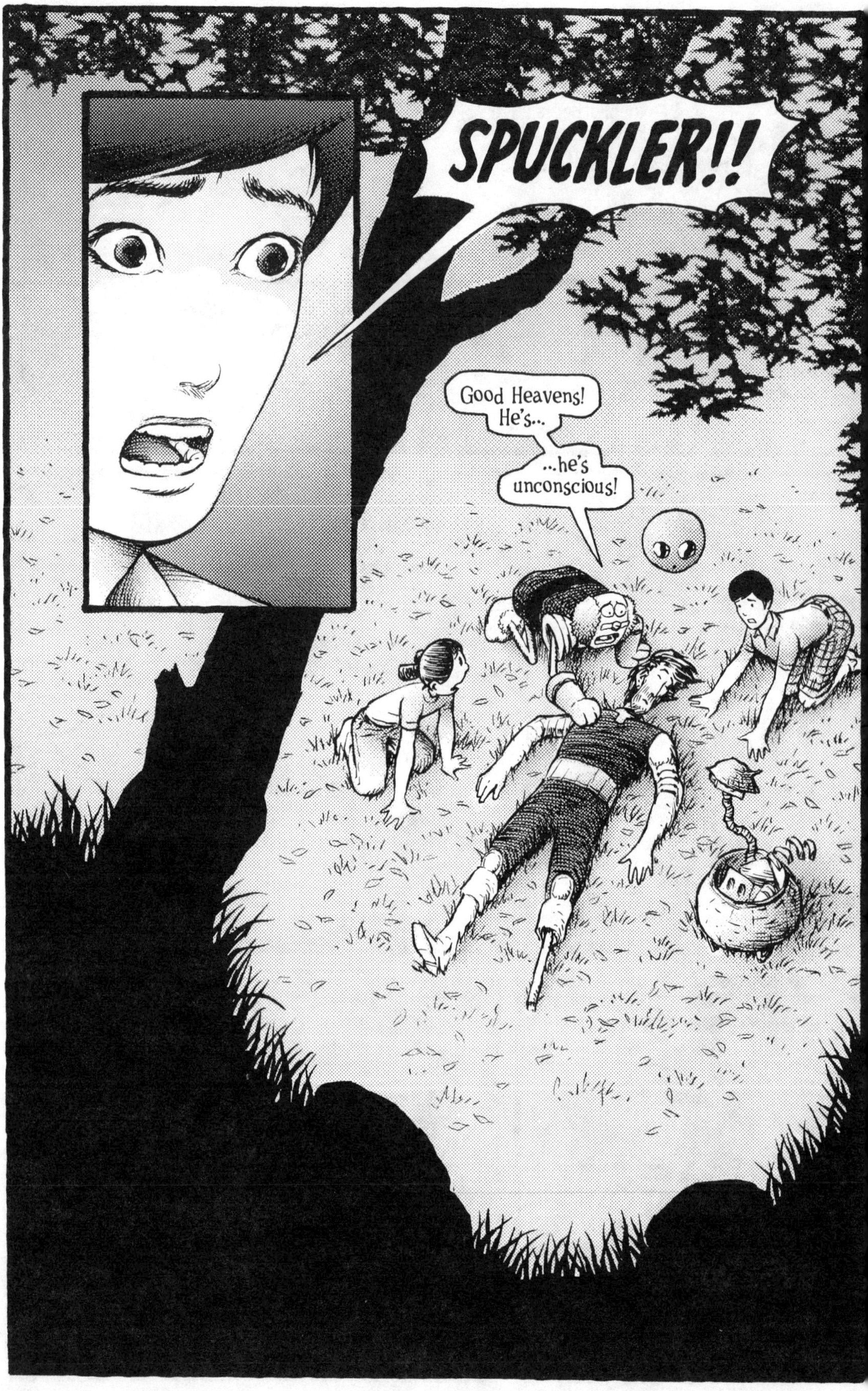
SPUCKLER!!
Good Heavens! He's...
...he's unconscious!

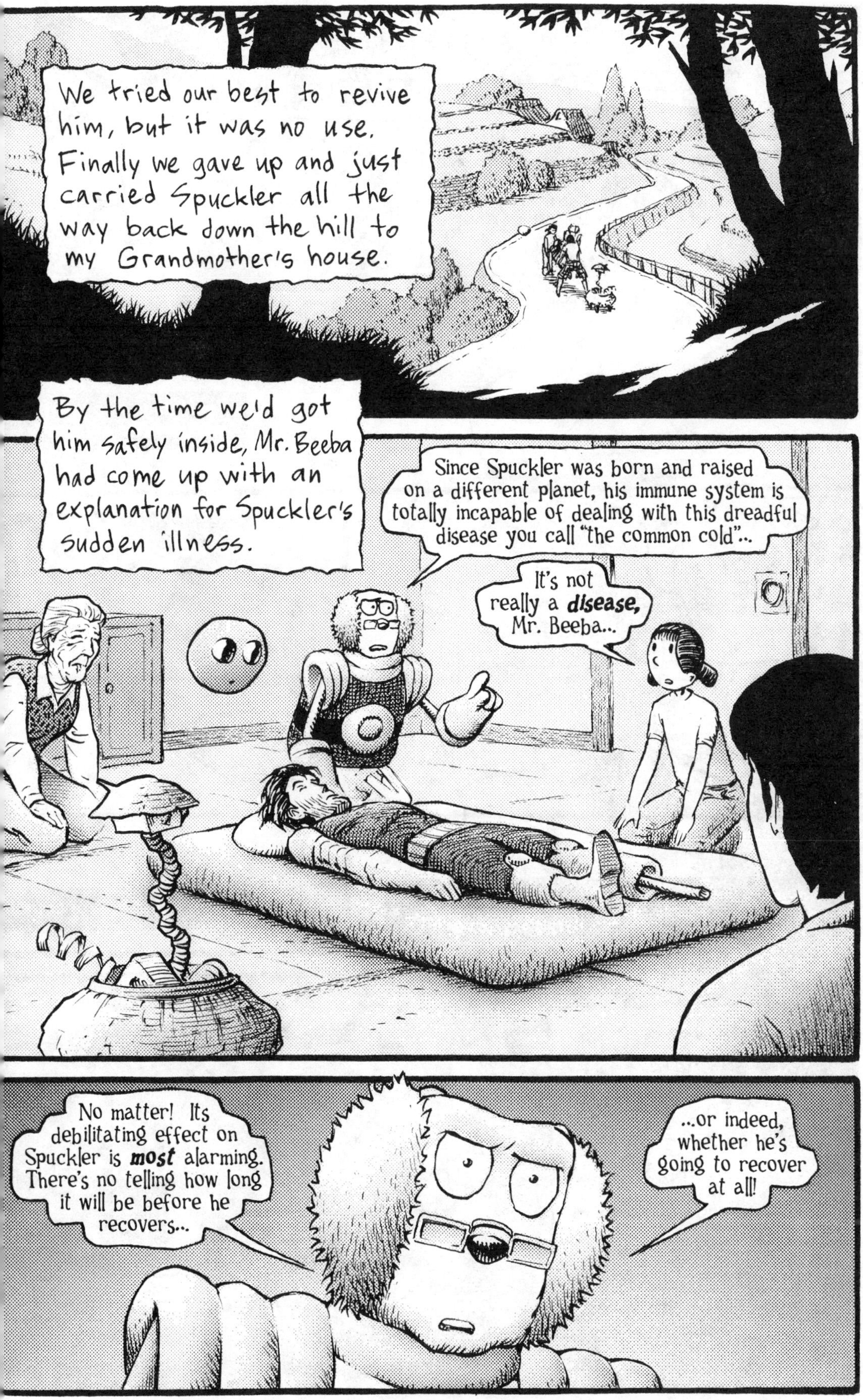

We tried our best to revive him, but it was no use. Finally we gave up and just carried Spuckler all the way back down the hill to my Grandmother's house.
By the time we'd got him safely inside, Mr. Beeba had come up with an explanation for Spuckler's sudden illness.
Since Spuckler was born and raised on a different planet, his immune system is totally incapable of dealing with this dreadful disease you call "the common cold"...
It's not really a ***disease,*** Mr. Beeba...
No matter! Its debilitating effect on Spuckler is ***most*** alarming. There's no telling how long it will be before he recovers...
...or indeed, whether he's going to recover at all!

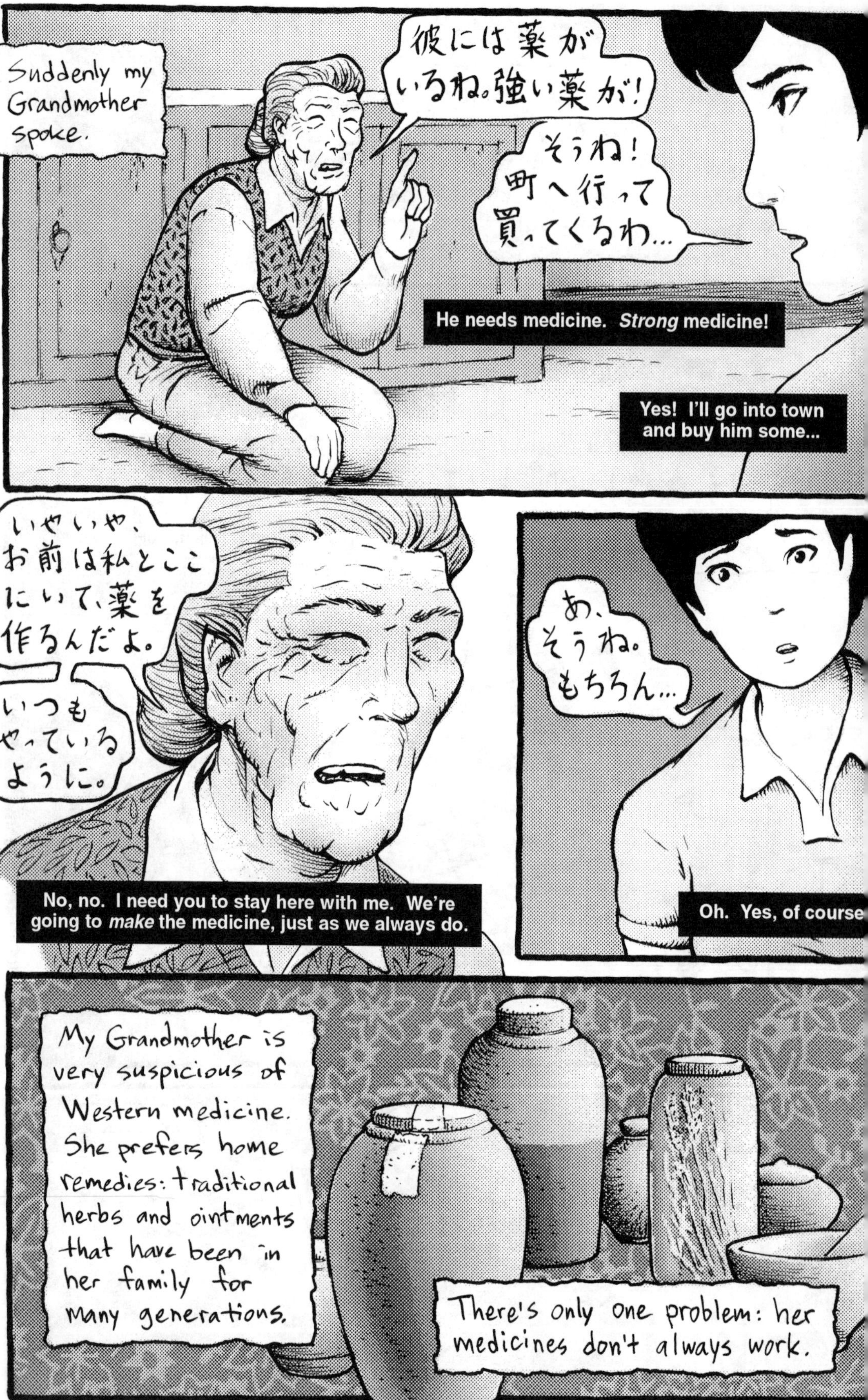
Suddenly my Grandmother spoke.
彼には薬がいるね。強い薬が!
He needs medicine. *Strong* medicine!
そうね!町へ行って買ってくるわ…
Yes! I'll go into town and buy him some...
いやいや、お前は私とここにいて、薬を作るんだよ。
いつもやっているように。
No, no. I need you to stay here with me. We're going to *make* the medicine, just as we always do.
あ、そうね。もちろん…
Oh. Yes, of course
My Grandmother is very suspicious of Western medicine. She prefers home remedies: traditional herbs and ointments that have been in her family for many generations.
There's only one problem: her medicines don't always work.

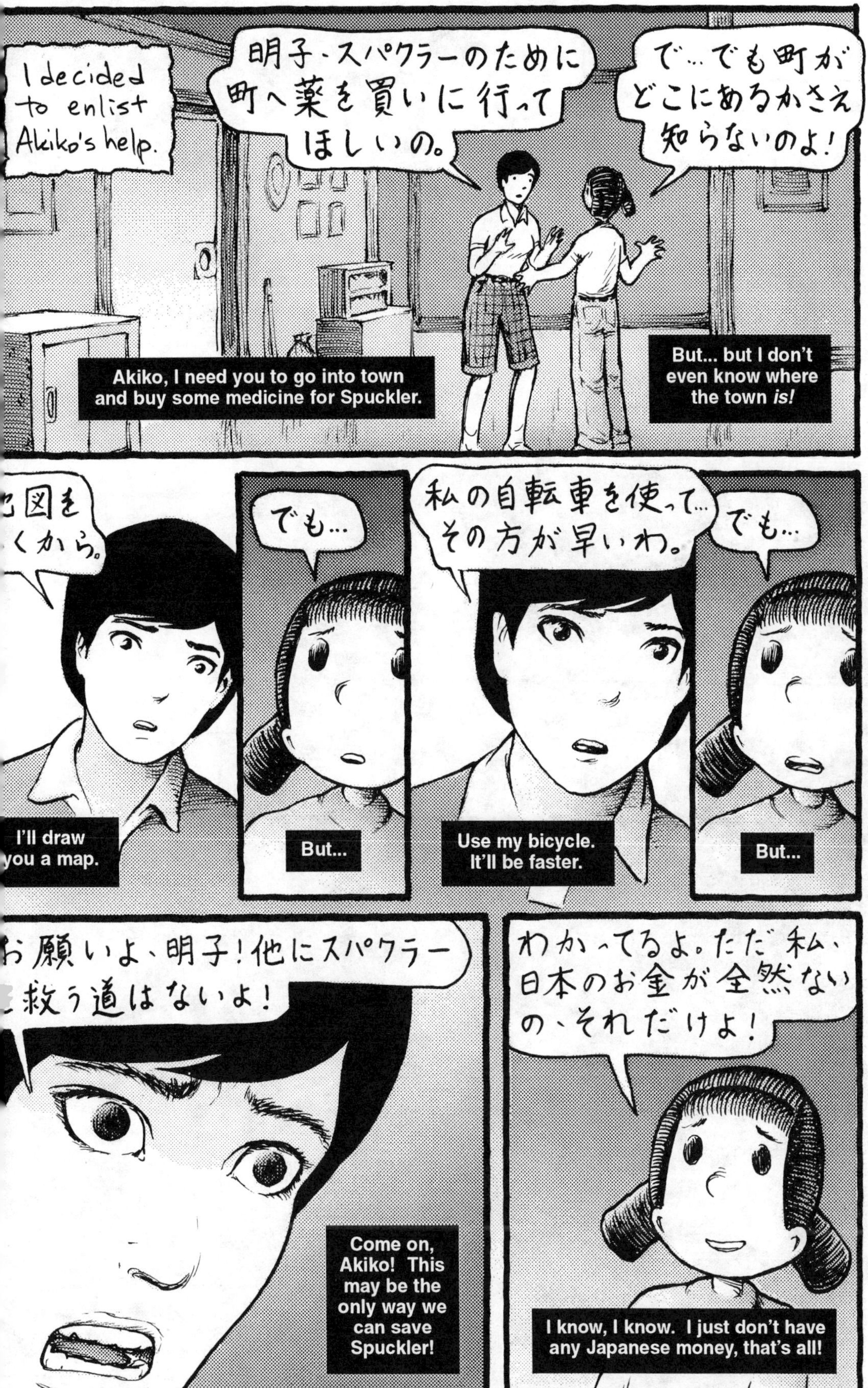

I decided to enlist Akiko's help.
明子・スパクラーのために町へ薬を買いに行ってほしいの。
で…でも町がどこにあるかさえ知らないのよ！
Akiko, I need you to go into town and buy some medicine for Spuckler.
But... but I don't even know where the town *is!*
図を
くから。
I'll draw you a map.
でも…
But...
私の自転車を使って…その方が早いわ。
Use my bicycle. It'll be faster.
でも…
But...
お願いよ、明子！他にスパクラー
救う道はないよ！
Come on, Akiko! This may be the only way we can save Spuckler!
わかってるよ。ただ私、日本のお金が全然ないの、それだけよ！
I know, I know. I just don't have any Japanese money, that's all!

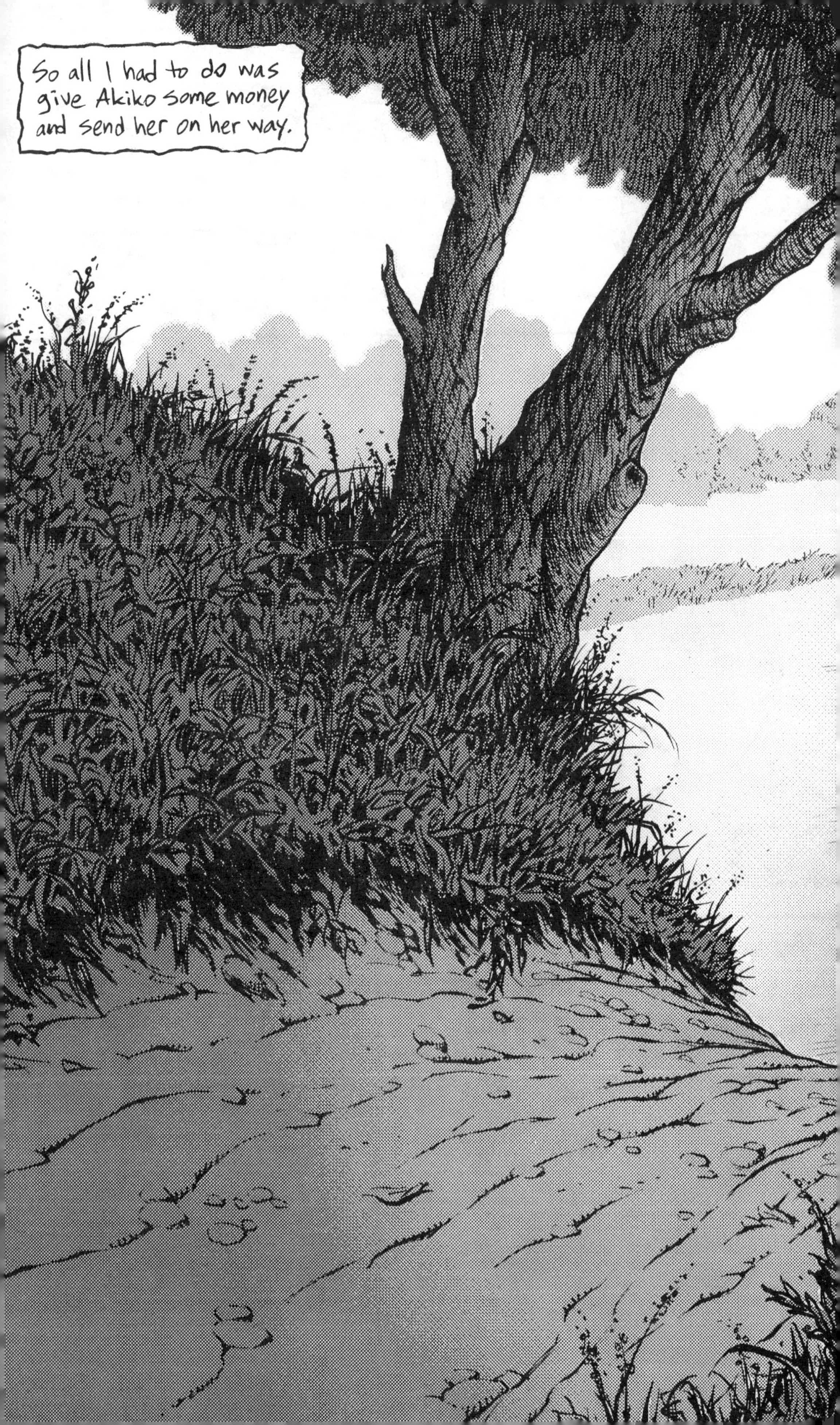
So all I had to do was give Akiko some money and send her on her way.

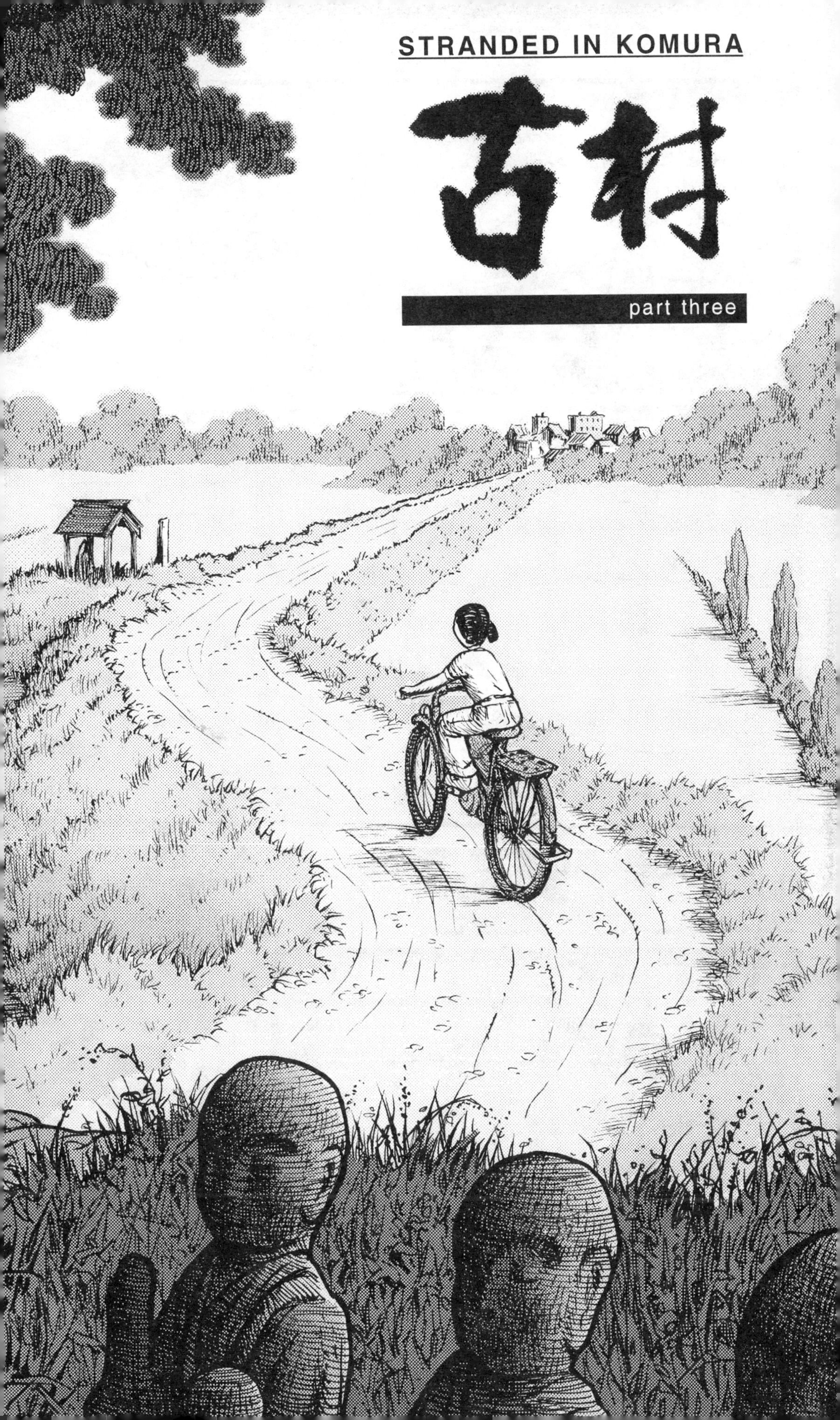
STRANDED IN KOMURA
古村
part three

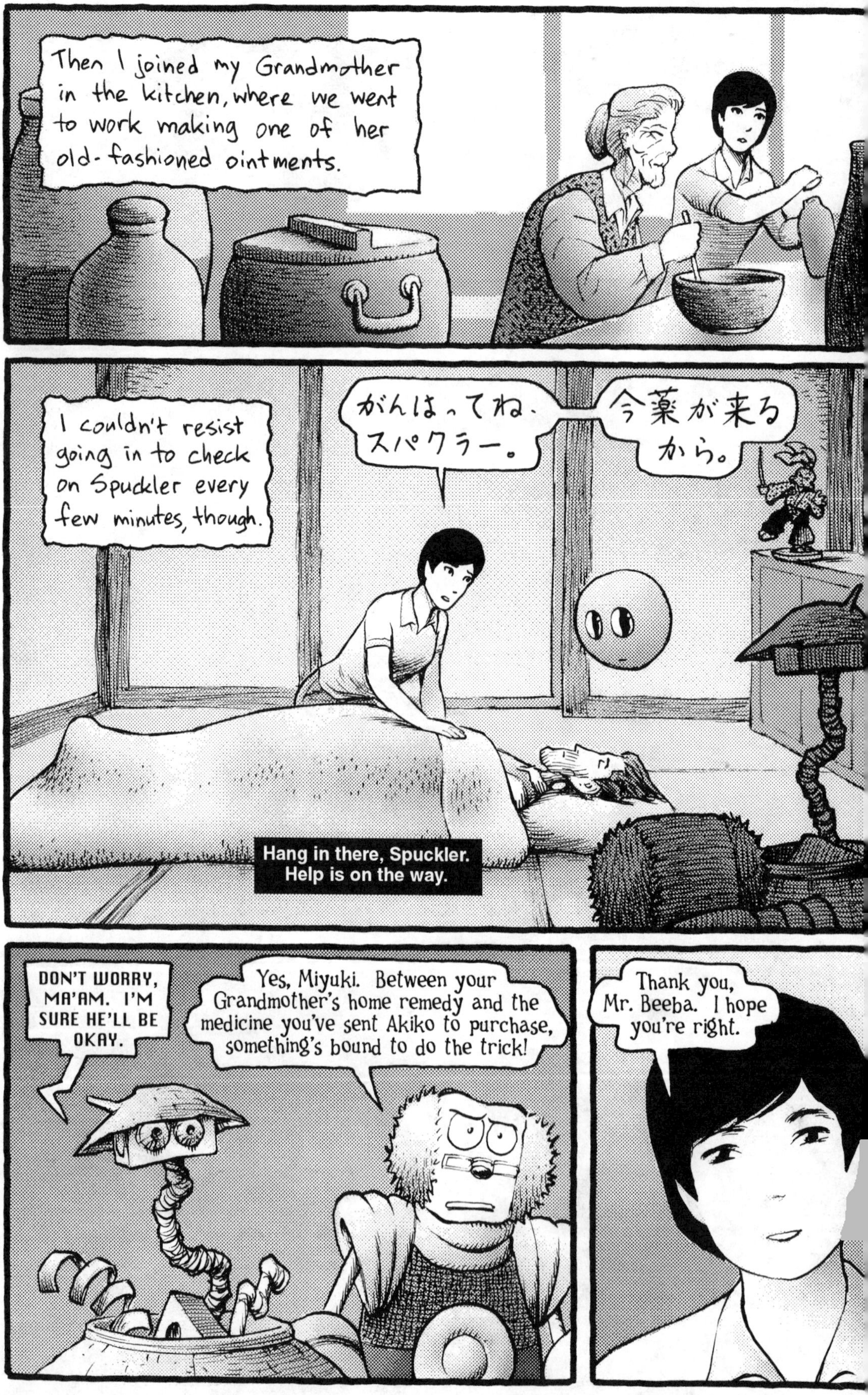
Then I joined my Grandmother in the kitchen, where we went to work making one of her old-fashioned ointments.
I couldn't resist going in to check on Spuckler every few minutes, though.
がんばってね、スパクラー。
今薬が来るから。
Hang in there, Spuckler. Help is on the way.
DON'T WORRY, MA'AM. I'M SURE HE'LL BE OKAY.
Yes, Miyuki. Between your Grandmother's home remedy and the medicine you've sent Akiko to purchase, something's bound to do the trick!
Thank you, Mr. Beeba. I hope you're right.

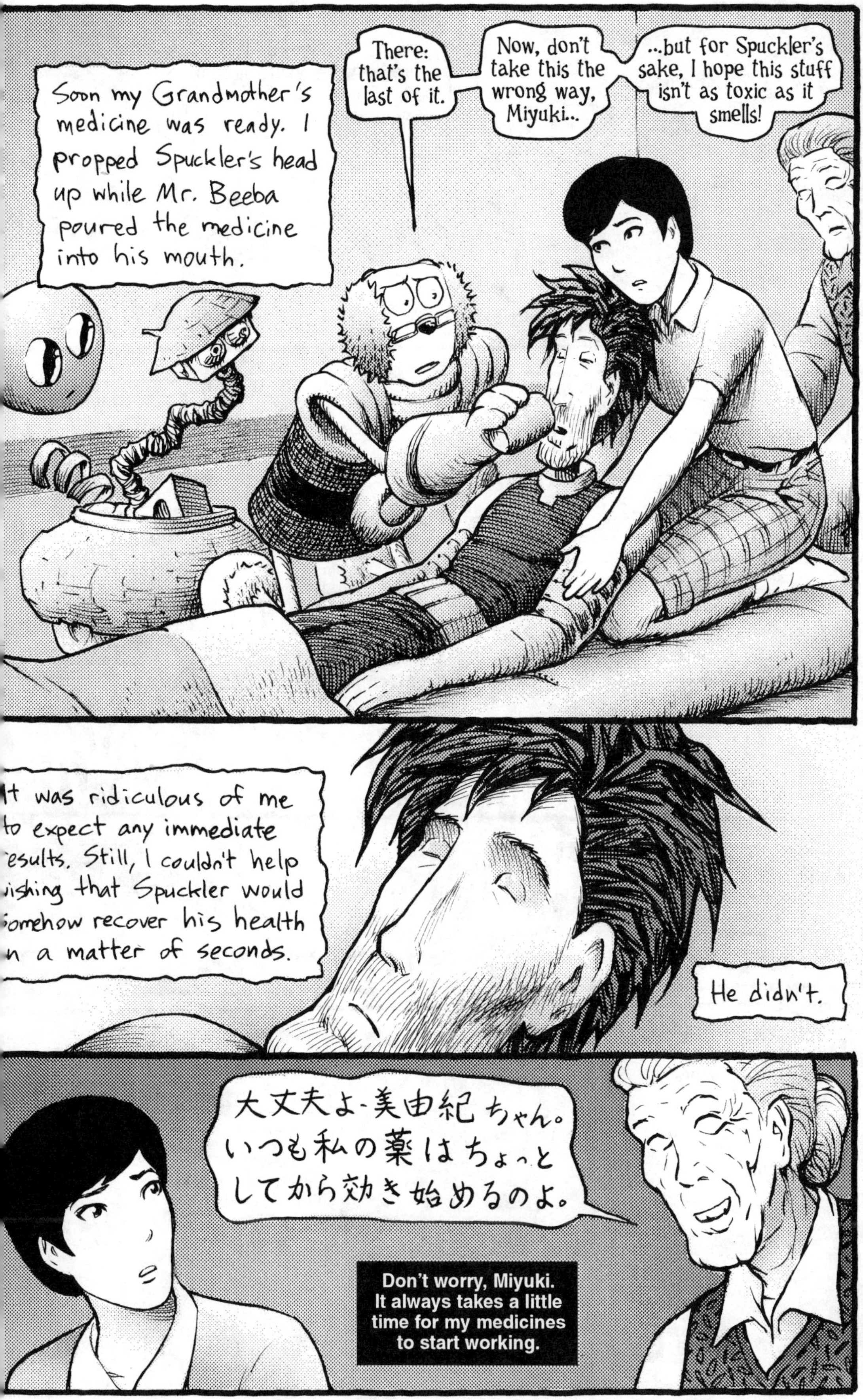

Soon my Grandmother's medicine was ready. I propped Spuckler's head up while Mr. Beeba poured the medicine into his mouth.
There: that's the last of it.
Now, don't take this the wrong way, Miyuki...
...but for Spuckler's sake, I hope this stuff isn't as toxic as it smells!
It was ridiculous of me to expect any immediate esults. Still, I couldn't help ishing that Spuckler would omehow recover his health n a matter of seconds.
He didn't.
大丈夫よ、美由紀ちゃん。いつも私の薬はちょっとしてから効き始めるのよ。
Don't worry, Miyuki. It always takes a little time for my medicines to start working.

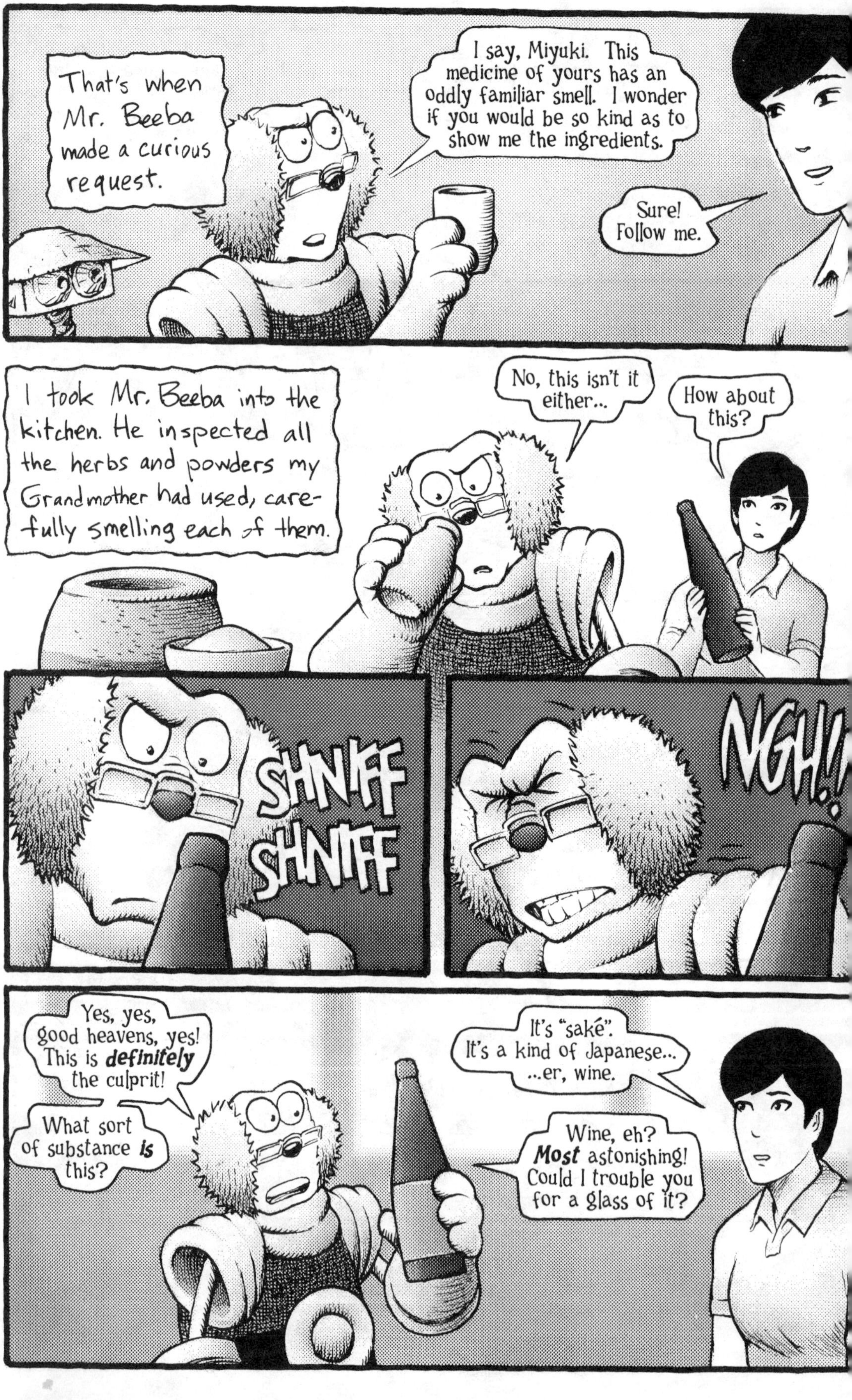
That's when Mr. Beeba made a curious request.
I say, Miyuki. This medicine of yours has an oddly familiar smell. I wonder if you would be so kind as to show me the ingredients.
Sure! Follow me.
I took Mr. Beeba into the kitchen. He inspected all the herbs and powders my Grandmother had used, carefully smelling each of them.
No, this isn't it either...
How about this?
SHNIFF SHNIFF
NGH!!
Yes, yes, good heavens, yes! This is **definitely** the culprit!
What sort of substance **is** this?
It's "saké". It's a kind of Japanese... ...er, wine.
Wine, eh? **Most** astonishing! Could I trouble you for a glass of it?

Have as much you like. But n't drink it too ickly. Saké is very strong!

Trust me, Miyuki. Drinking is **not** what I have in mind.

A few minutes later Akiko returned with a bag full of all sorts of medicine.

うわあ！お店のあらゆる種類の薬を買ってきたのね！

Wow! You must have bought every kind of medicine in the whole store!

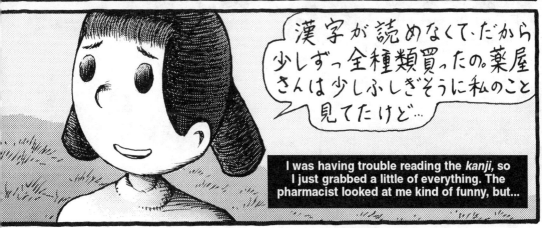

漢字が読めなくて。だから少しずつ全種類買ったの。薬屋さんは少しふしぎそうに私のこと見てたけど…

I was having trouble reading the *kanji*, so I just grabbed a little of everything. The pharmacist looked at me kind of funny, but...

明子!これ下剤じゃない!

なるほど。それで彼変な目で私を見てたんだ…

Akiko! This is a *laxative!*

No *wonder* he looked at me funny...

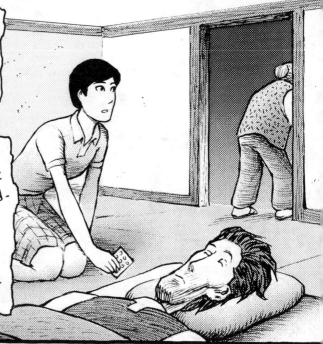

Fortunately, at least one of the medicines Akiko bought was the kind of thing I was looking for.

It wouldn't have been so hard to give Spuckler the medicine without my Grandmother knowing, but I didn't want to take any chances. I waited until she left the room before I made my move.

But just as I was about to put the medicine in Spuckler's mouth, I realized that I was being watched.

It was Poog.

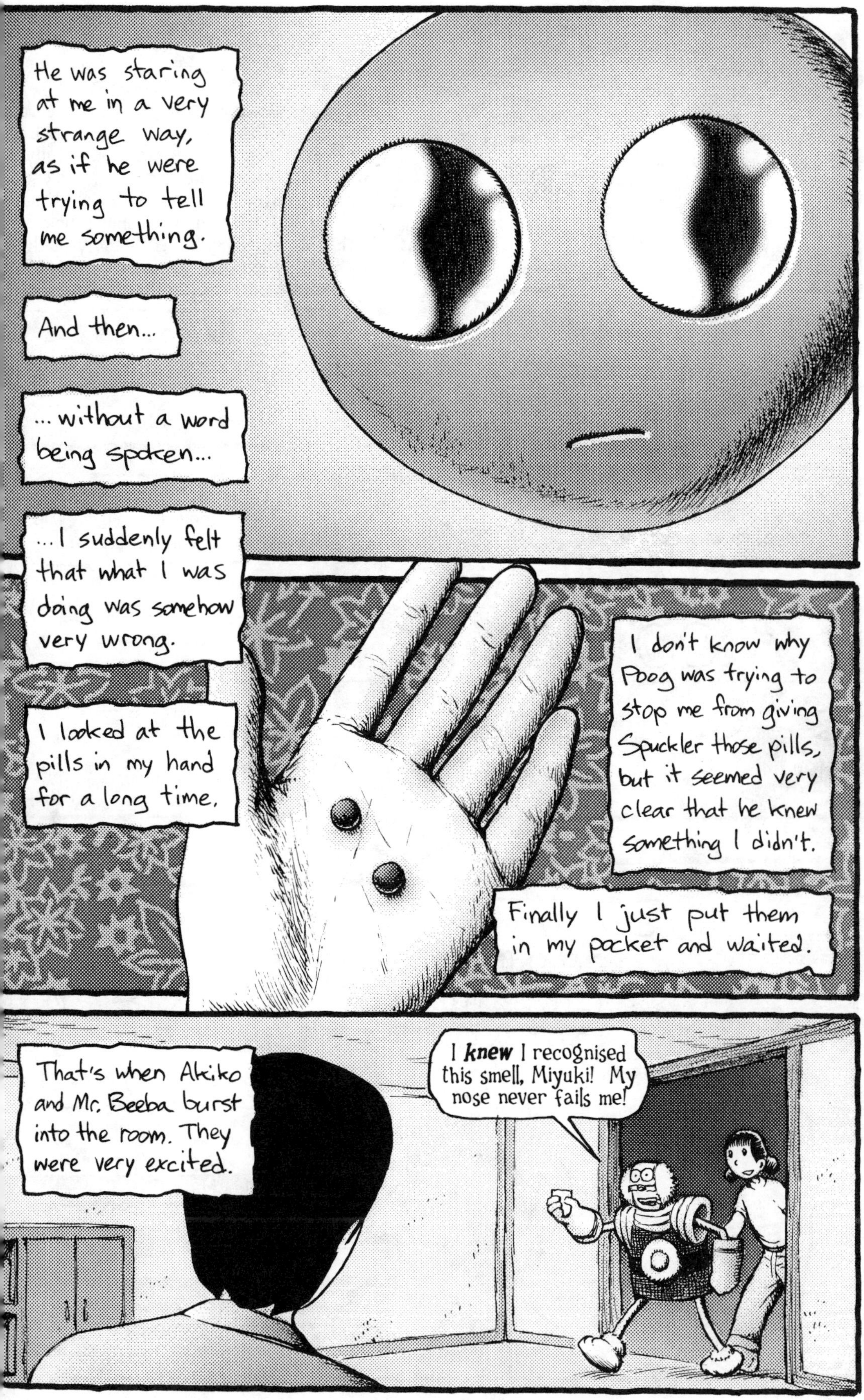
He was staring at me in a very strange way, as if he were trying to tell me something.
And then...
... without a word being spoken...
...I suddenly felt that what I was doing was somehow very wrong.
I looked at the pills in my hand for a long time.
I don't know why Poog was trying to stop me from giving Spuckler those pills, but it seemed very clear that he knew something I didn't.
Finally I just put them in my pocket and waited.
That's when Akiko and Mr. Beeba burst into the room. They were very excited.
I **knew** I recognised this smell, Miyuki! My nose never fails me!

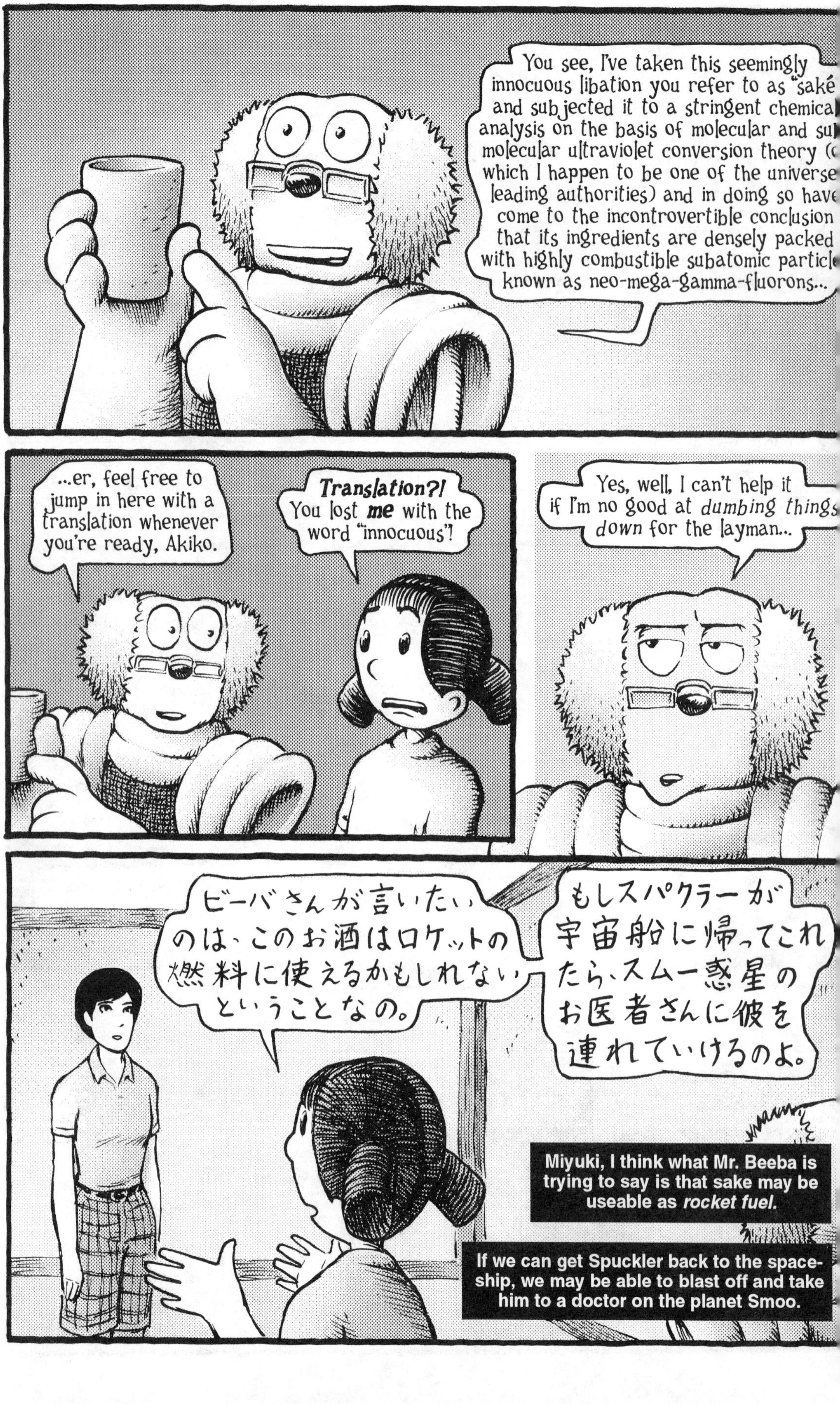
You see, I've taken this seemingly innocuous libation you refer to as "saké and subjected it to a stringent chemica analysis on the basis of molecular and su molecular ultraviolet conversion theory (c which I happen to be one of the universe leading authorities) and in doing so have come to the incontrovertible conclusion that its ingredients are densely packed with highly combustible subatomic particl known as neo-mega-gamma-fluorons...
...er, feel free to jump in here with a translation whenever you're ready, Akiko.
Translation?! You lost **me** with the word "innocuous"!
Yes, well, I can't help it if I'm no good at *dumbing things down* for the layman...
ビーバさんが言いたいのは、このお酒はロケットの燃料に使えるかもしれないということなの。
もしスパクラーが宇宙船に帰ってこれたら、スムー惑星のお医者さんに彼を連れていけるのよ。
Miyuki, I think what Mr. Beeba is trying to say is that sake may be useable as *rocket fuel.*
If we can get Spuckler back to the spaceship, we may be able to blast off and take him to a doctor on the planet Smoo.

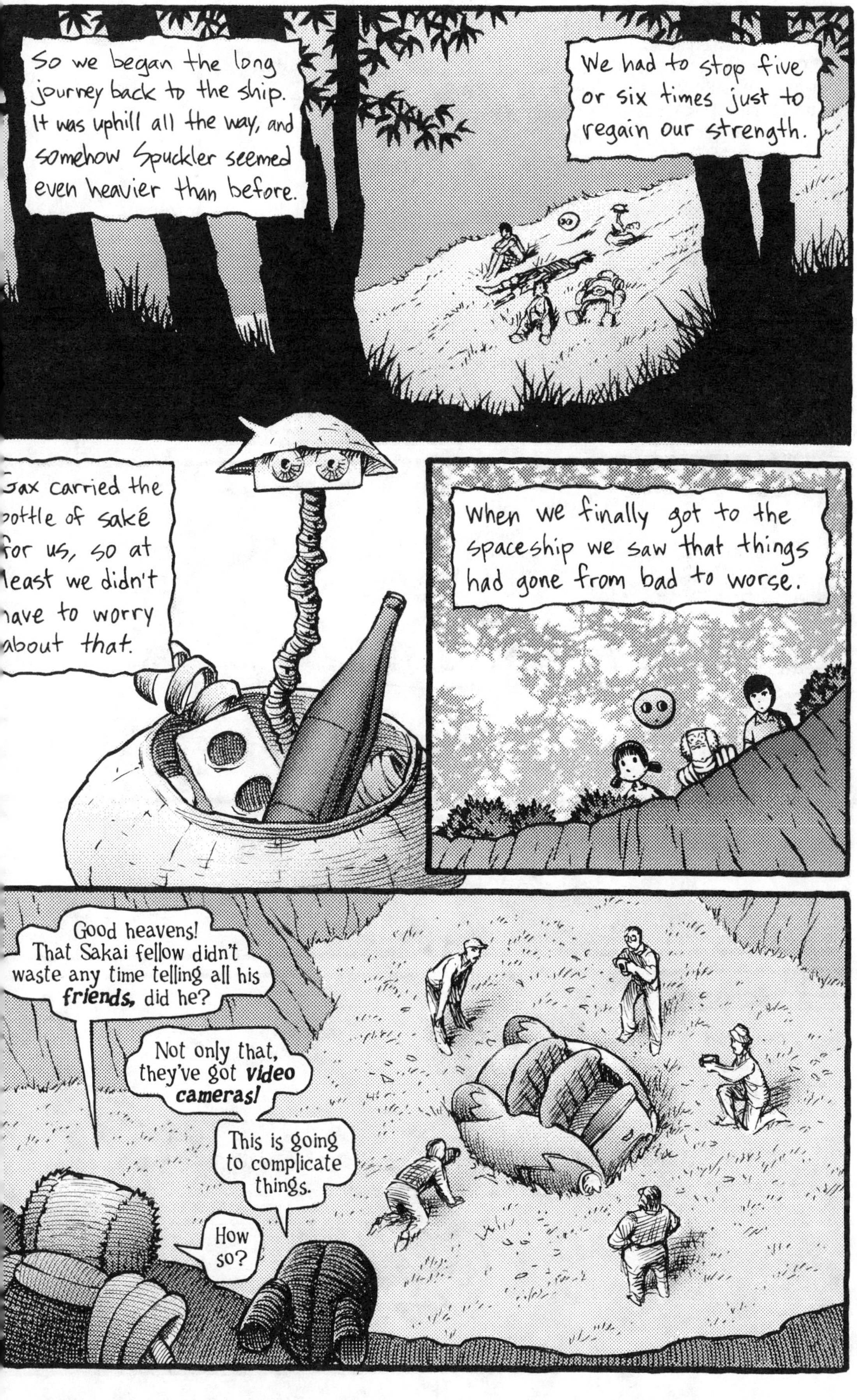

So we began the long journey back to the ship. It was uphill all the way, and somehow Spuckler seemed even heavier than before.
We had to stop five or six times just to regain our strength.
Gax carried the bottle of saké for us, so at least we didn't have to worry about that.
When we finally got to the spaceship we saw that things had gone from bad to worse.
Good heavens! That Sakai fellow didn't waste any time telling all his friends, did he?
Not only that, they've got video cameras!
This is going to complicate things.
How so?

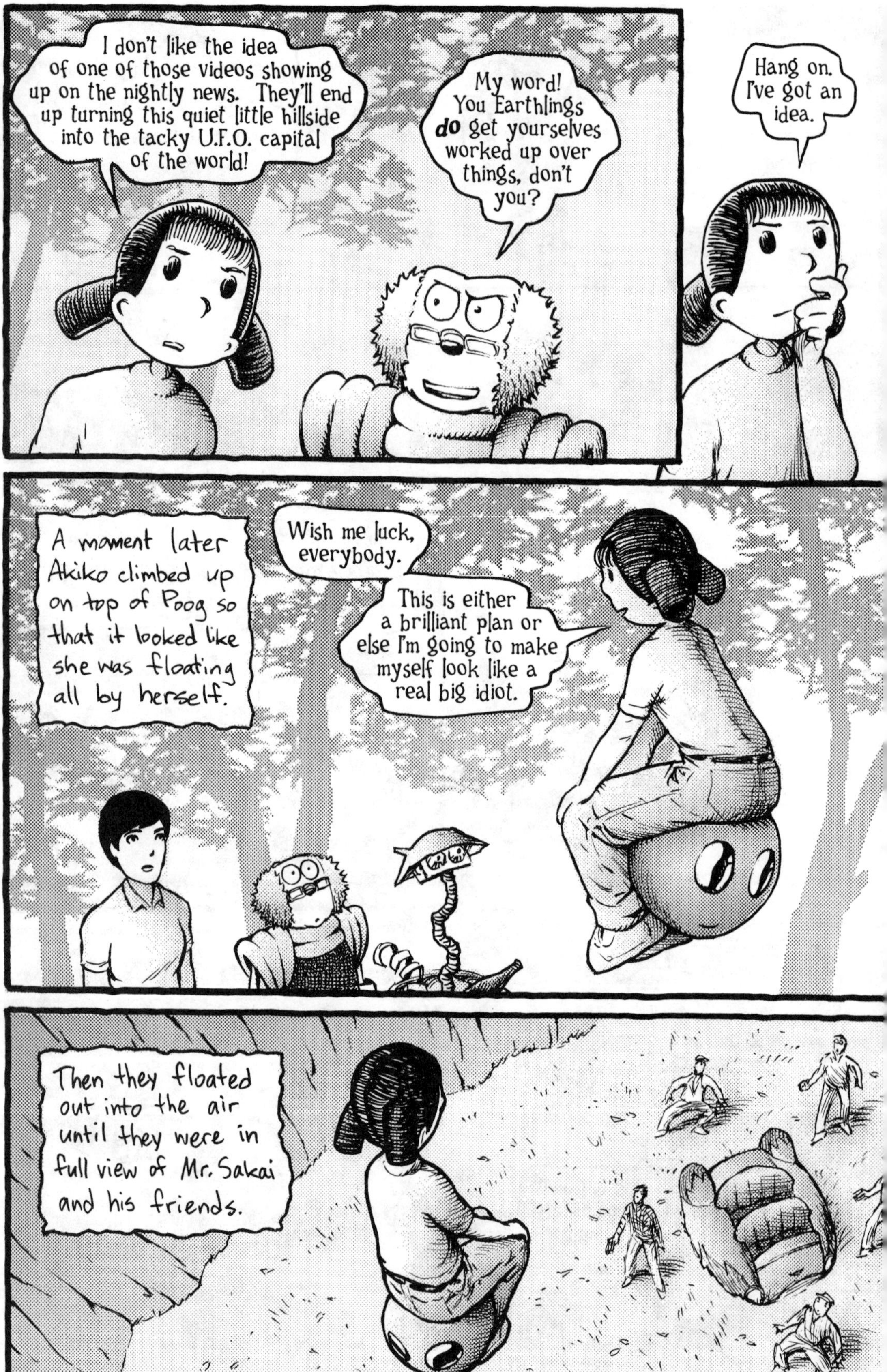
I don't like the idea of one of those videos showing up on the nightly news. They'll end up turning this quiet little hillside into the tacky U.F.O. capital of the world!
My word! You Earthlings **do** get yourselves worked up over things, don't you?
Hang on. I've got an idea.
A moment later Akiko climbed up on top of Poog so that it looked like she was floating all by herself.
Wish me luck, everybody.
This is either a brilliant plan or else I'm going to make myself look like a real big idiot.
Then they floated out into the air until they were in full view of Mr. Sakai and his friends.

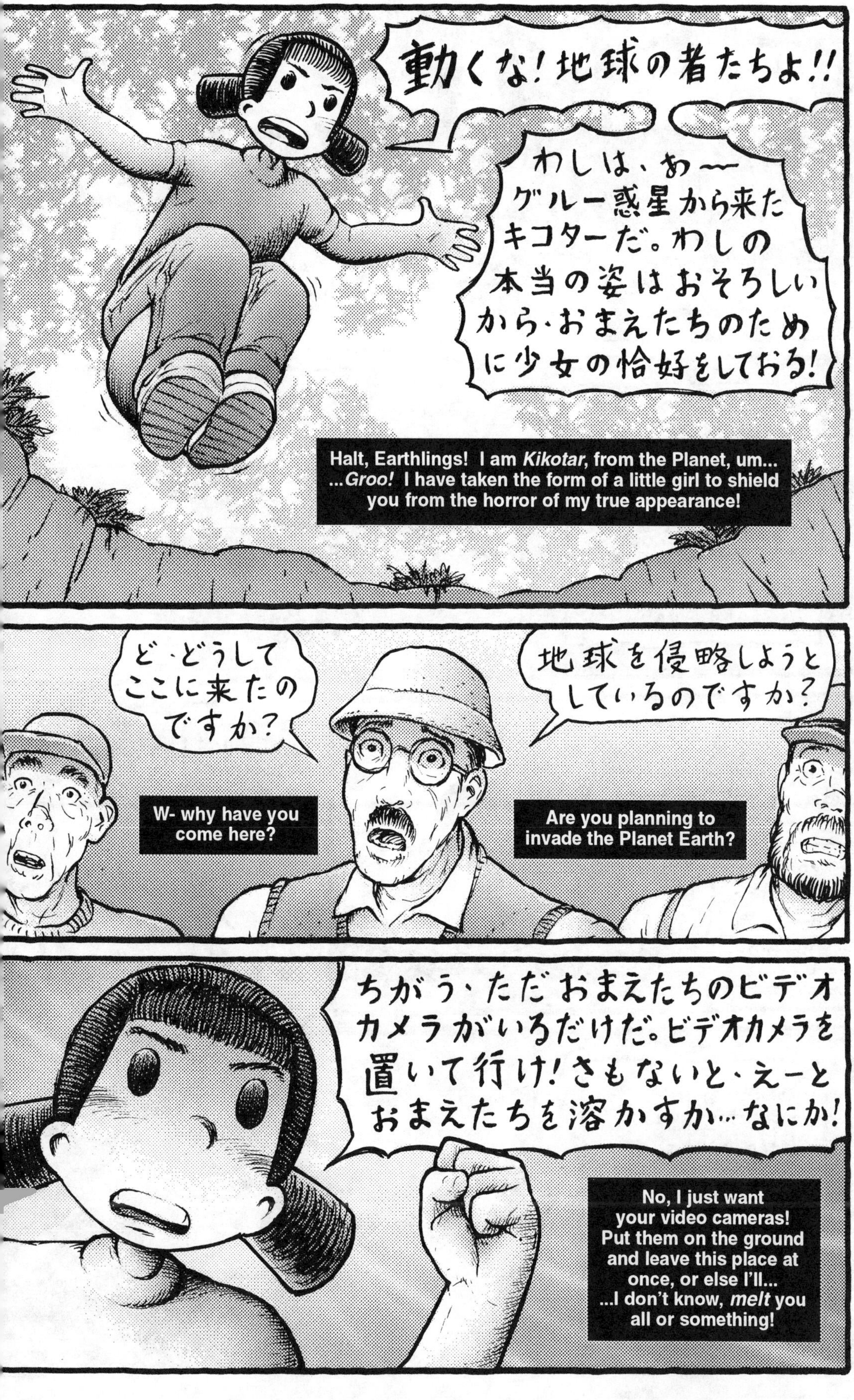

動くな！地球の者たちよ！！
わしは、あ〜〜グルー惑星から来たキコターだ。わしの本当の姿はおそろしいから・おまえたちのために少女の恰好をしておる！
Halt, Earthlings! I am *Kikotar*, from the Planet, um... ...*Groo!* I have taken the form of a little girl to shield you from the horror of my true appearance!
ど・どうしてここに来たのですか？
W- why have you come here?
地球を侵略しようとしているのですか？
Are you planning to invade the Planet Earth?
ちがう、ただおまえたちのビデオカメラがいるだけだ。ビデオカメラを置いて行け！さもないと、えーとおまえたちを溶かすか…なにか！
No, I just want your video cameras! Put them on the ground and leave this place at once, or else I'll... ...I don't know, *melt* you all or something!

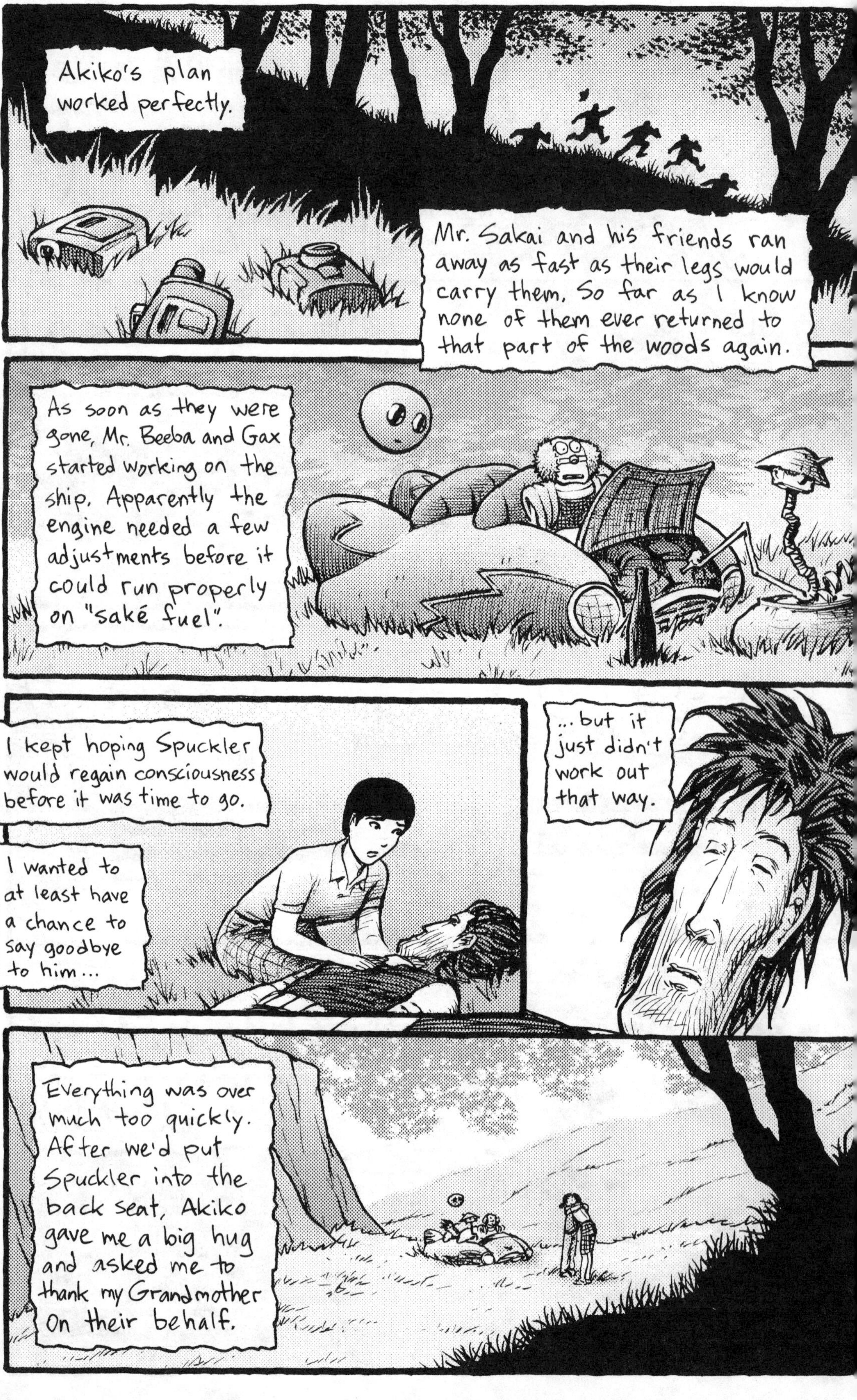
Akiko's plan worked perfectly.
Mr. Sakai and his friends ran away as fast as their legs would carry them. So far as I know none of them ever returned to that part of the woods again.
As soon as they were gone, Mr. Beeba and Gax started working on the ship. Apparently the engine needed a few adjustments before it could run properly on "saké fuel".
I kept hoping Spuckler would regain consciousness before it was time to go.
I wanted to at least have a chance to say goodbye to him...
...but it just didn't work out that way.
Everything was over much too quickly. After we'd put Spuckler into the back seat, Akiko gave me a big hug and asked me to thank my Grandmother on their behalf.

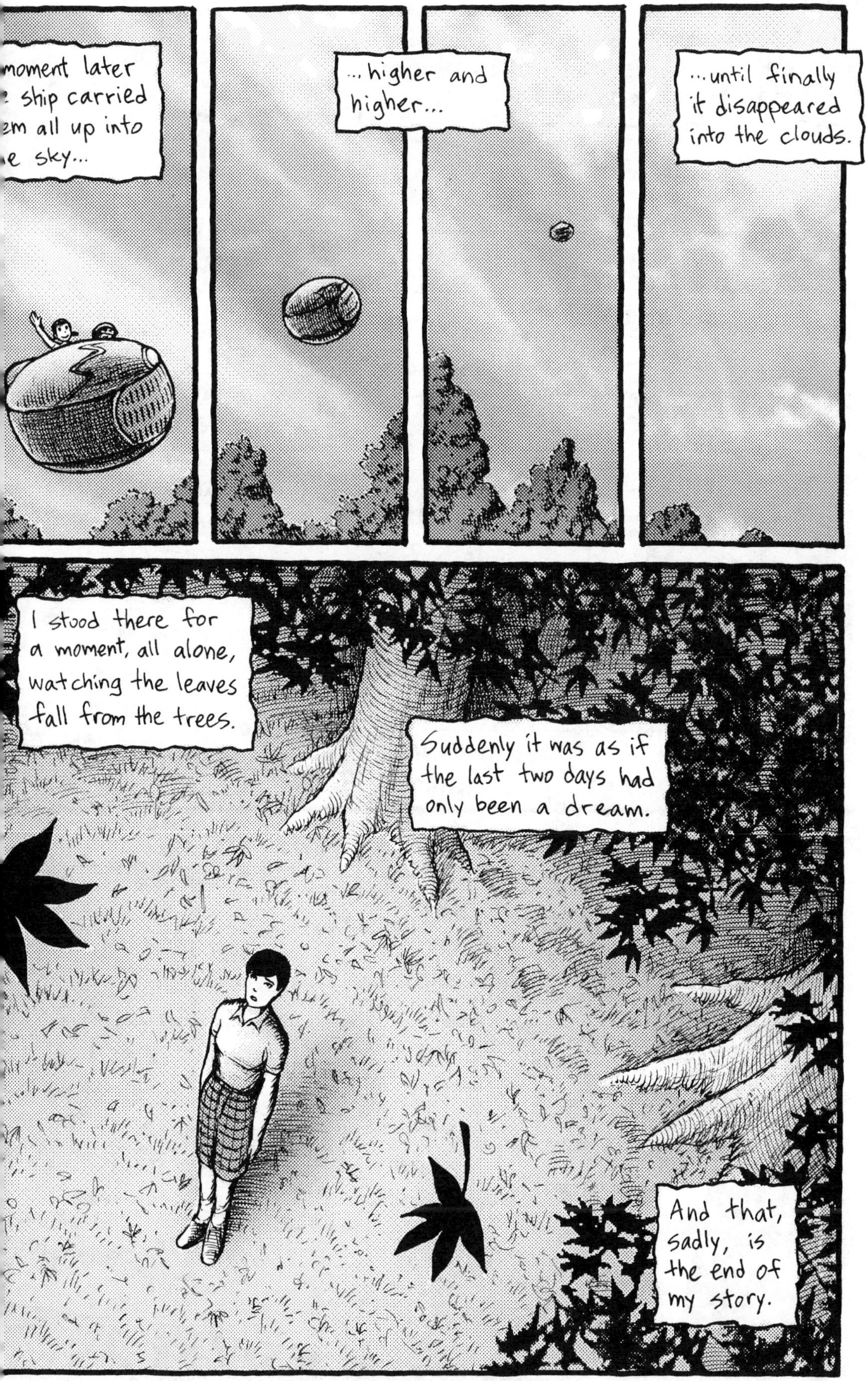
moment later
ship carried
em all up into
e sky...
...higher and
higher...
...until finally
it disappeared
into the clouds.
I stood there for
a moment, all alone,
watching the leaves
fall from the trees.
Suddenly it was as if
the last two days had
only been a dream.
And that,
sadly, is
the end of
my story.

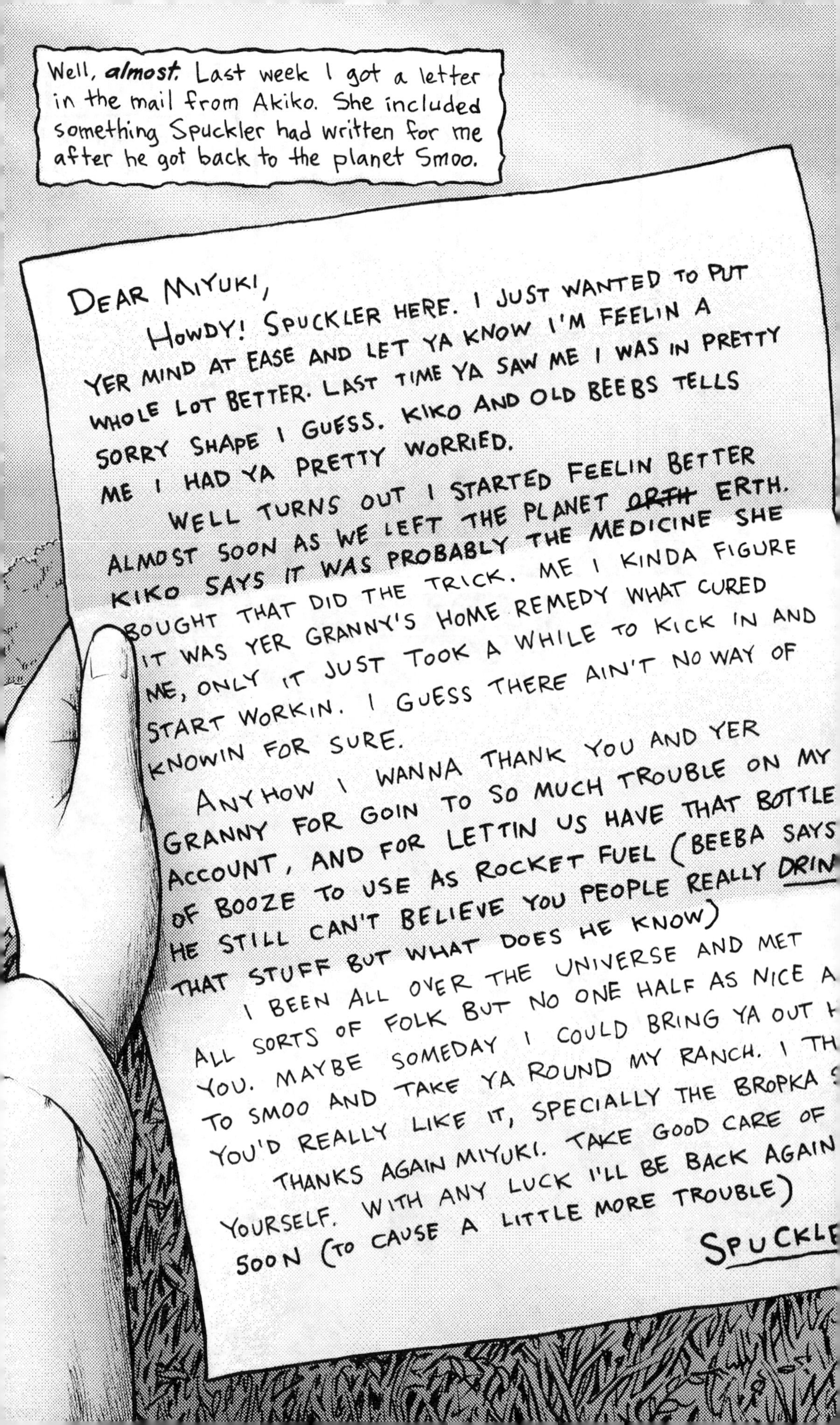
Well, *almost.* Last week I got a letter in the mail from Akiko. She included something Spuckler had written for me after he got back to the planet Smoo.
DEAR MIYUKI,
HOWDY! SPUCKLER HERE. I JUST WANTED TO PUT
YER MIND AT EASE AND LET YA KNOW I'M FEELIN A
WHOLE LOT BETTER. LAST TIME YA SAW ME I WAS IN PRETTY
SORRY SHAPE I GUESS. KIKO AND OLD BEEBS TELLS
ME I HAD YA PRETTY WORRIED.
WELL TURNS OUT I STARTED FEELIN BETTER
ALMOST SOON AS WE LEFT THE PLANET ~~ORTH~~ ERTH.
KIKO SAYS IT WAS PROBABLY THE MEDICINE SHE
BOUGHT THAT DID THE TRICK. ME I KINDA FIGURE
IT WAS YER GRANNY'S HOME REMEDY WHAT CURED
ME, ONLY IT JUST TOOK A WHILE TO KICK IN AND
START WORKIN. I GUESS THERE AIN'T NO WAY OF
KNOWIN FOR SURE.
ANYHOW I WANNA THANK YOU AND YER
GRANNY FOR GOIN TO SO MUCH TROUBLE ON MY
ACCOUNT, AND FOR LETTIN US HAVE THAT BOTTLE
OF BOOZE TO USE AS ROCKET FUEL (BEEBA SAYS
HE STILL CAN'T BELIEVE YOU PEOPLE REALLY DRIN
THAT STUFF BUT WHAT DOES HE KNOW)
I BEEN ALL OVER THE UNIVERSE AND MET
ALL SORTS OF FOLK BUT NO ONE HALF AS NICE A
YOU. MAYBE SOMEDAY I COULD BRING YA OUT
TO SMOO AND TAKE YA ROUND MY RANCH. I TH
YOU'D REALLY LIKE IT, SPECIALLY THE BROPKA
THANKS AGAIN MIYUKI. TAKE GOOD CARE OF
YOURSELF. WITH ANY LUCK I'LL BE BACK AGAIN
SOON (TO CAUSE A LITTLE MORE TROUBLE)
SPUCKLE

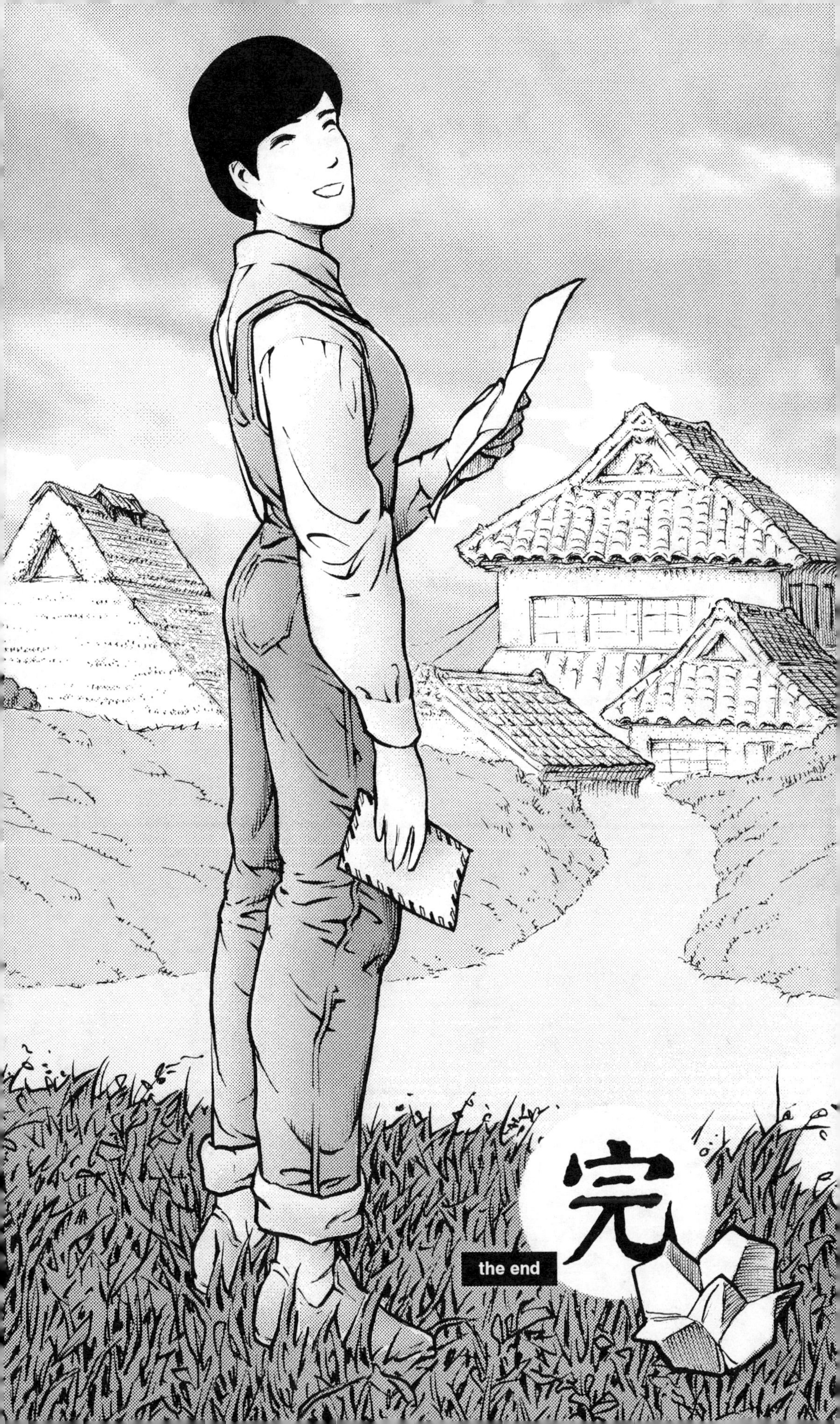
完
the end

Moonshopping

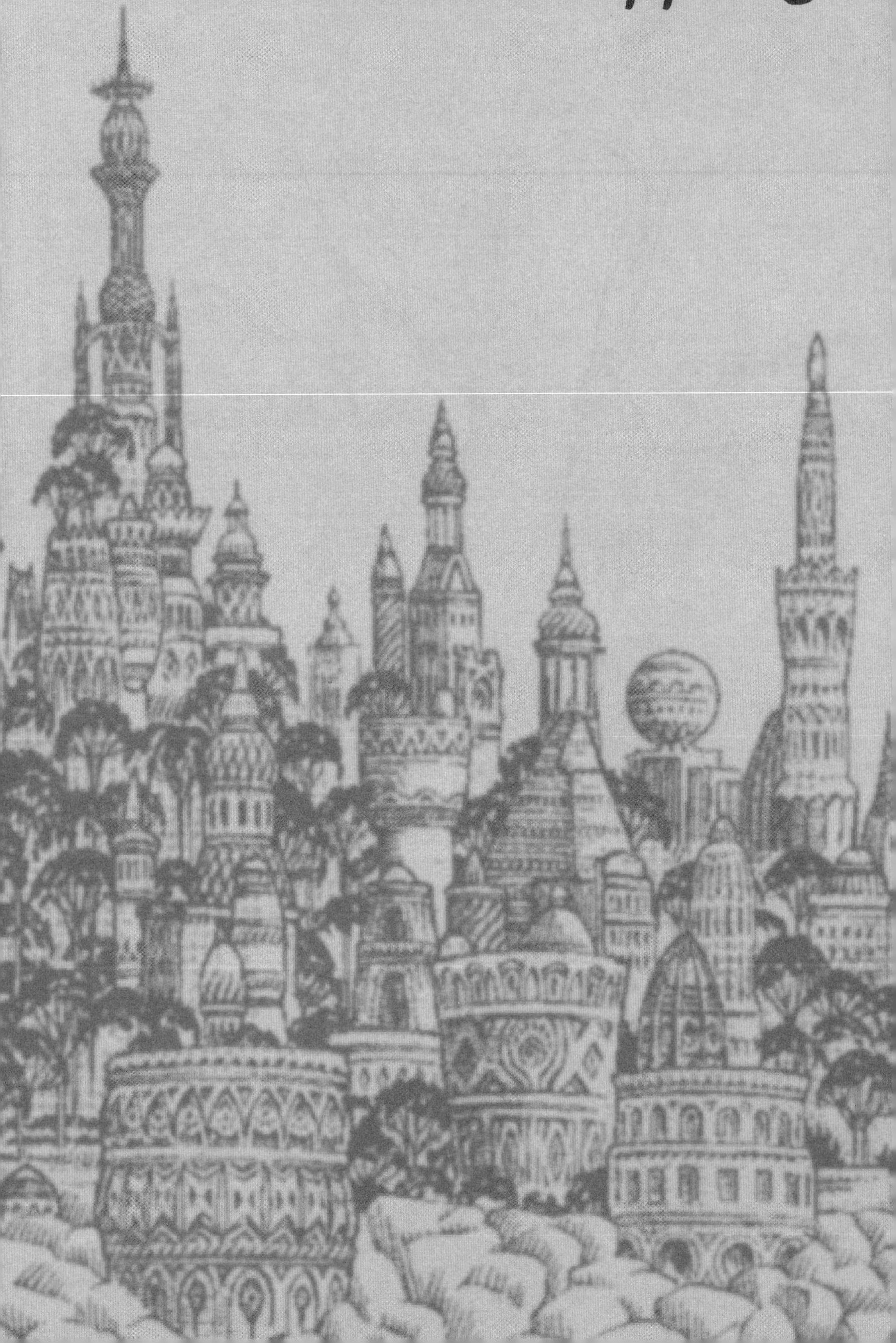

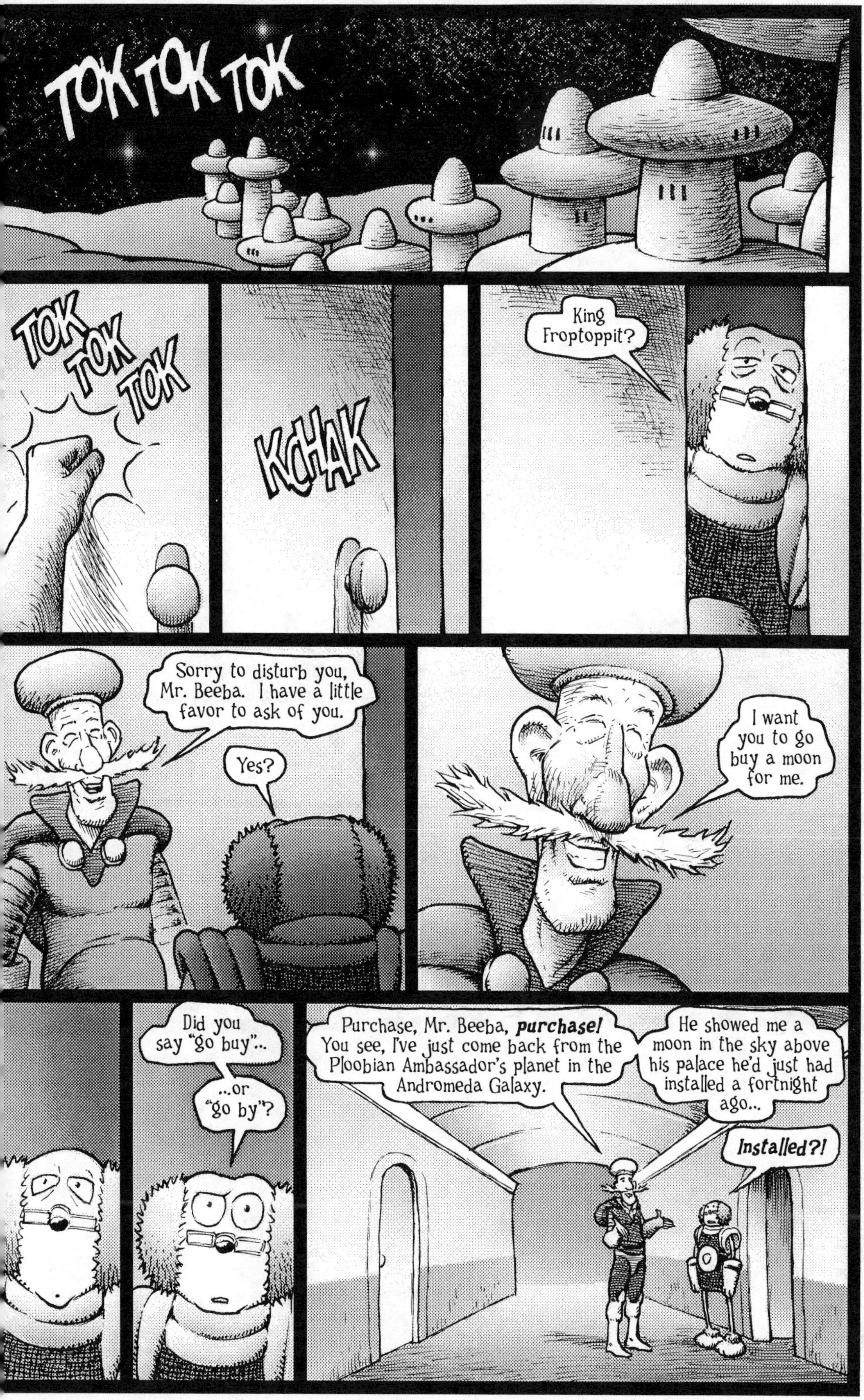
TOK TOK TOK
TOK TOK TOK
KCHAK
King Froptoppit?
Sorry to disturb you, Mr. Beeba. I have a little favor to ask of you.
Yes?
I want you to go buy a moon for me.
Did you say "go buy"...
...or "go by"?
Purchase, Mr. Beeba, *purchase!* You see, I've just come back from the Ploobian Ambassador's planet in the Andromeda Galaxy.
He showed me a moon in the sky above his palace he'd just had installed a fortnight ago...
Installed?!

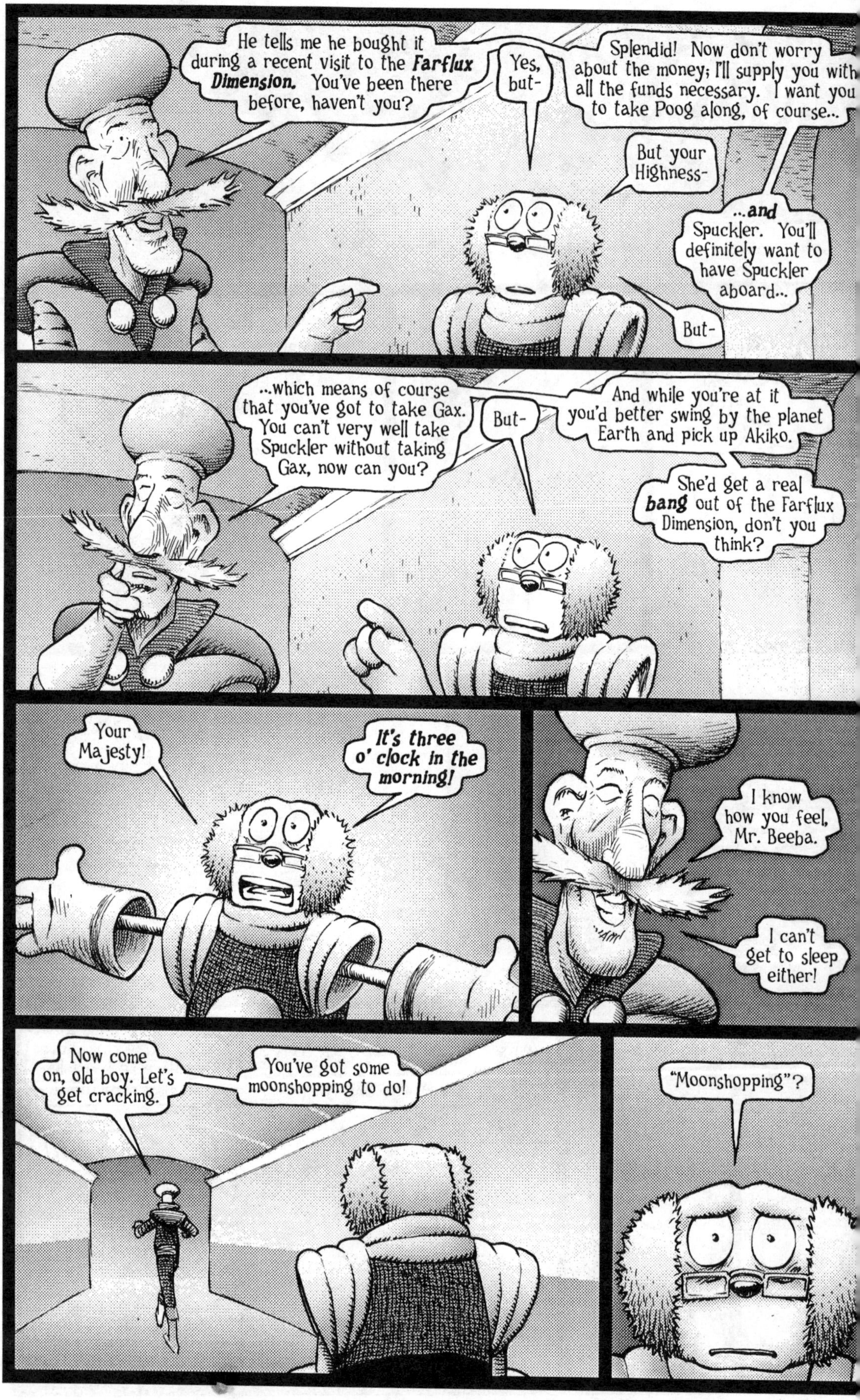
He tells me he bought it during a recent visit to the **Farflux Dimension.** You've been there before, haven't you?
Yes, but-
Splendid! Now don't worry about the money; I'll supply you with all the funds necessary. I want you to take Poog along, of course...
But your Highness-
...and Spuckler. You'll definitely want to have Spuckler aboard...
But-
...which means of course that you've got to take Gax. You can't very well take Spuckler without taking Gax, now can you?
But-
And while you're at it you'd better swing by the planet Earth and pick up Akiko.
She'd get a real **bang** out of the Farflux Dimension, don't you think?
Your Majesty!
It's three o' clock in the morning!
I know how you feel, Mr. Beeba.
I can't get to sleep either!
Now come on, old boy. Let's get cracking.
You've got some moonshopping to do!
"Moonshopping"?

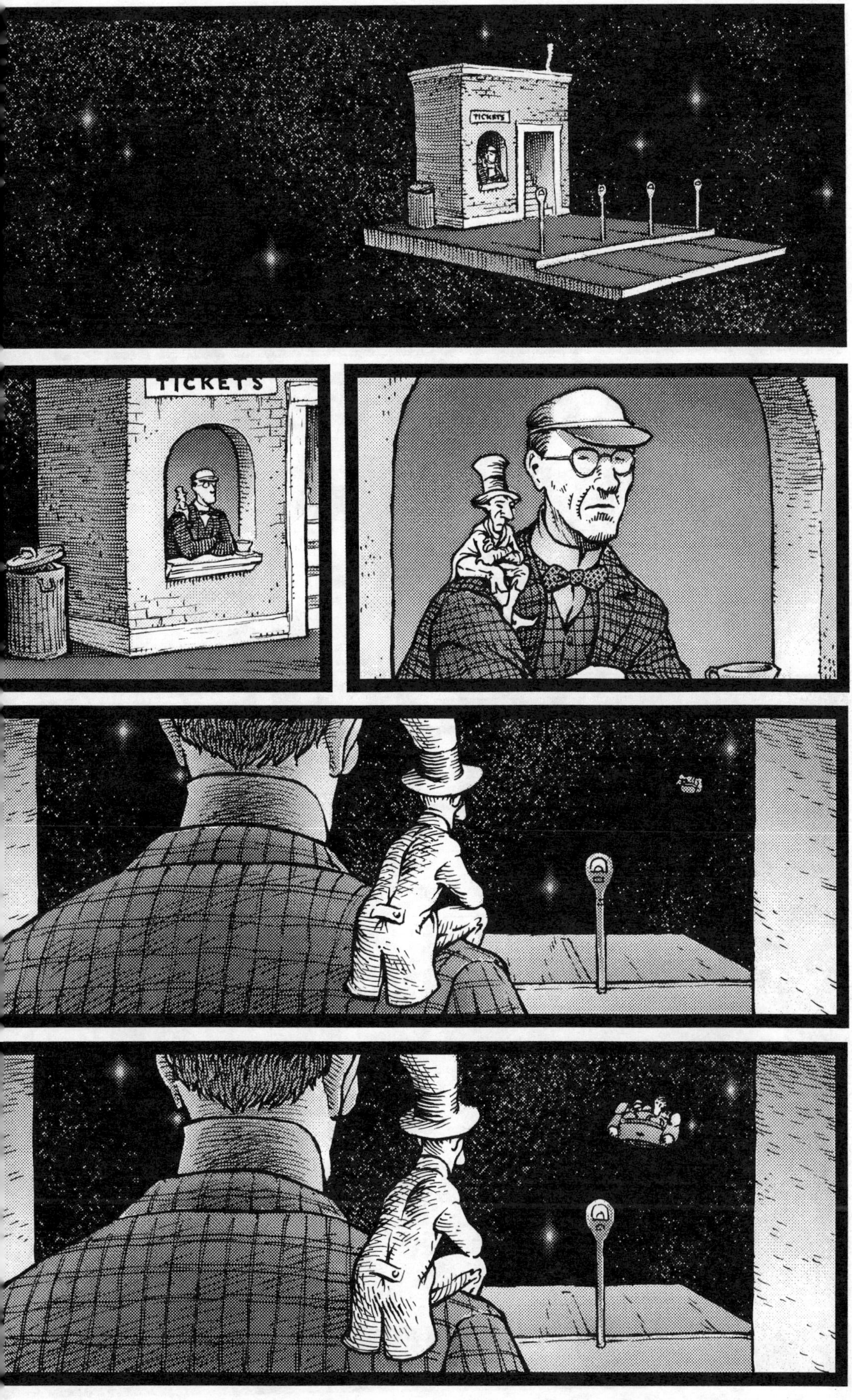
TICKETS
TICKETS

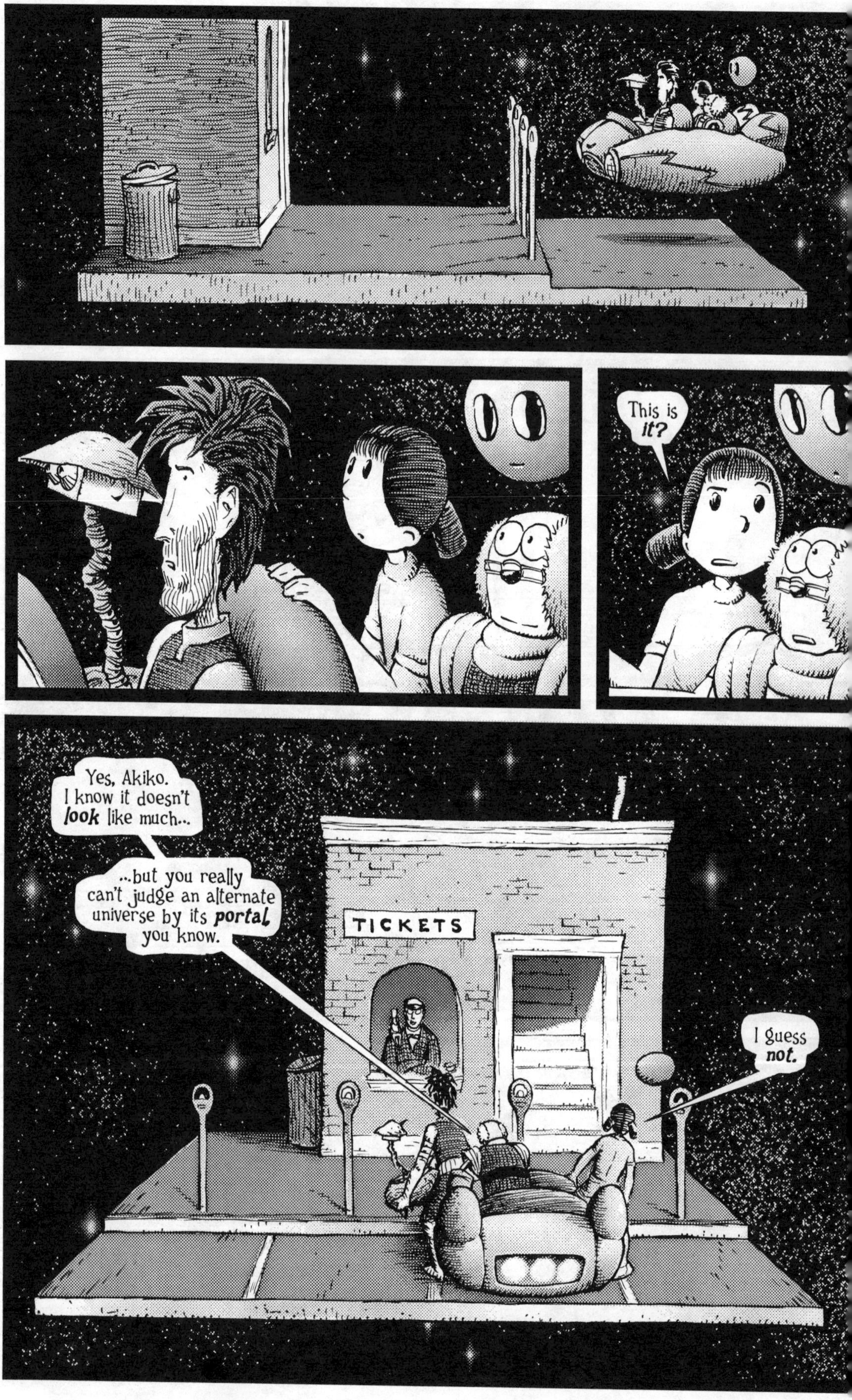
This is *it?*
Yes, Akiko. I know it doesn't ***look*** like much...
...but you really can't judge an alternate universe by its ***portal,*** you know.
TICKETS
I guess ***not.***

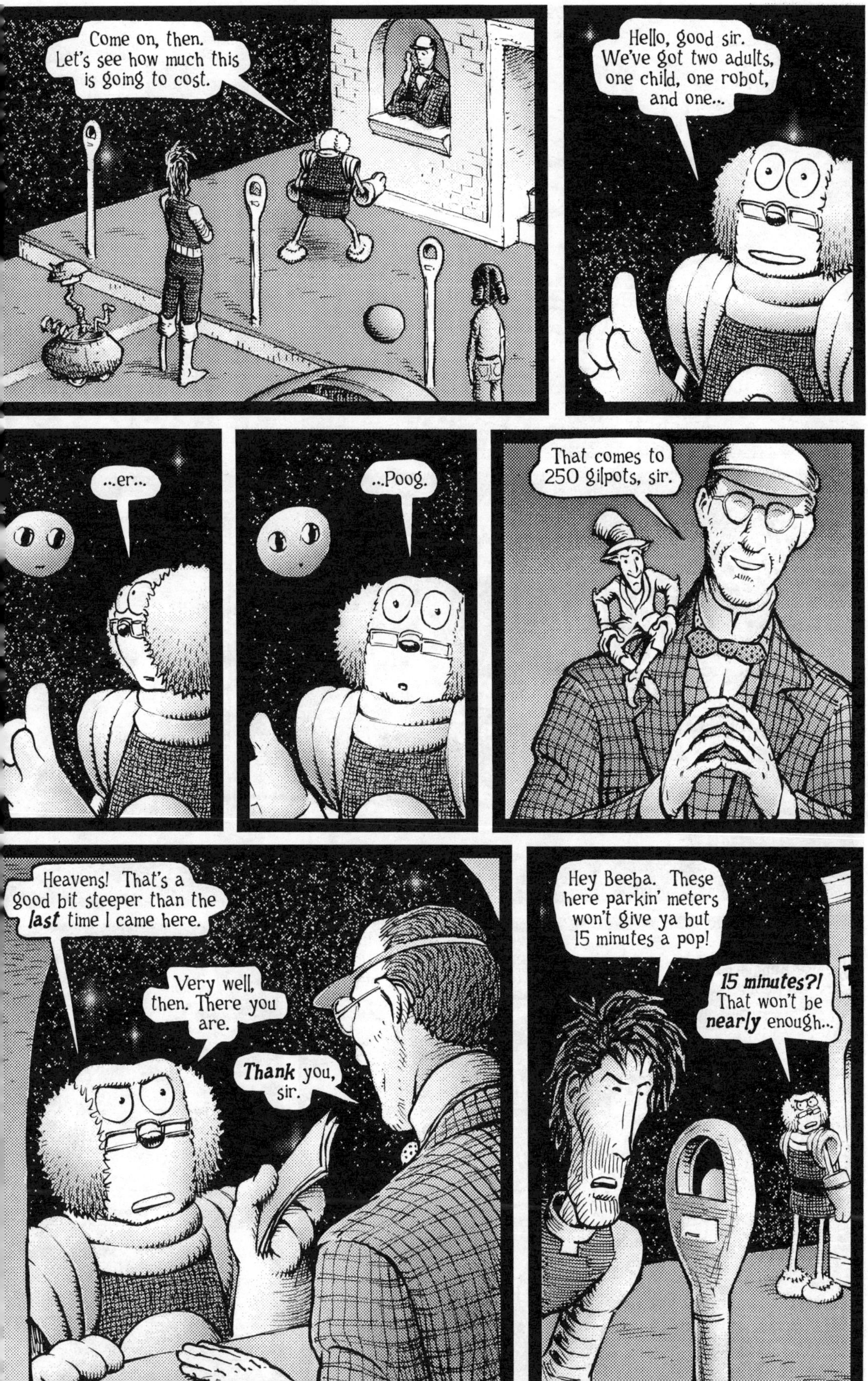
Come on, then. Let's see how much this is going to cost.
Hello, good sir. We've got two adults, one child, one robot, and one...
...er...
...Poog.
That comes to 250 gilpots, sir.
Heavens! That's a good bit steeper than the *last* time I came here.
Very well, then. There you are.
Thank you, sir.
Hey Beeba. These here parkin' meters won't give ya but 15 minutes a pop!
15 minutes?! That won't be **nearly** enough...

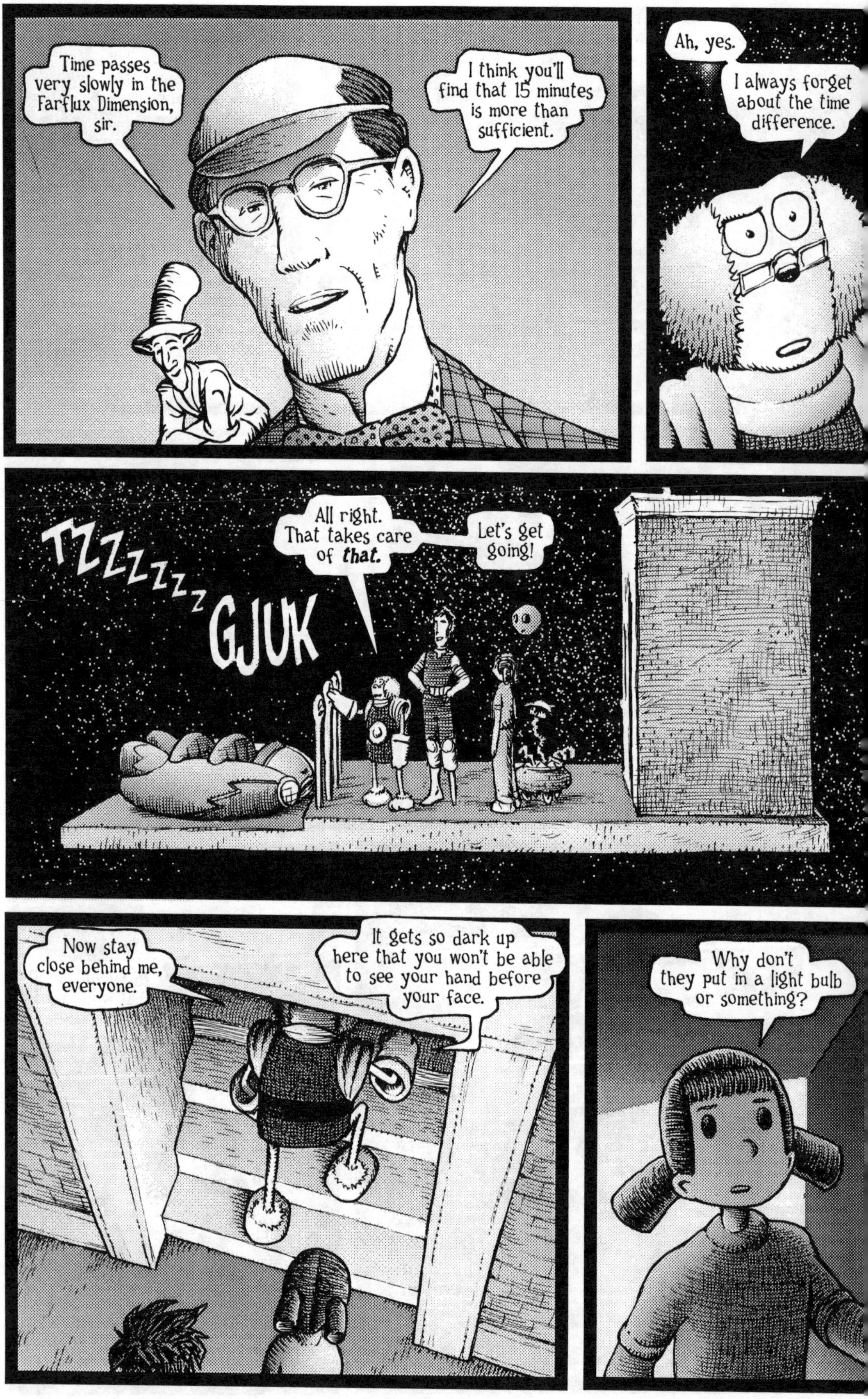
Time passes very slowly in the Farflux Dimension, sir.
I think you'll find that 15 minutes is more than sufficient.
Ah, yes.
I always forget about the time difference.
TZZZZZZZ
GJUK
All right. That takes care of *that.*
Let's get going!
Now stay close behind me, everyone.
It gets so dark up here that you won't be able to see your hand before your face.
Why don't they put in a light bulb or something?

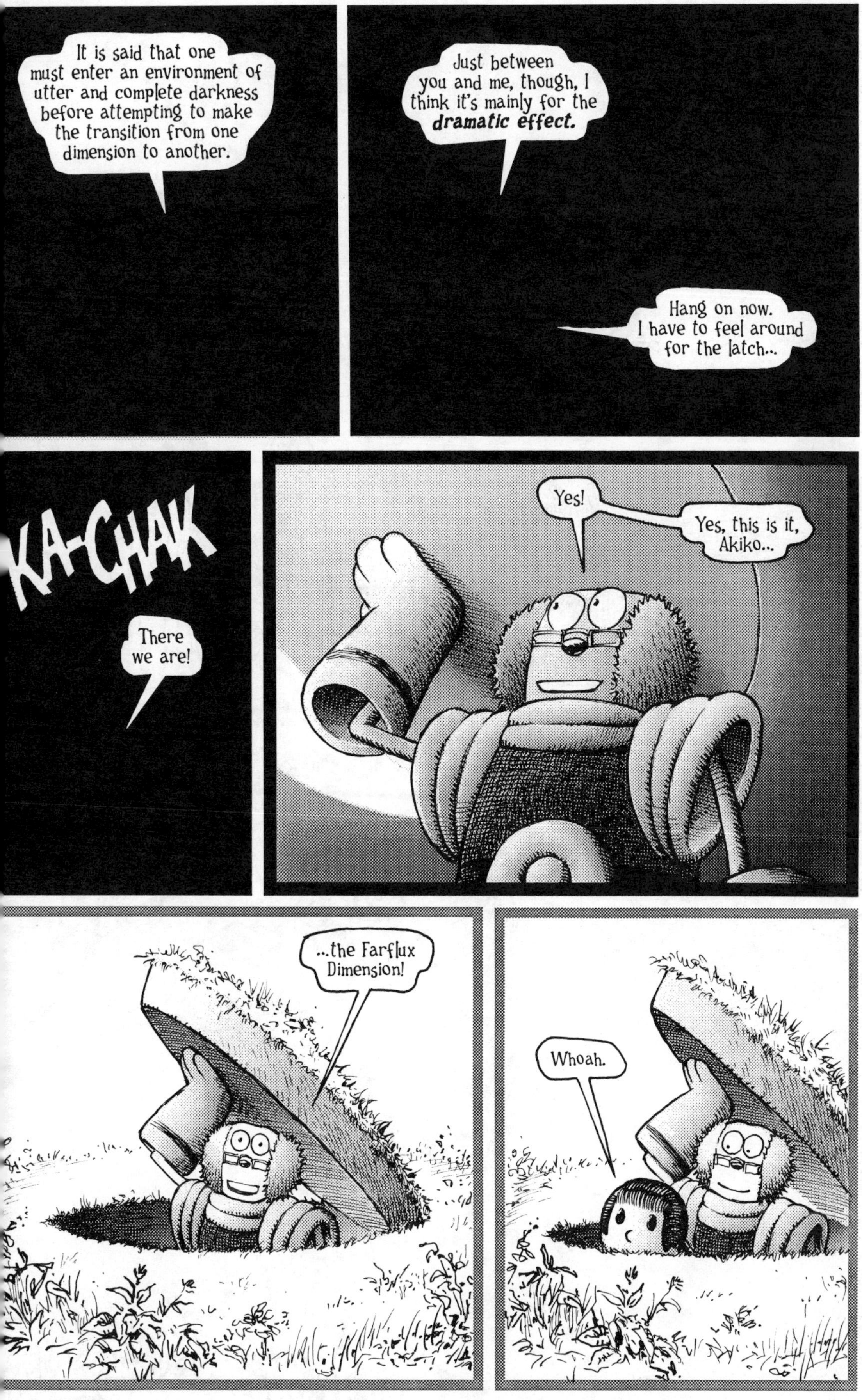

It is said that one must enter an environment of utter and complete darkness before attempting to make the transition from one dimension to another.
Just between you and me, though, I think it's mainly for the ***dramatic effect.***
Hang on now. I have to feel around for the latch...
KA-CHAK
There we are!
Yes!
Yes, this is it, Akiko...
...the Farflux Dimension!
Whoah.

Moonshopping

part one

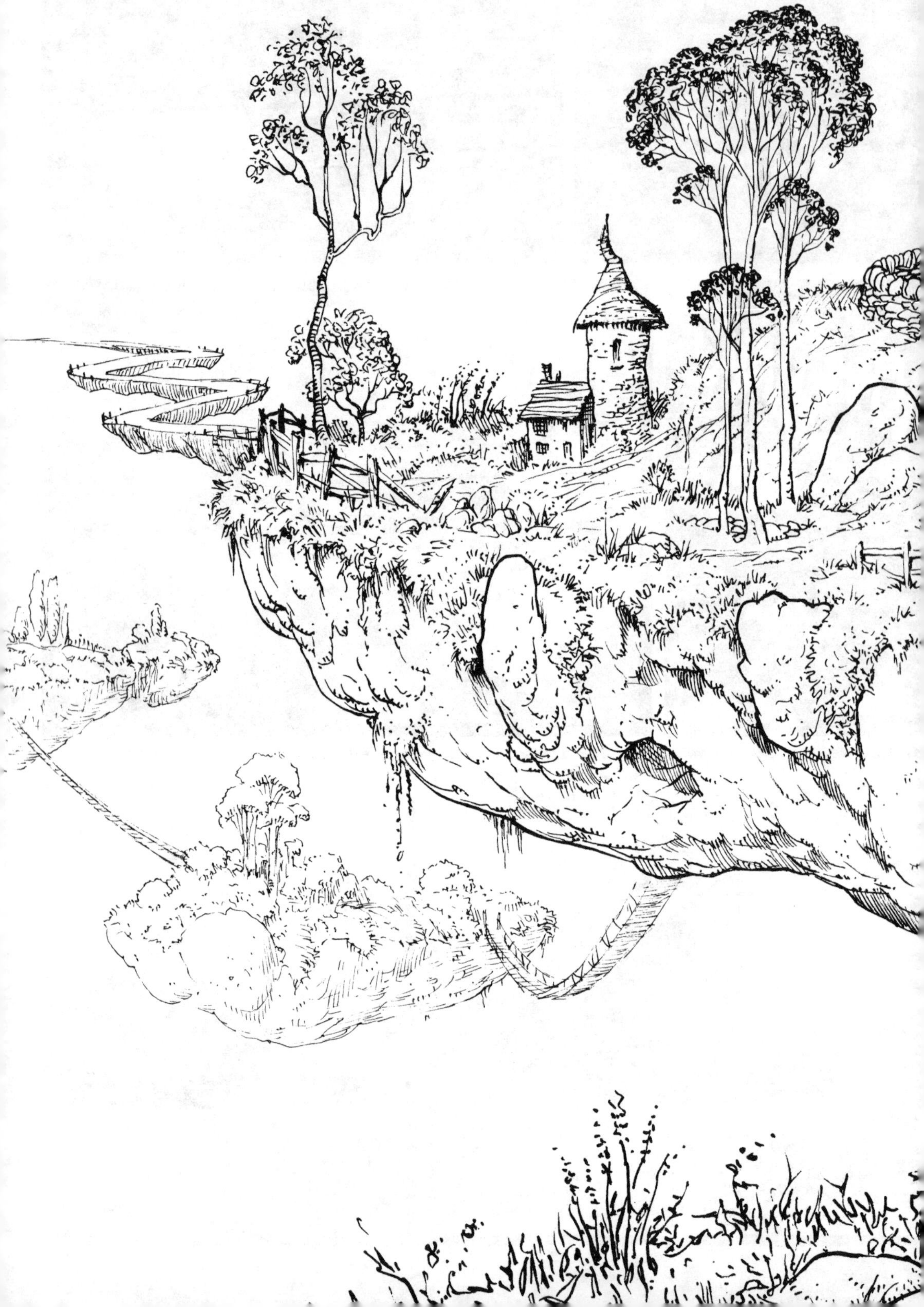

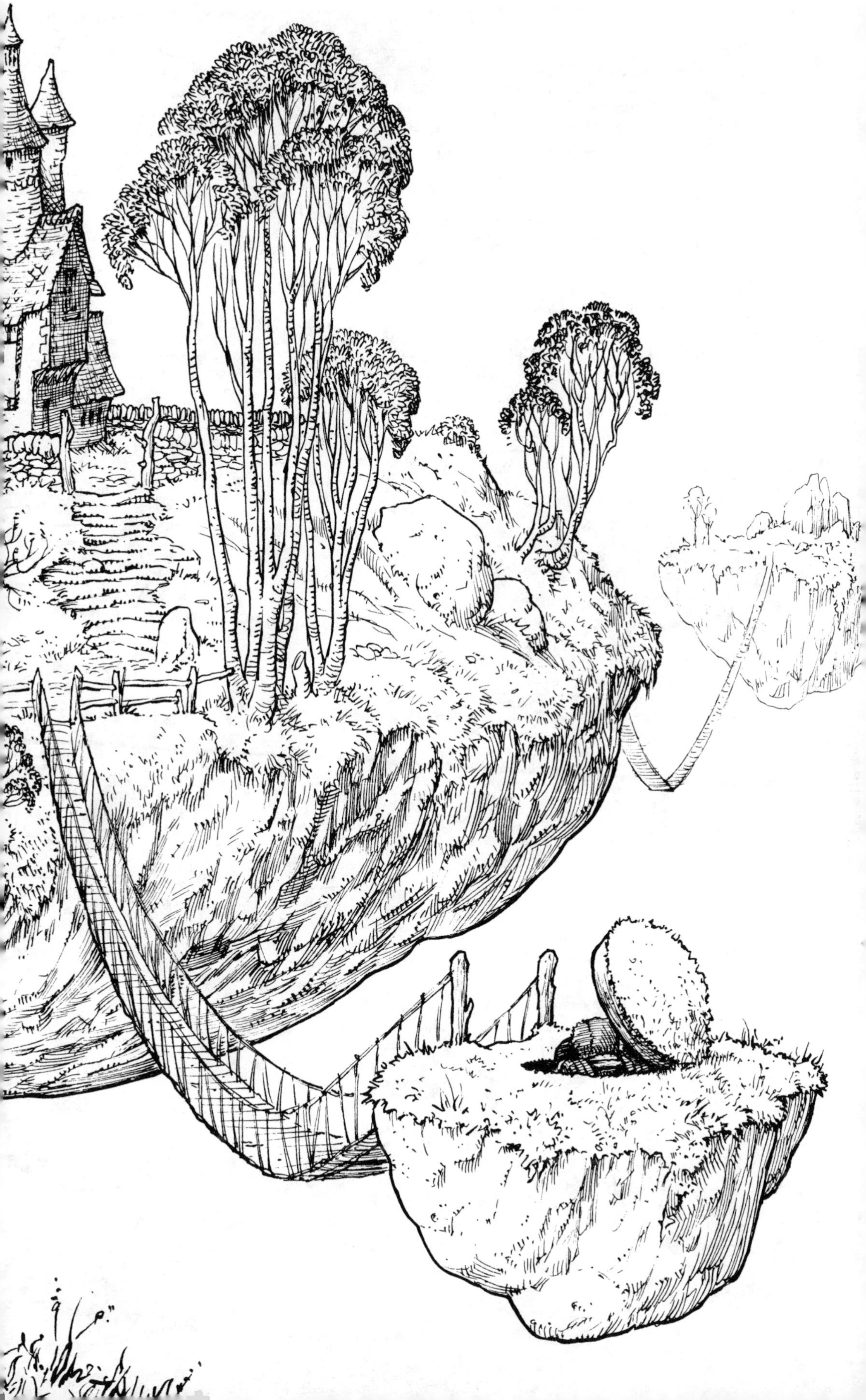

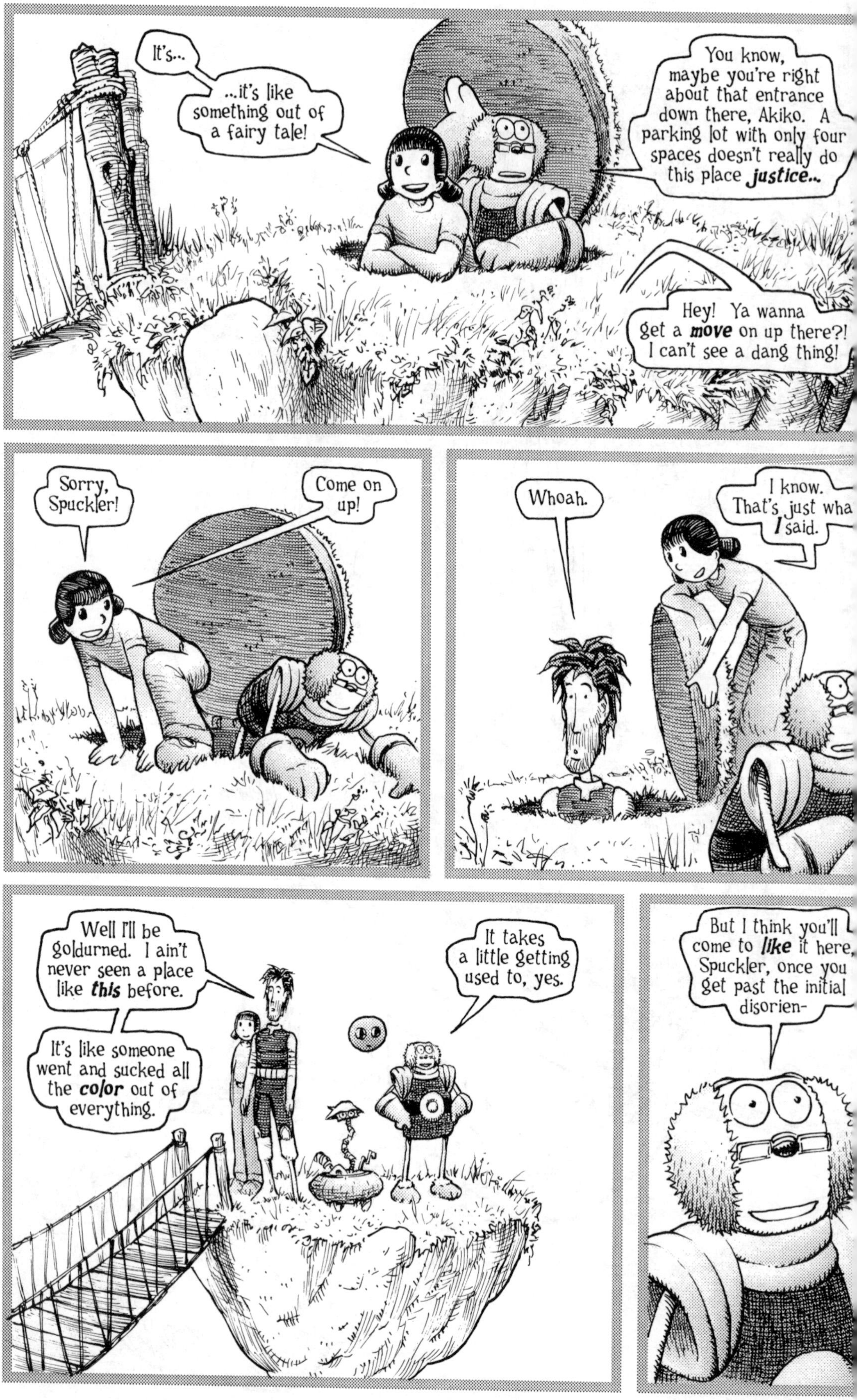

It's...
...it's like something out of a fairy tale!
You know, maybe you're right about that entrance down there, Akiko. A parking lot with only four spaces doesn't really do this place **justice**..
Hey! Ya wanna get a **move** on up there?! I can't see a dang thing!
Sorry, Spuckler!
Come on up!
Whoah.
I know. That's just wha *I* said.
Well I'll be goldurned. I ain't never seen a place like **this** before.
It's like someone went and sucked all the **color** out of everything.
It takes a little getting used to, yes.
But I think you'll come to **like** it here, Spuckler, once you get past the initial disorien-

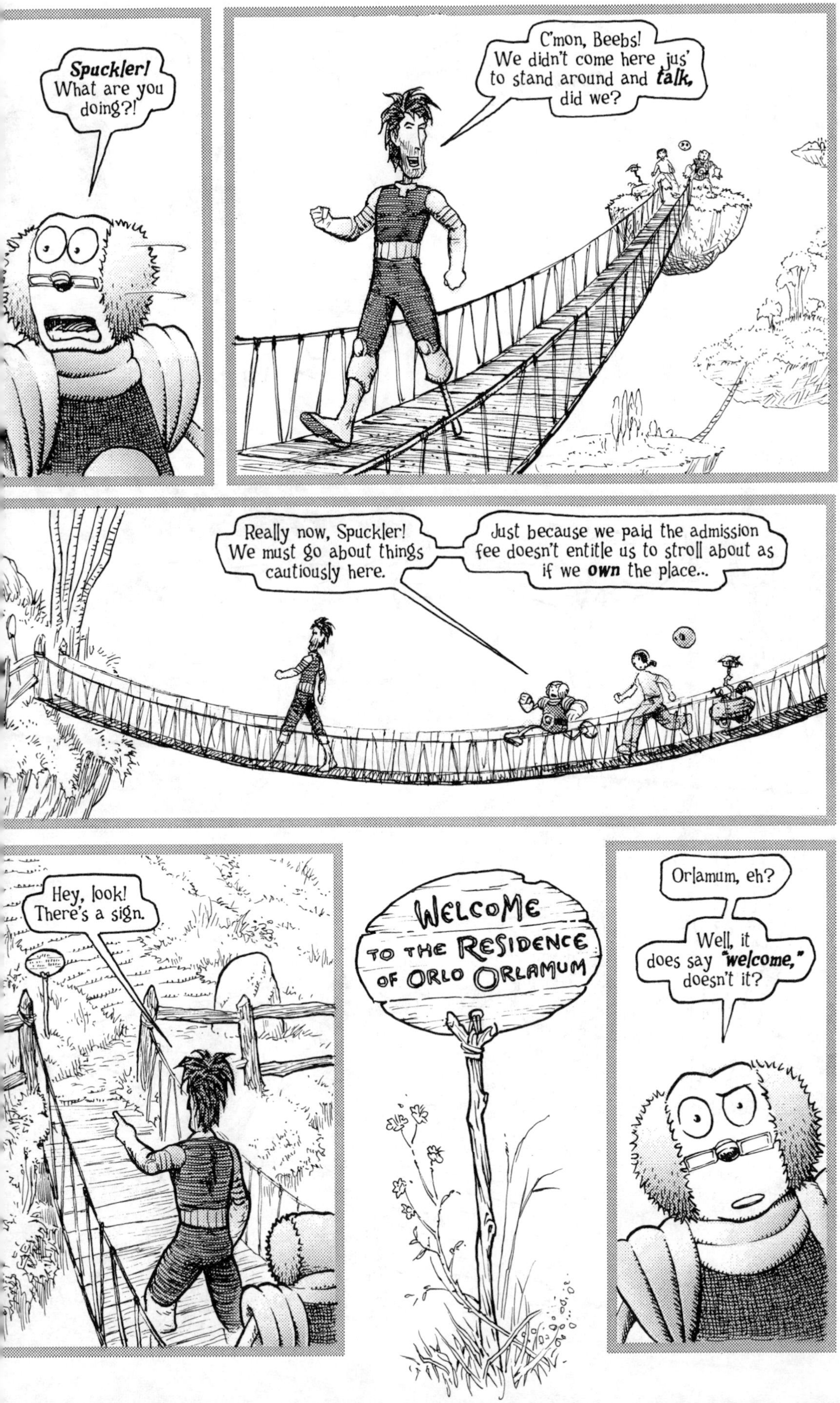
Spuckler! What are you doing?!
C'mon, Beebs! We didn't come here jus' to stand around and talk, did we?
Really now, Spuckler! We must go about things cautiously here.
Just because we paid the admission fee doesn't entitle us to stroll about as if we own the place..
Hey, look! There's a sign.
WELCOME TO THE RESIDENCE OF ORLO ORLAMUM
Orlamum, eh?
Well, it does say "welcome," doesn't it?

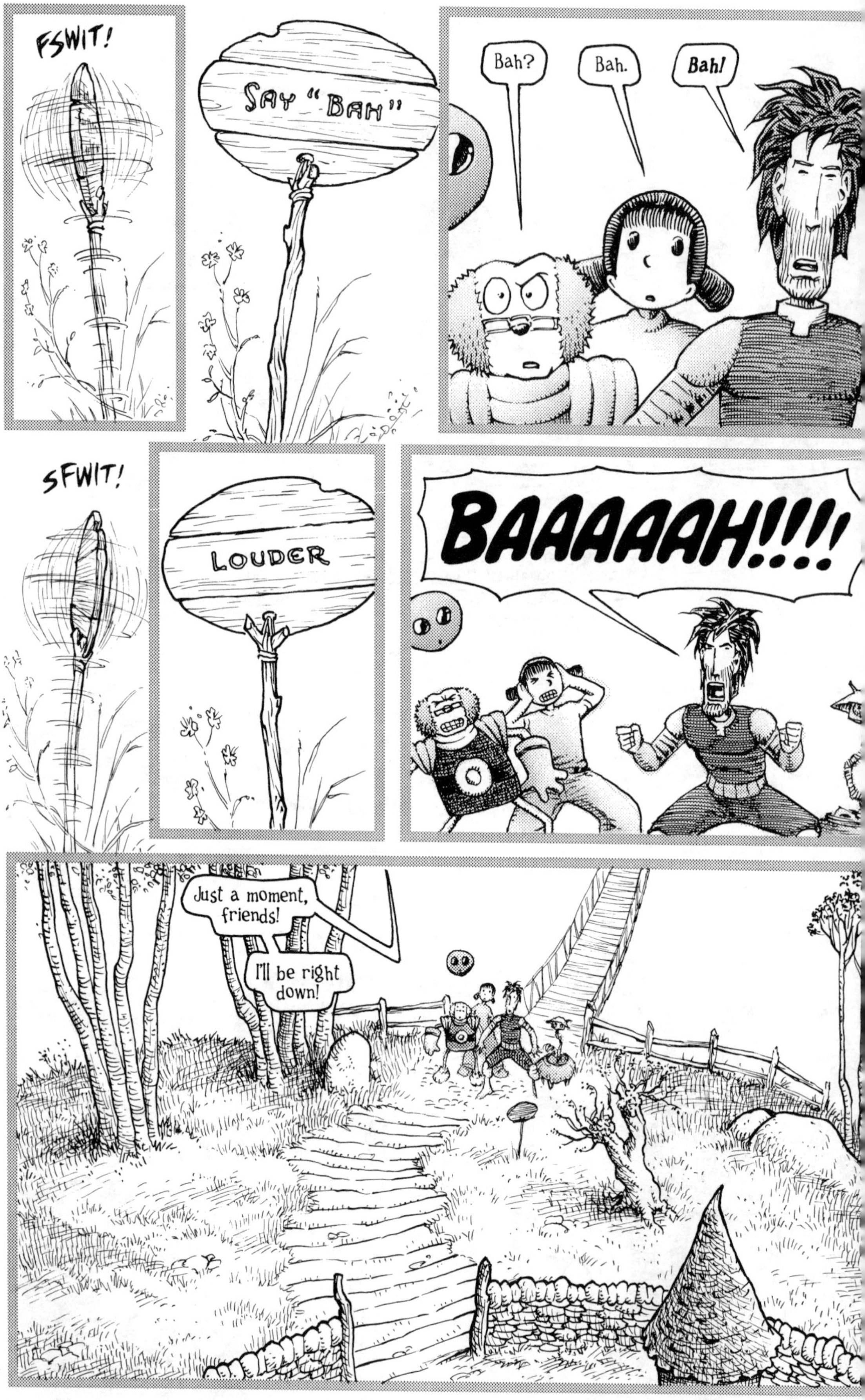
FSWIT!
SAY "BAH"
Bah?
Bah.
Bah!
SFWIT!
LOUDER
BAAAAAH!!!!
Just a moment, friends!
I'll be right down!

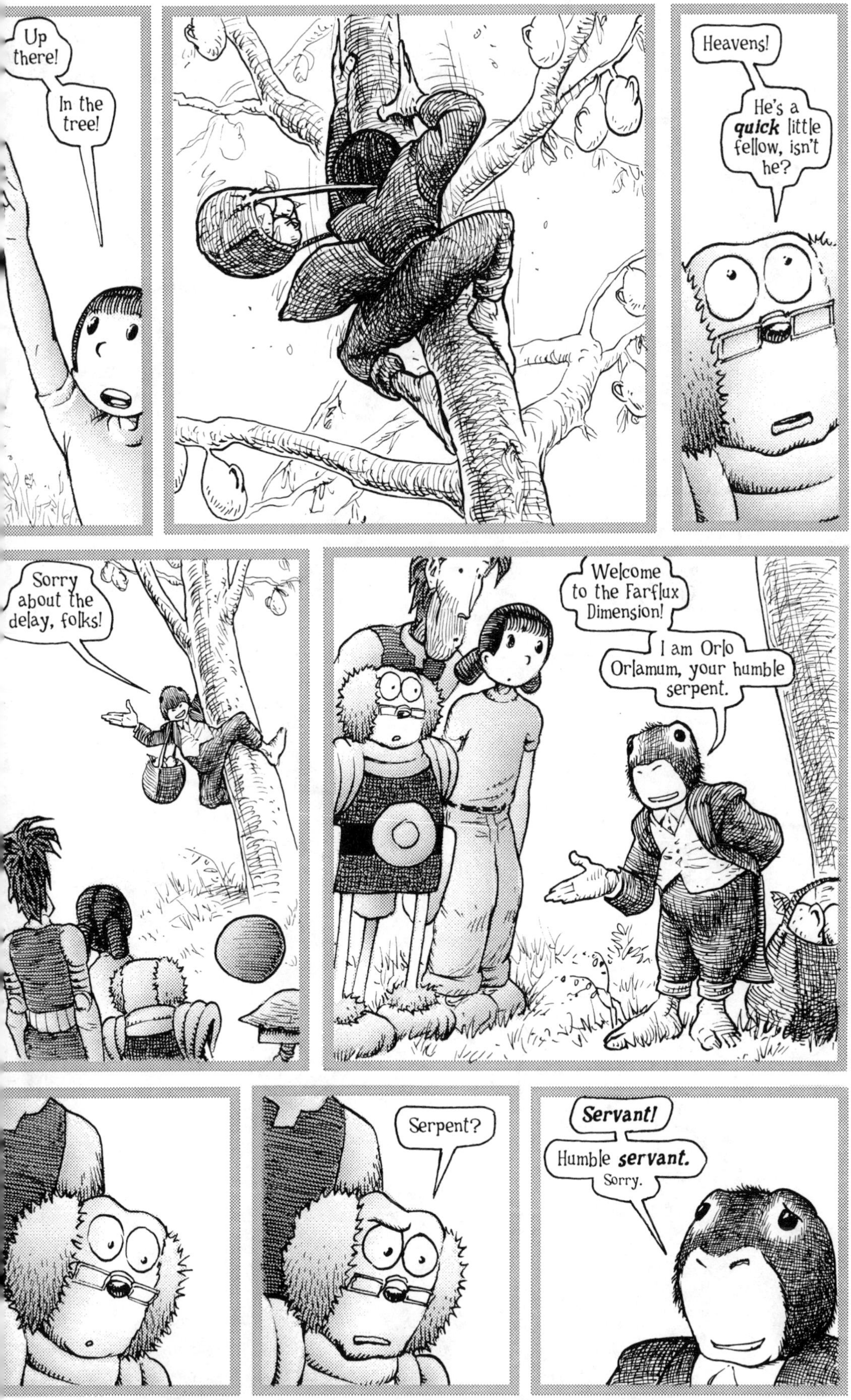
Up there!
In the tree!
Heavens!
He's a **quick** little fellow, isn't he?
Sorry about the delay, folks!
Welcome to the Farflux Dimension!
I am Orlo Orlamum, your humble serpent.
Serpent?
Servant!
Humble **servant.**
Sorry.

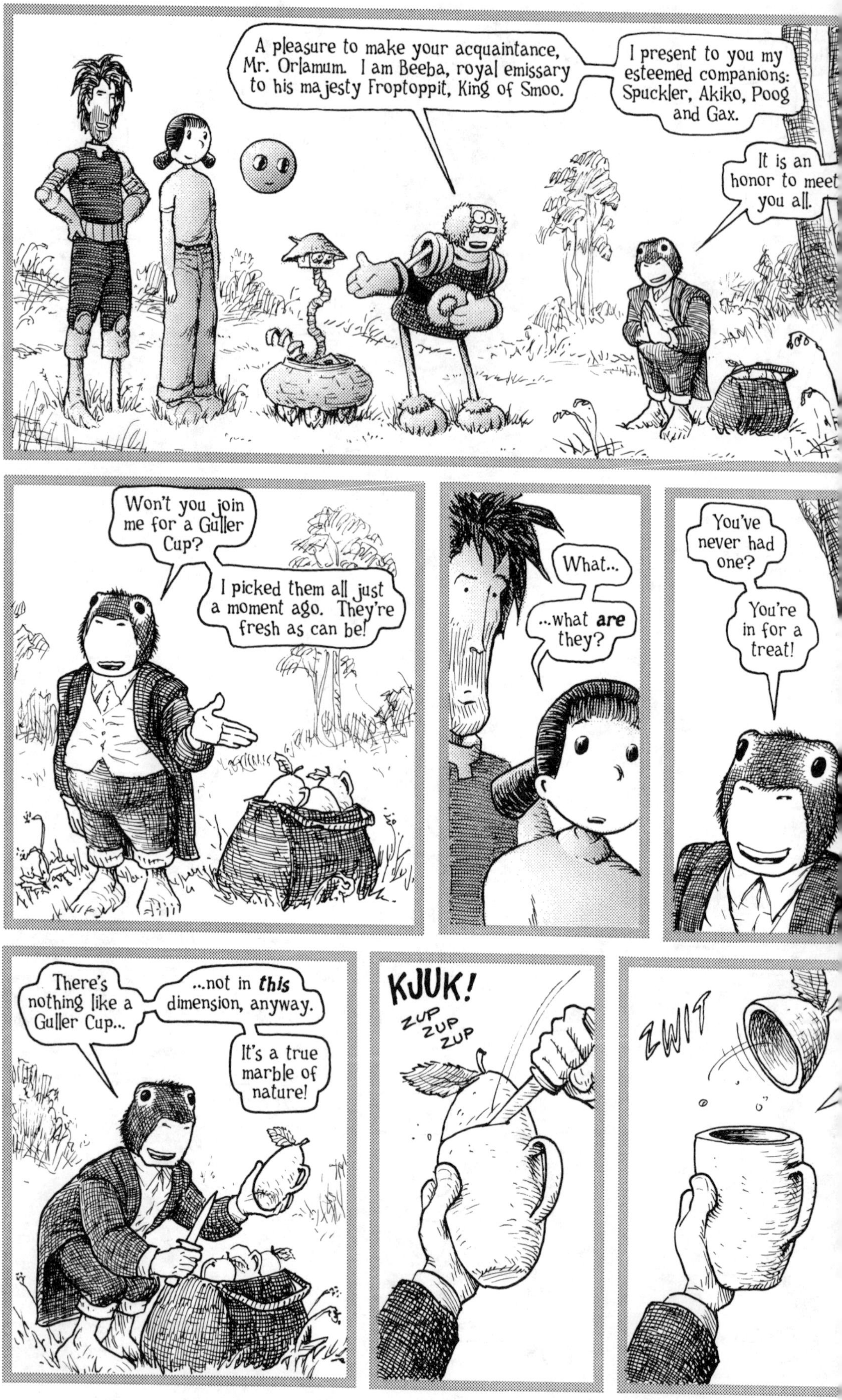

A pleasure to make your acquaintance, Mr. Orlamum. I am Beeba, royal emissary to his majesty Froptoppit, King of Smoo.
I present to you my esteemed companions: Spuckler, Akiko, Poog and Gax.
It is an honor to meet you all.
Won't you join me for a Guller Cup?
I picked them all just a moment ago. They're fresh as can be!
What...
...what **are** they?
You've never had one?
You're in for a treat!
There's nothing like a Guller Cup...
...not in ***this*** dimension, anyway.
It's a true marble of nature!
KJUK!
ZUP ZUP ZUP
ZWIT

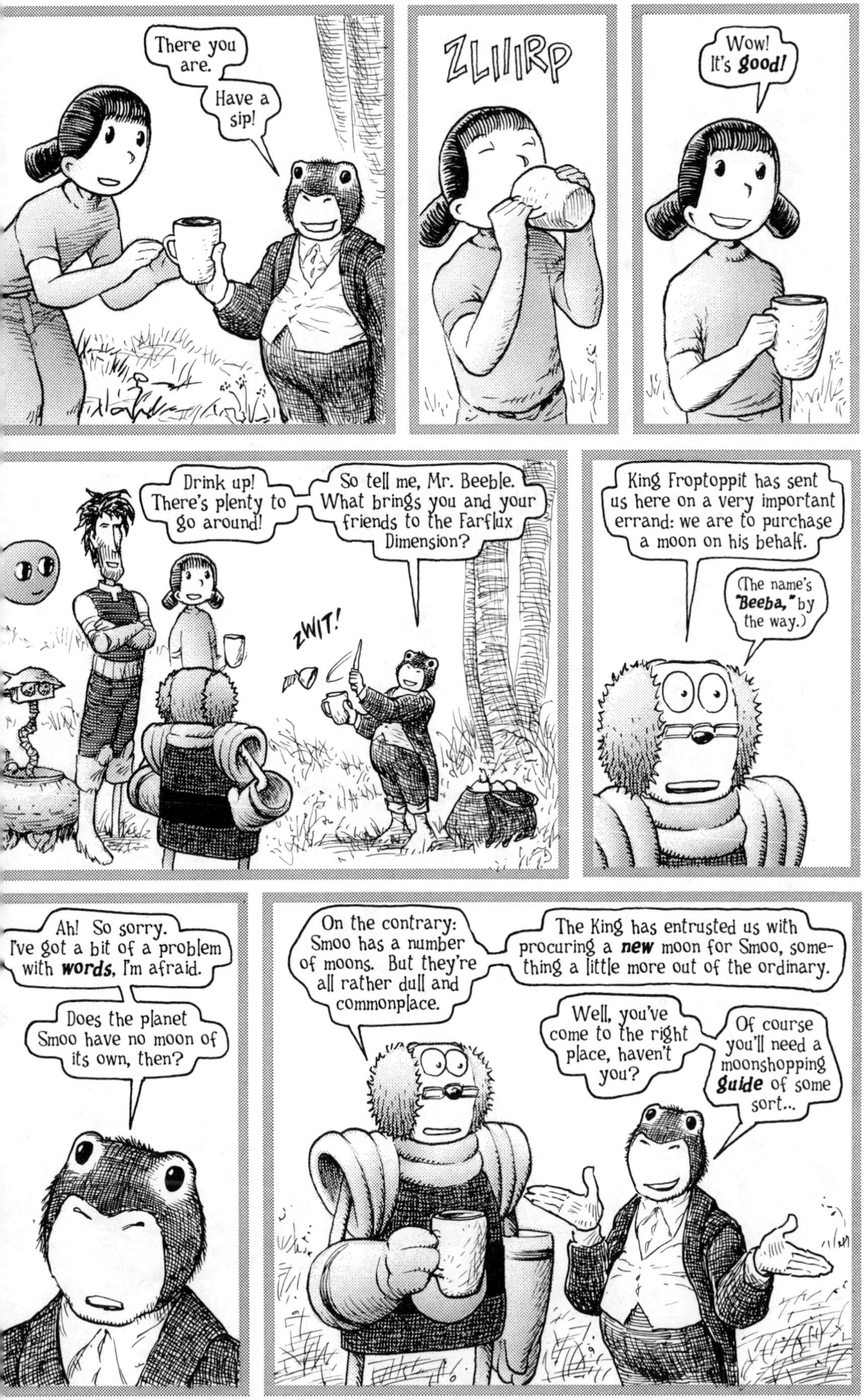
There you are.
Have a sip!
ZLIIIRP
Wow! It's **good!**
Drink up! There's plenty to go around!
So tell me, Mr. Beeble. What brings you and your friends to the Farflux Dimension?
ZWIT!
King Froptoppit has sent us here on a very important errand: we are to purchase a moon on his behalf.
(The name's **"Beeba,"** by the way.)
Ah! So sorry. I've got a bit of a problem with **words**, I'm afraid.
Does the planet Smoo have no moon of its own, then?
On the contrary: Smoo has a number of moons. But they're all rather dull and commonplace.
The King has entrusted us with procuring a **new** moon for Smoo, something a little more out of the ordinary.
Well, you've come to the right place, haven't you?
Of course you'll need a moonshopping **guide** of some sort...

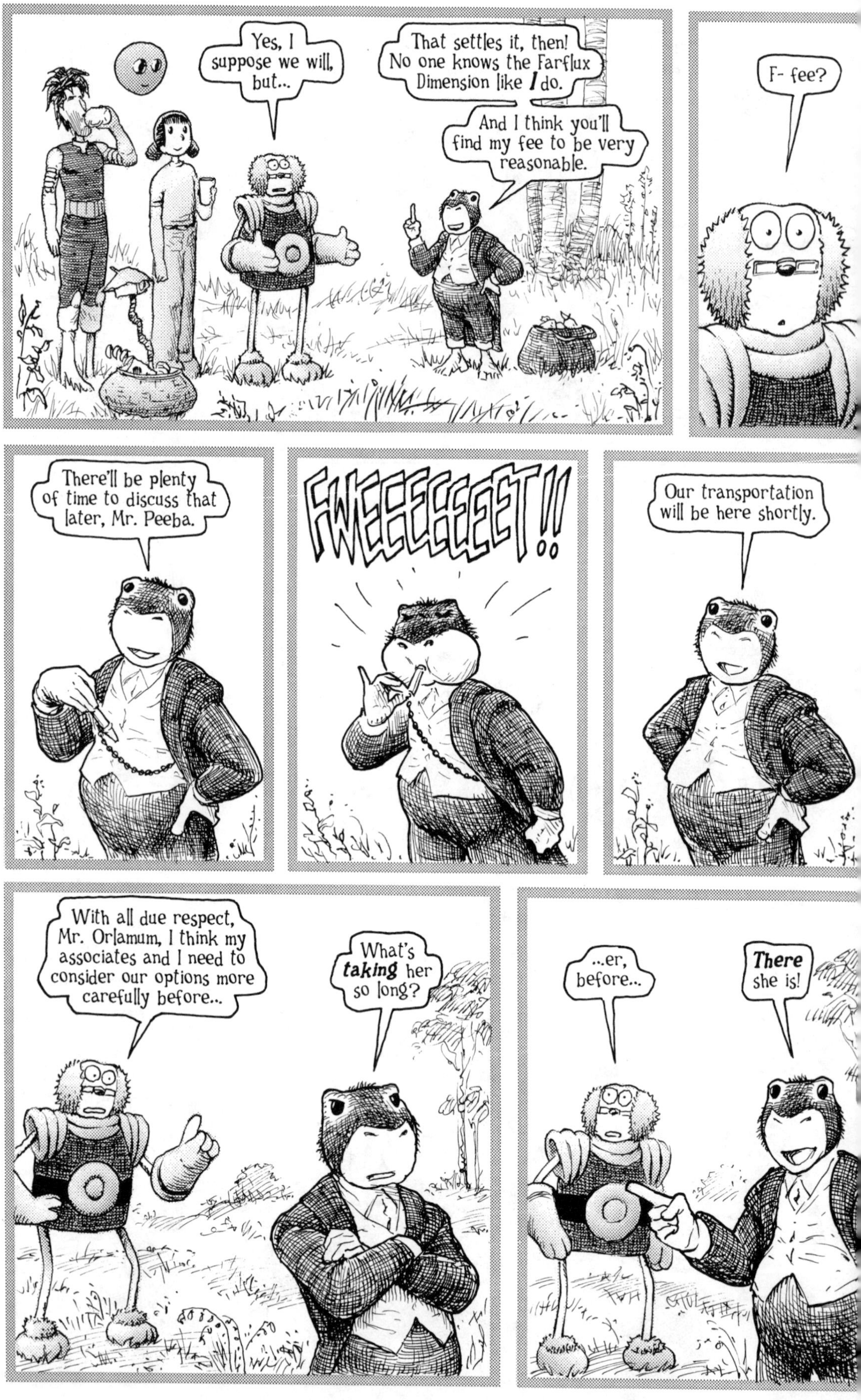

Yes, I suppose we will, but...
That settles it, then! No one knows the Farflux Dimension like *I* do.
And I think you'll find my fee to be very reasonable.
F- fee?
There'll be plenty of time to discuss that later, Mr. Peeba.
FWEEEEEEEET!!
Our transportation will be here shortly.
With all due respect, Mr. Orlamum, I think my associates and I need to consider our options more carefully before...
What's *taking* her so long?
...er, before...
There she is!

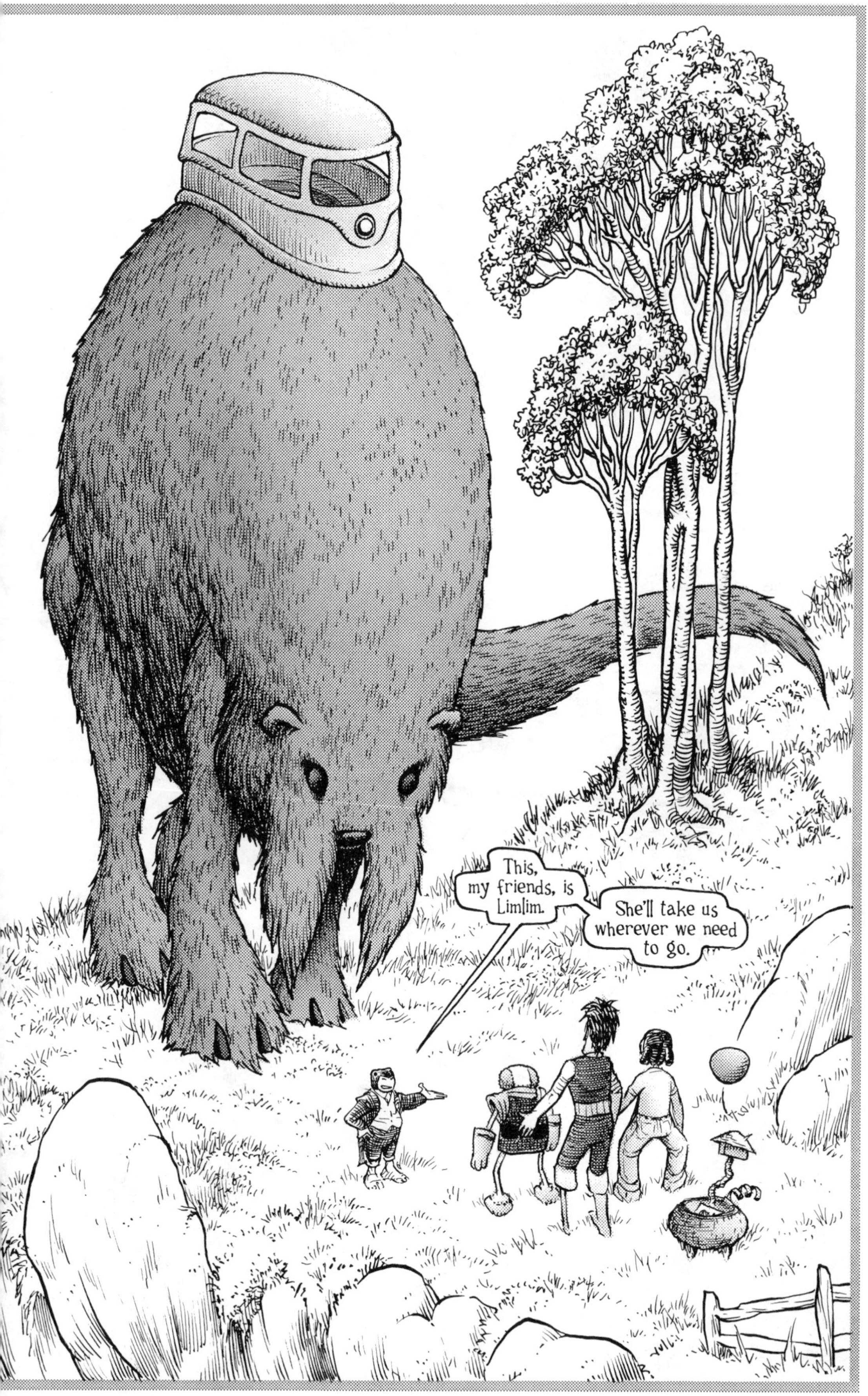
This, my friends, is Limlim.
She'll take us wherever we need to go.

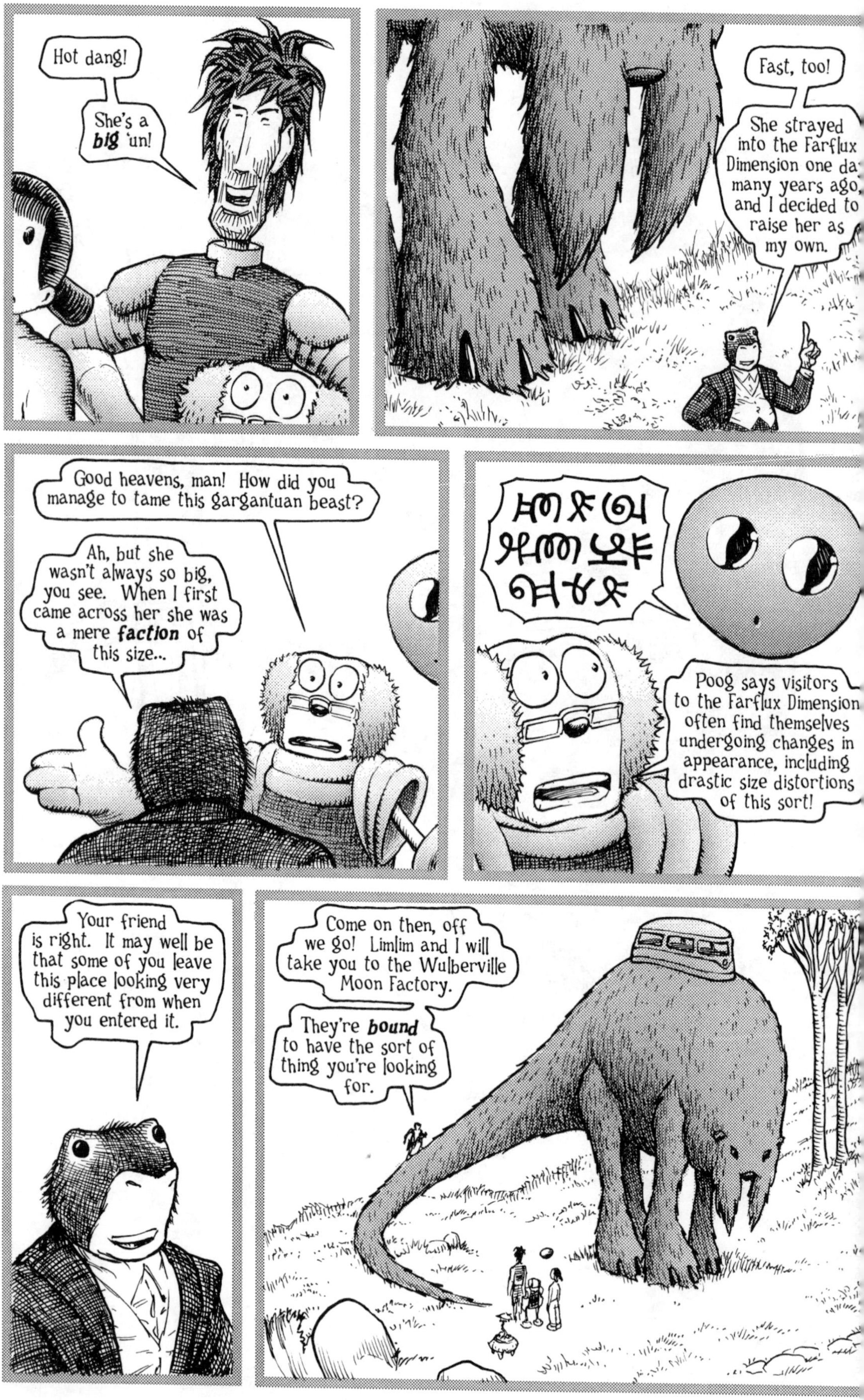
Hot dang!
She's a ***big*** 'un!
Fast, too!
She strayed into the Farflux Dimension one da many years ago, and I decided to raise her as my own.
Good heavens, man! How did you manage to tame this gargantuan beast?
Ah, but she wasn't always so big, you see. When I first came across her she was a mere ***faction*** of this size...
Poog says visitors to the Farflux Dimension often find themselves undergoing changes in appearance, including drastic size distortions of this sort!
Your friend is right. It may well be that some of you leave this place looking very different from when you entered it.
Come on then, off we go! Limlim and I will take you to the Wulberville Moon Factory.
They're ***bound*** to have the sort of thing you're looking for.

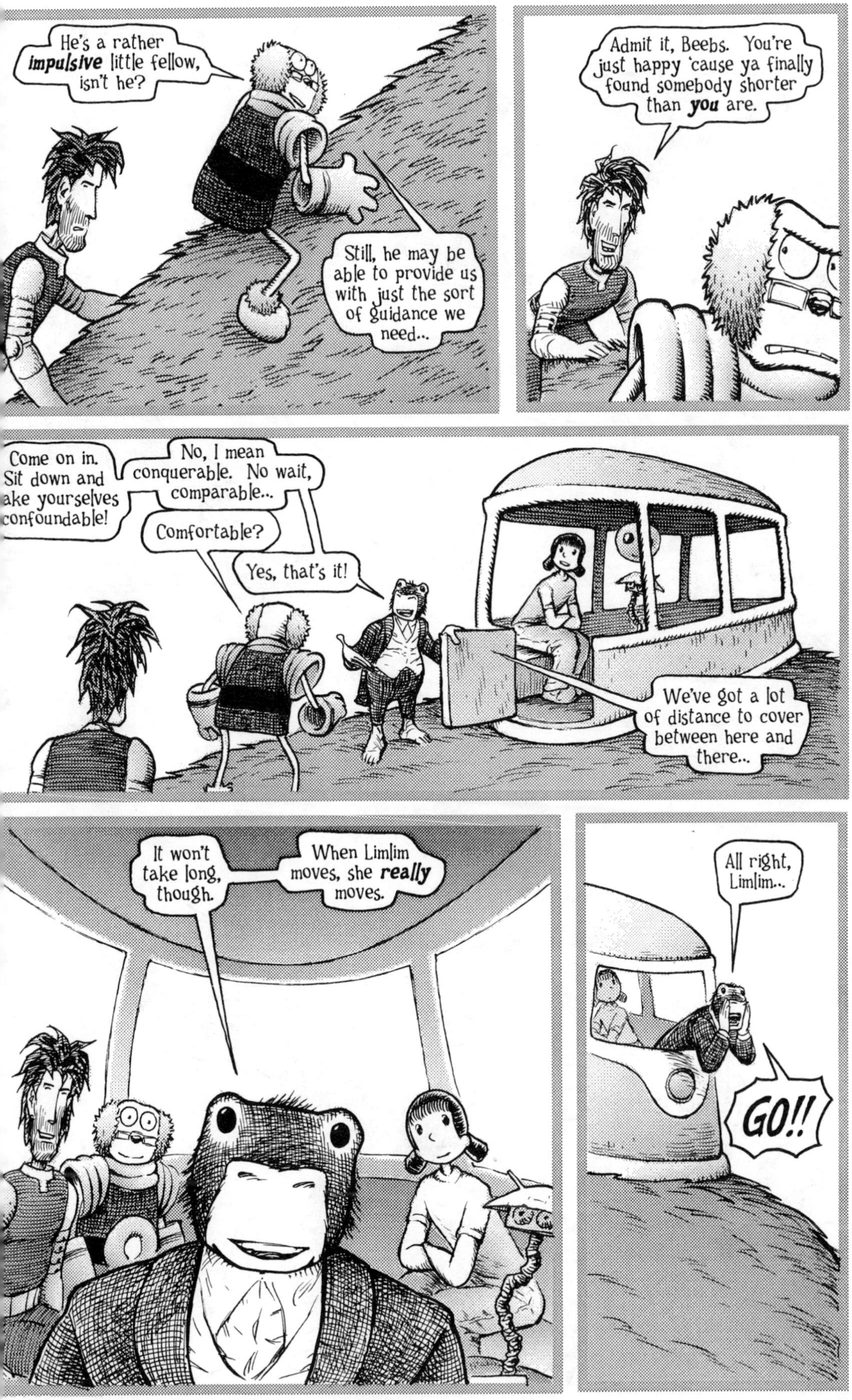
He's a rather **impulsive** little fellow, isn't he?
Still, he may be able to provide us with just the sort of guidance we need...
Admit it, Beebs. You're just happy 'cause ya finally found somebody shorter than **you** are.
Come on in. Sit down and ake yourselves confoundable!
No, I mean conquerable. No wait, comparable...
Comfortable?
Yes, that's it!
We've got a lot of distance to cover between here and there...
It won't take long, though.
When Limlim moves, she **really** moves.
All right, Limlim...
GO!!

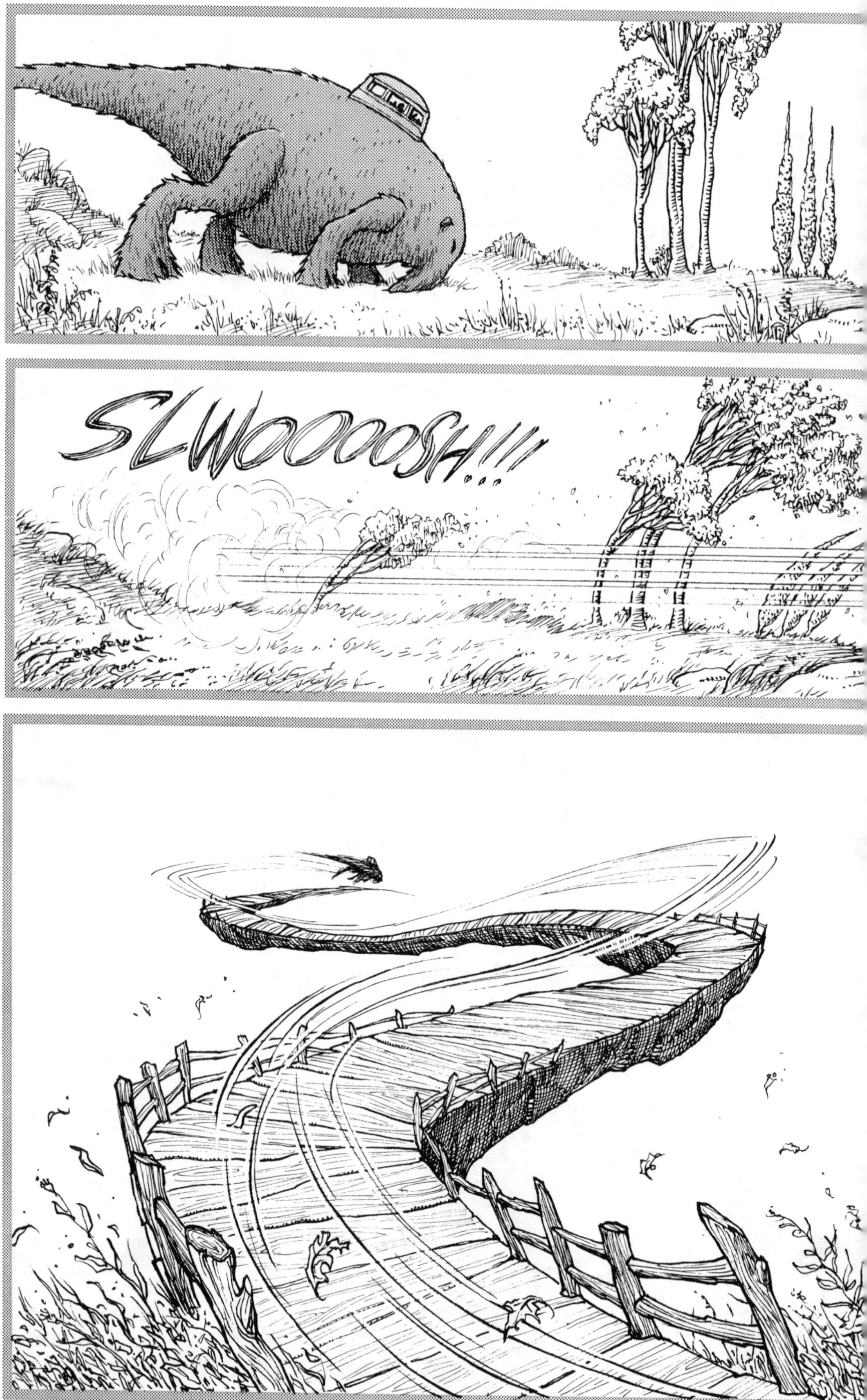
SLWOOOOOSH!!!

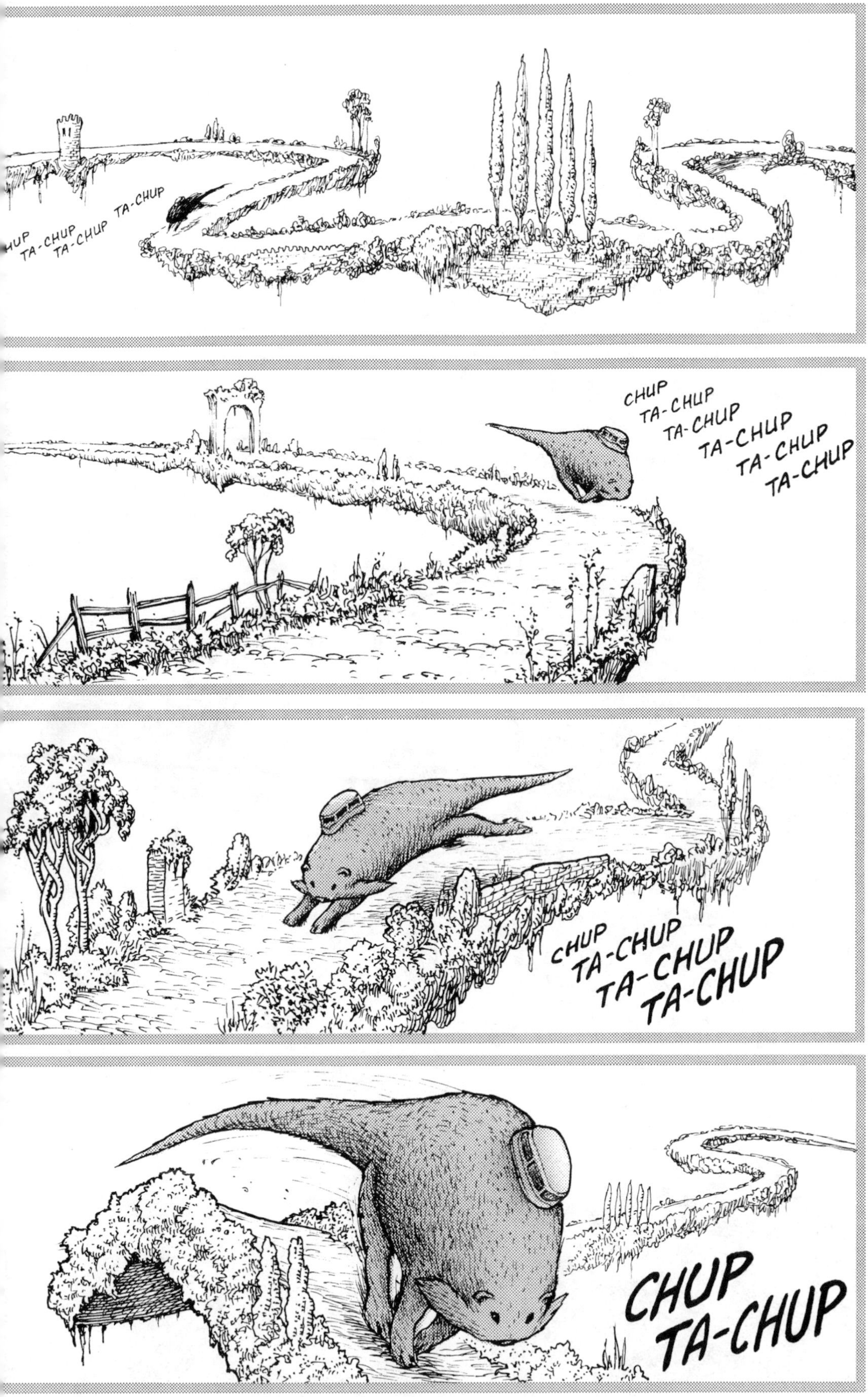

HUP
TA-CHUP
TA-CHUP
TA-CHUP
CHUP
TA-CHUP
TA-CHUP
TA-CHUP
TA-CHUP
TA-CHUP
CHUP
TA-CHUP
TA-CHUP
TA-CHUP
CHUP
TA-CHUP

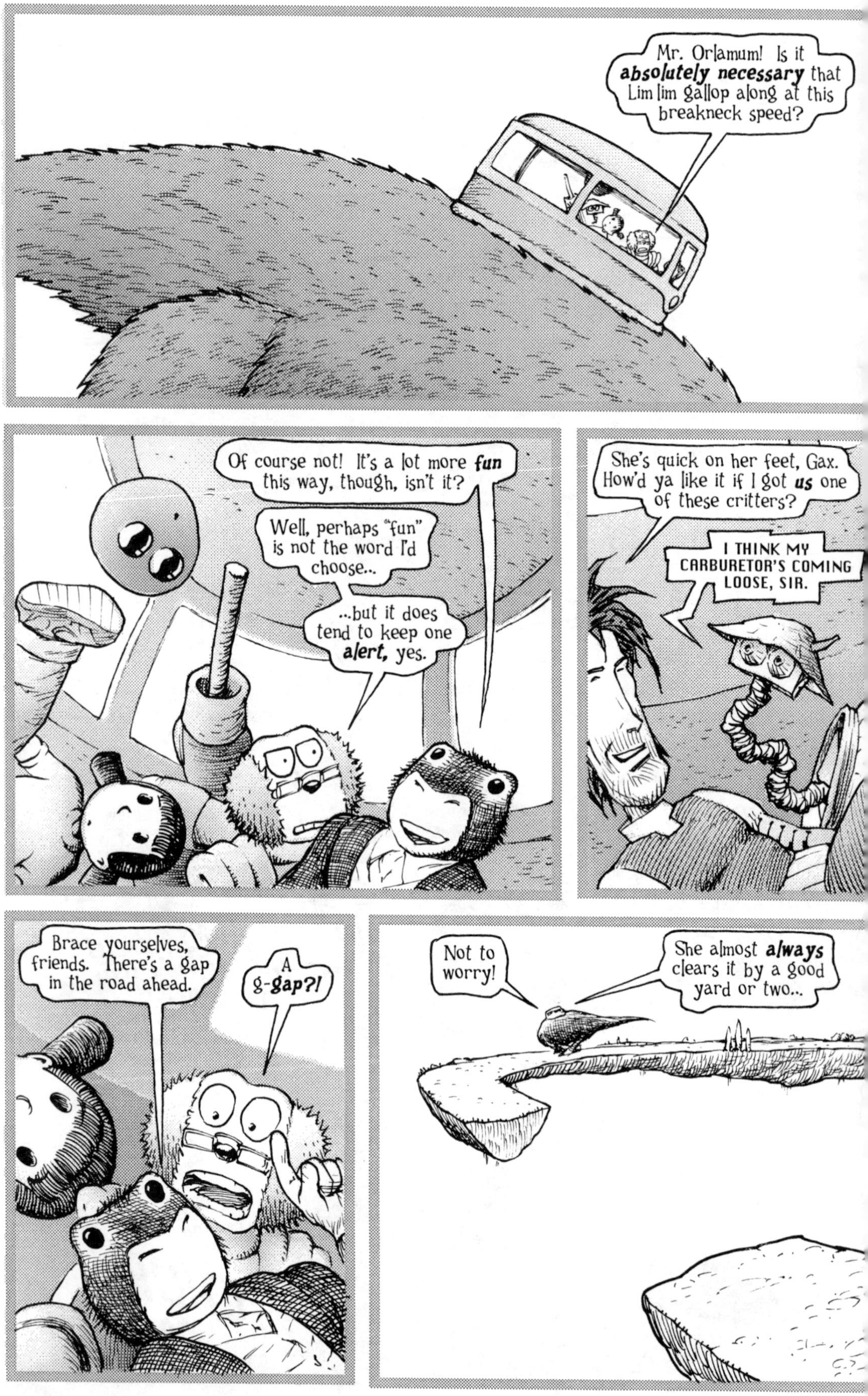

Mr. Orlamum! Is it **absolutely necessary** that Limlim gallop along at this breakneck speed?
Of course not! It's a lot more **fun** this way, though, isn't it?
Well, perhaps "fun" is not the word I'd choose...
...but it does tend to keep one **alert,** yes.
She's quick on her feet, Gax. How'd ya like it if I got **us** one of these critters?
I THINK MY CARBURETOR'S COMING LOOSE, SIR.
Brace yourselves, friends. There's a gap in the road ahead.
A g-**gap?!**
Not to worry!
She almost **always** clears it by a good yard or two...

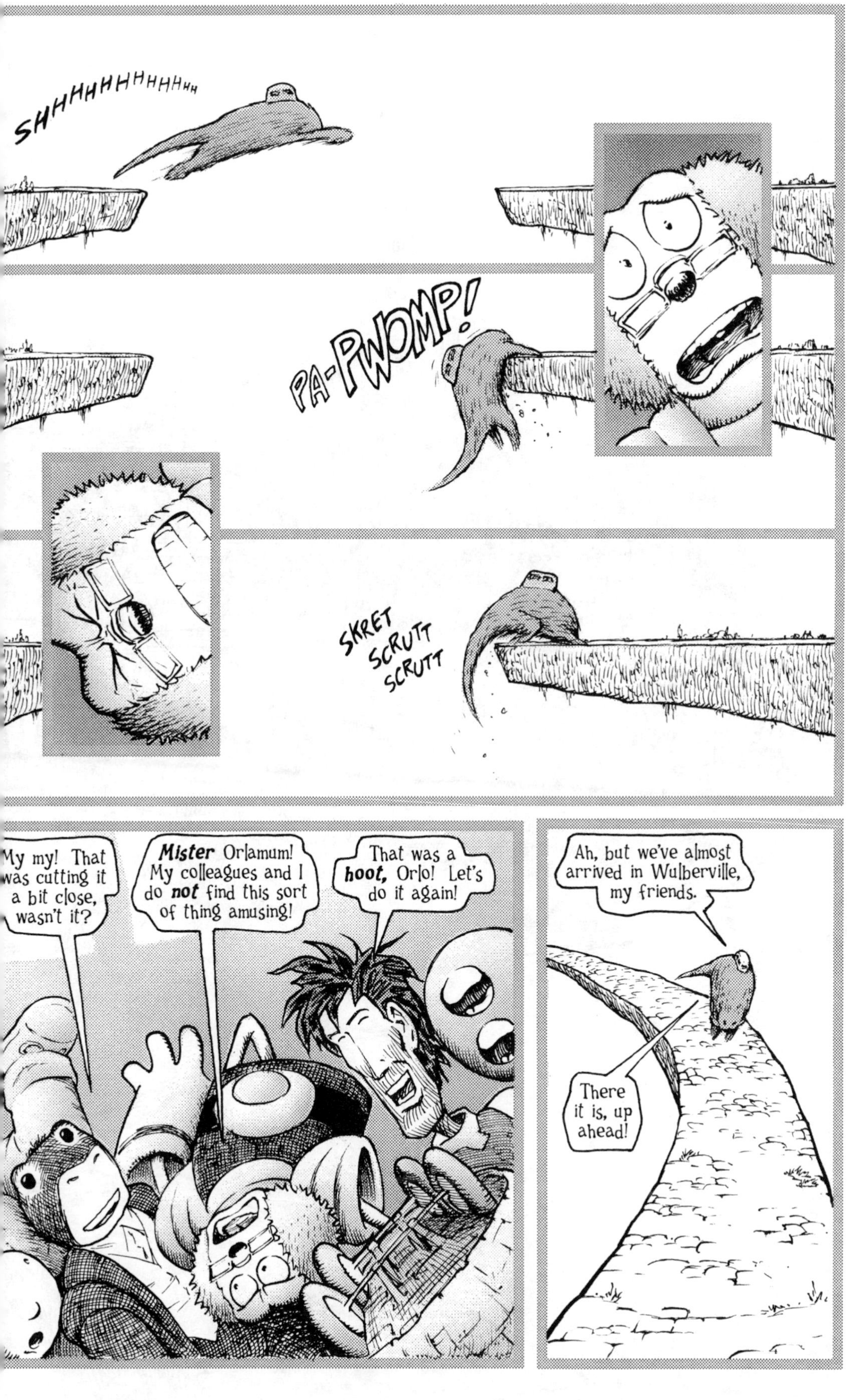
SHHHHHHHHHHHhh
PA-PWOMP!
SKRET SCRUTT SCRUTT
My my! That was cutting it a bit close, wasn't it?
Mister Orlamum! My colleagues and I do not find this sort of thing amusing!
That was a hoot, Orlo! Let's do it again!
Ah, but we've almost arrived in Wulberville, my friends.
There it is, up ahead!

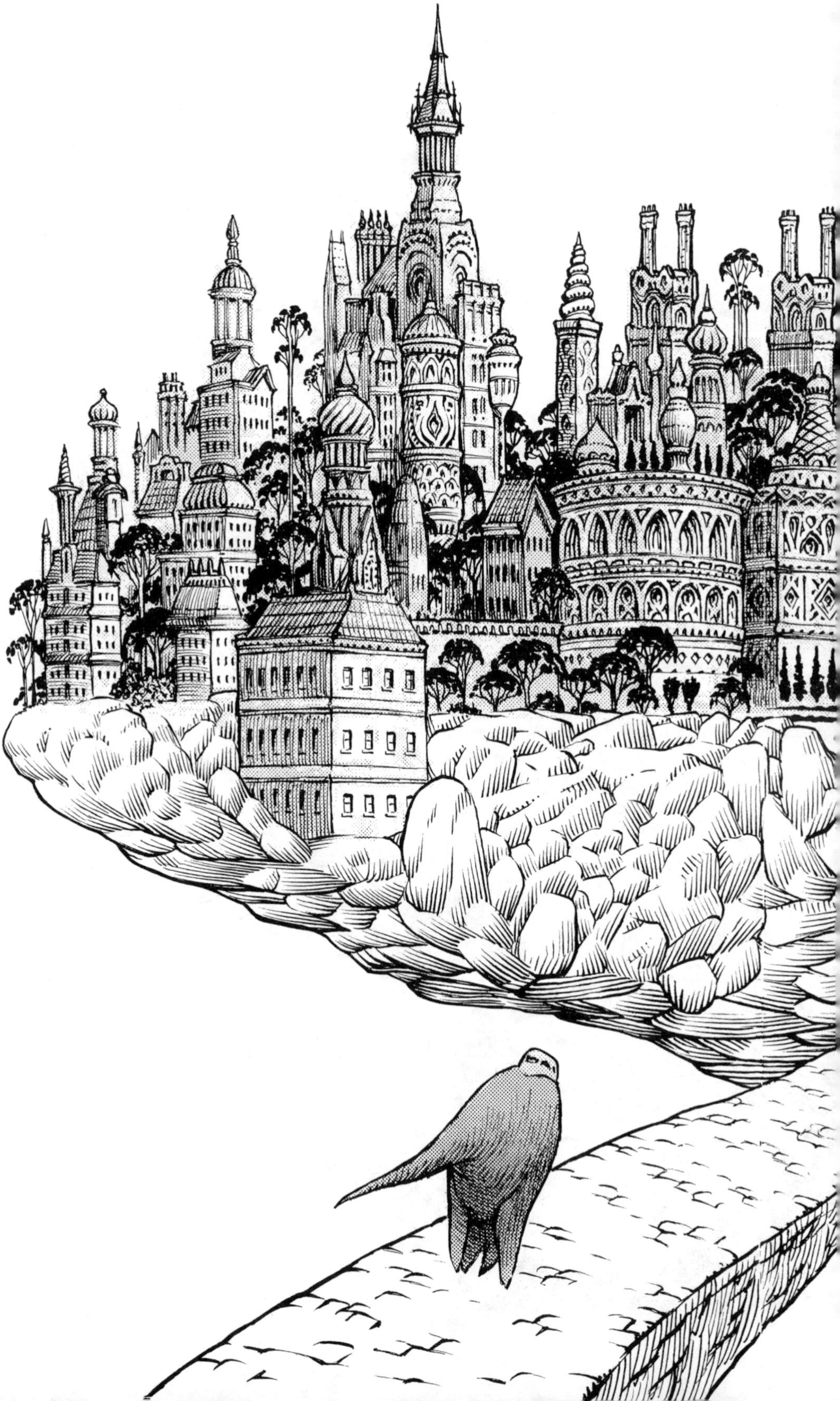

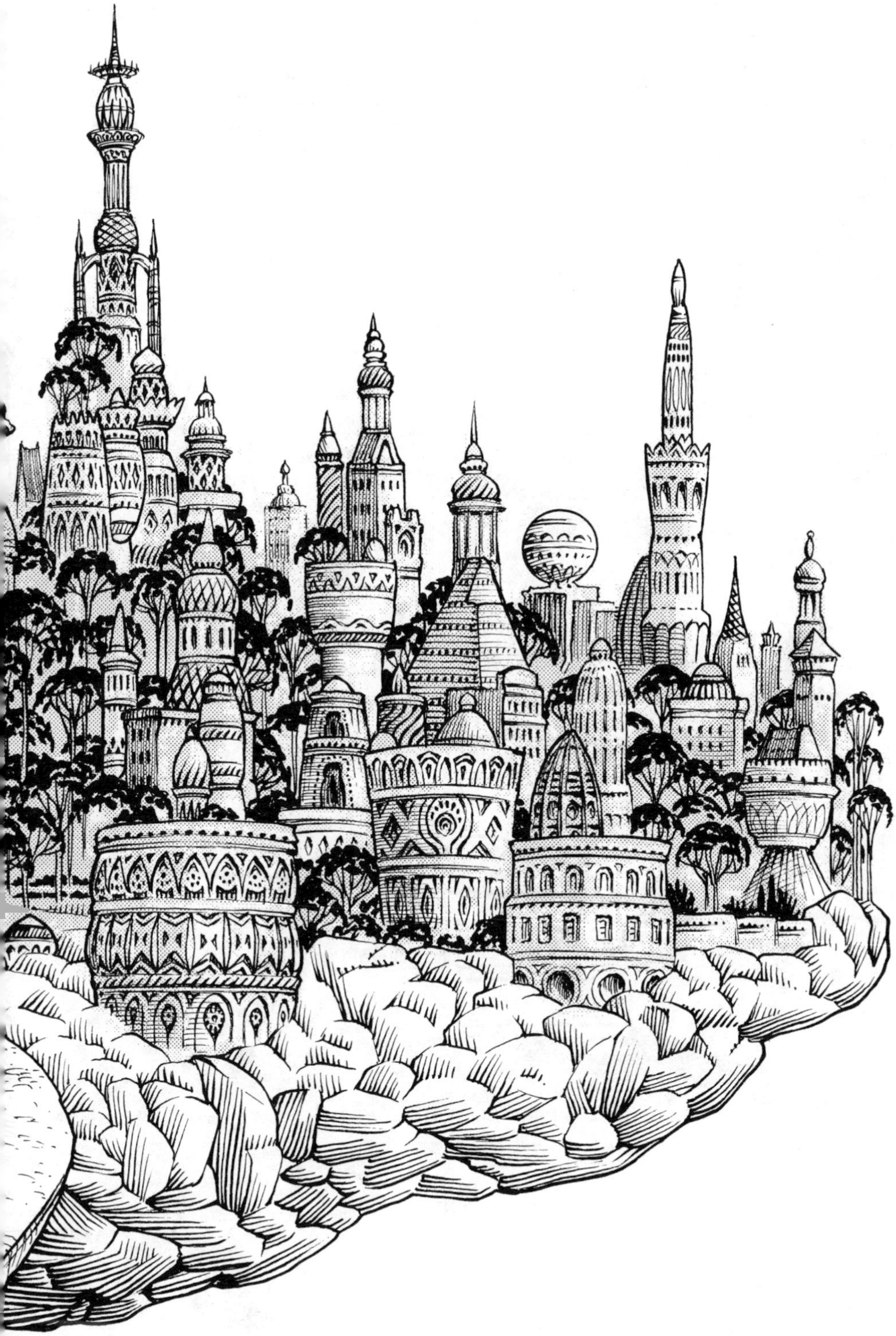

Moonshopping

part two

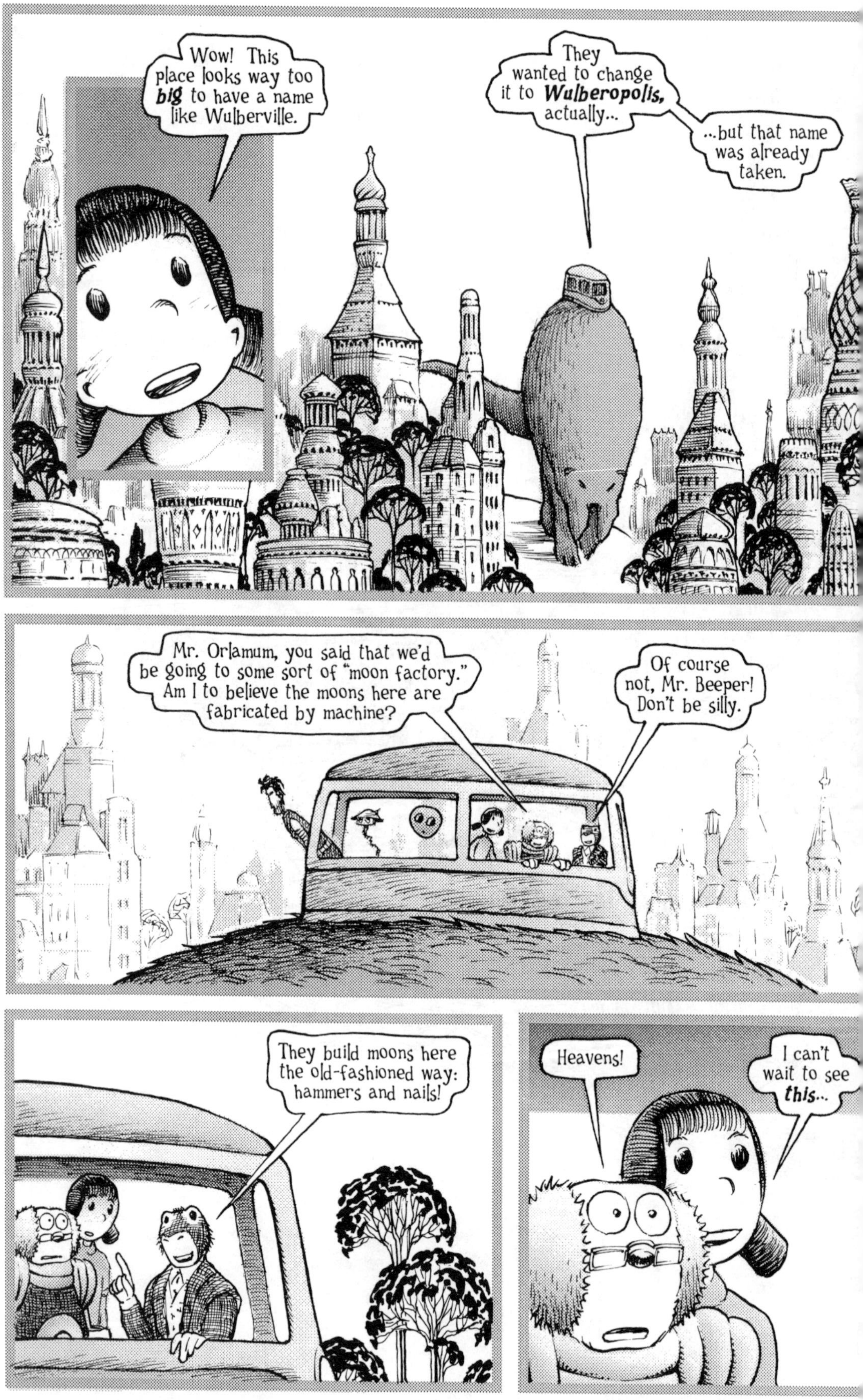
Wow! This place looks way too **big** to have a name like Wulberville.
They wanted to change it to **Wulberopolis,** actually...
...but that name was already taken.
Mr. Orlamum, you said that we'd be going to some sort of "moon factory." Am I to believe the moons here are fabricated by machine?
Of course not, Mr. Beeper! Don't be silly.
They build moons here the old-fashioned way: hammers and nails!
Heavens!
I can't wait to see **this**...

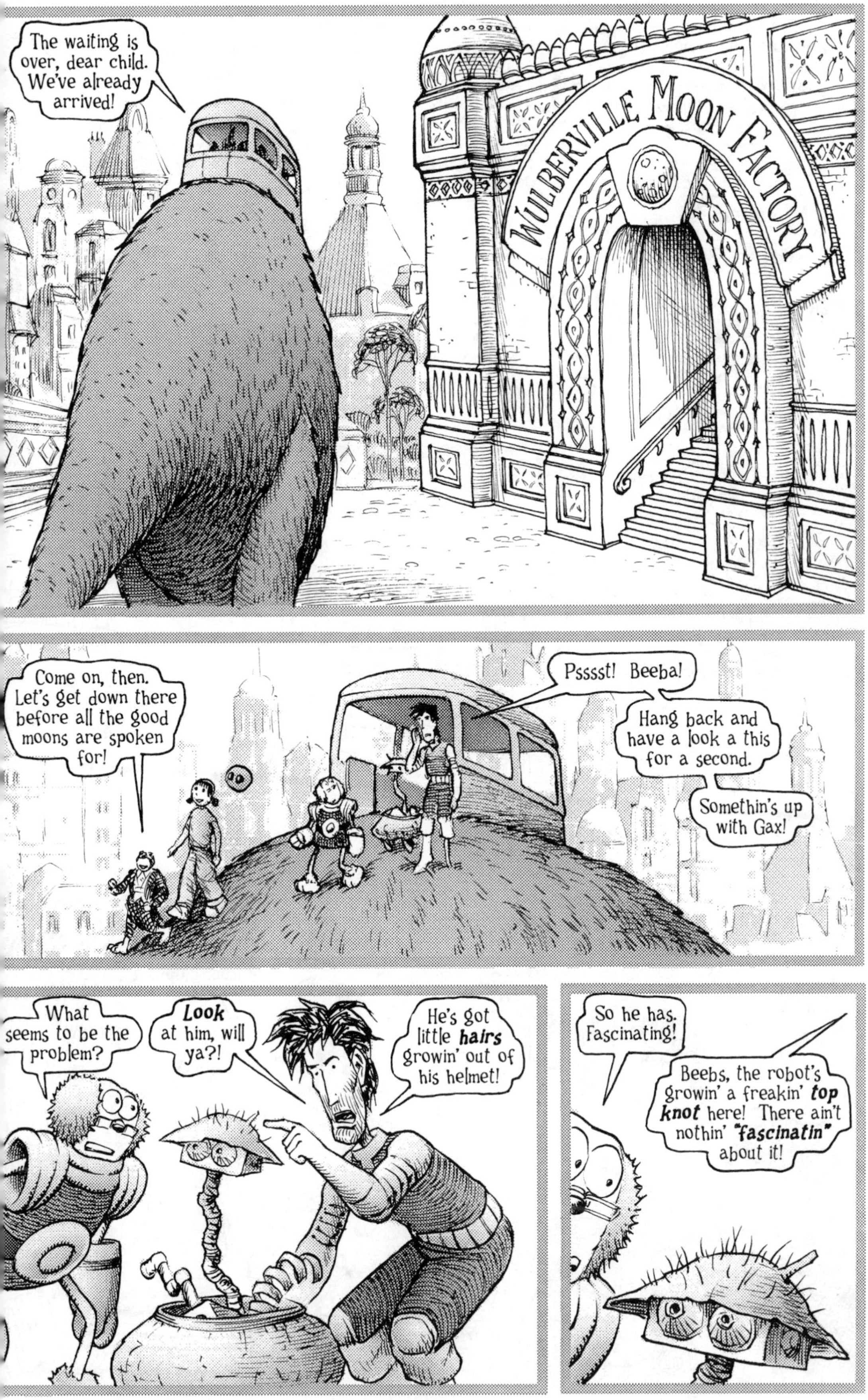
The waiting is over, dear child. We've already arrived!
WULBERVILLE MOON FACTORY
Come on, then. Let's get down there before all the good moons are spoken for!
Psssst! Beeba!
Hang back and have a look a this for a second.
Somethin's up with Gax!
What seems to be the problem?
Look at him, will ya?!
He's got little **hairs** growin' out of his helmet!
So he has. Fascinating!
Beebs, the robot's growin' a freakin' **top knot** here! There ain't nothin' **"fascinatin"** about it!

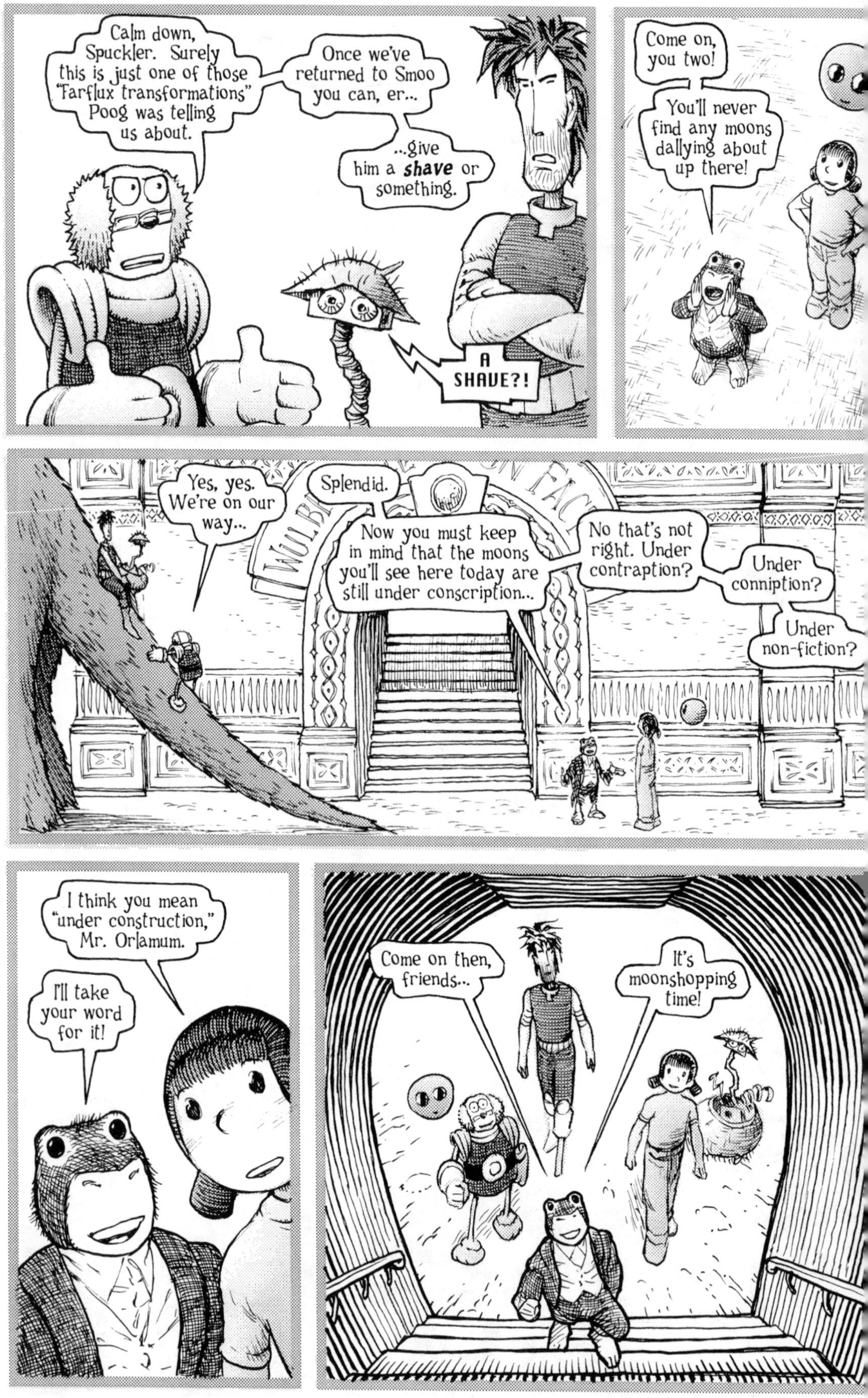
Calm down, Spuckler. Surely this is just one of those "Farflux transformations" Poog was telling us about.
Once we've returned to Smoo you can, er...
...give him a **shave** or something.
A SHAVE?!
Come on, you two!
You'll never find any moons dallying about up there!
Yes, yes. We're on our way...
Splendid.
Now you must keep in mind that the moons you'll see here today are still under conscription...
No that's not right. Under contraption?
Under conniption?
Under non-fiction?
I think you mean "under construction," Mr. Orlamum.
I'll take your word for it!
Come on then, friends...
It's moonshopping time!

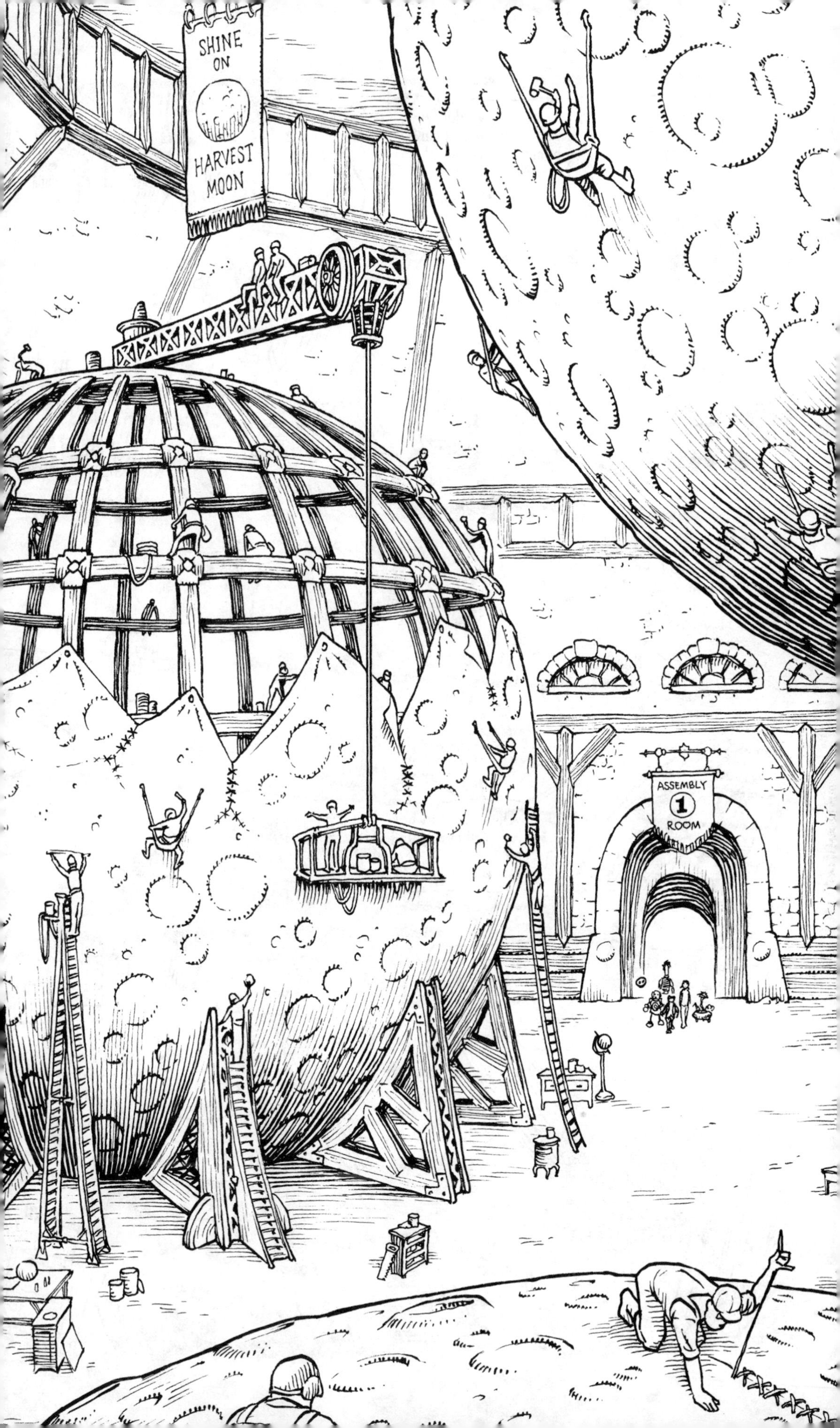
SHINE ON
HARVEST MOON
ASSEMBLY 1 ROOM

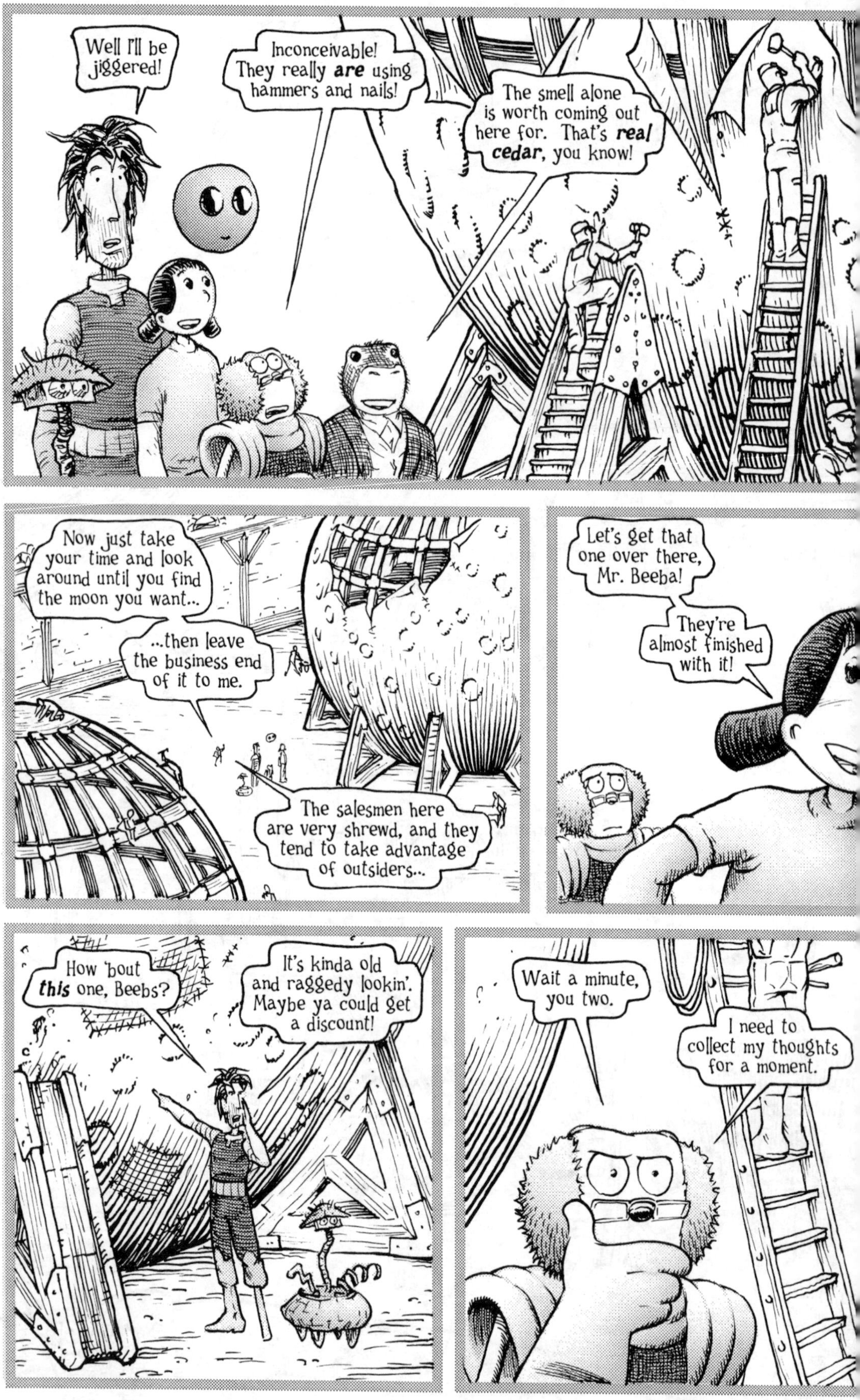
Well I'll be jiggered!
Inconceivable! They really **are** using hammers and nails!
The smell alone is worth coming out here for. That's **real cedar**, you know!
Now just take your time and look around until you find the moon you want...
...then leave the business end of it to me.
The salesmen here are very shrewd, and they tend to take advantage of outsiders...
Let's get that one over there, Mr. Beeba!
They're almost finished with it!
How 'bout **this** one, Beebs?
It's kinda old and raggedy lookin'. Maybe ya could get a discount!
Wait a minute, you two.
I need to collect my thoughts for a moment.

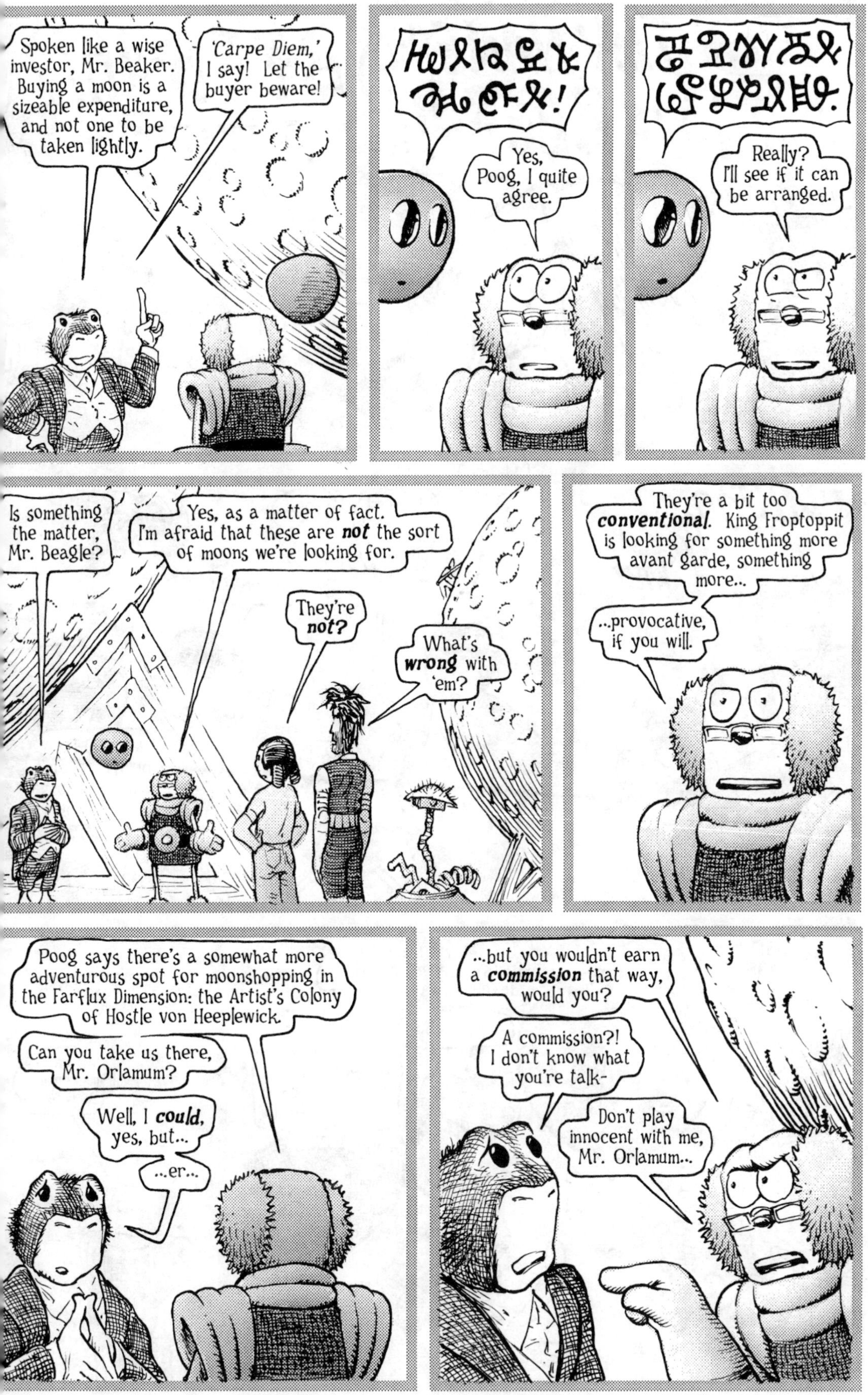
Spoken like a wise investor, Mr. Beaker. Buying a moon is a sizeable expenditure, and not one to be taken lightly.
'Carpe Diem,' I say! Let the buyer beware!
Yes, Poog, I quite agree.
Really? I'll see if it can be arranged.
Is something the matter, Mr. Beagle?
Yes, as a matter of fact. I'm afraid that these are **not** the sort of moons we're looking for.
They're **not?**
What's **wrong** with 'em?
They're a bit too **conventional**. King Froptoppit is looking for something more avant garde, something more...
...provocative, if you will.
Poog says there's a somewhat more adventurous spot for moonshopping in the Farflux Dimension: the Artist's Colony of Hostle von Heeplewick.
Can you take us there, Mr. Orlamum?
Well, I **could**, yes, but...
...er...
...but you wouldn't earn a **commission** that way, would you?
A commission?! I don't know what you're talk-
Don't play innocent with me, Mr. Orlamum...

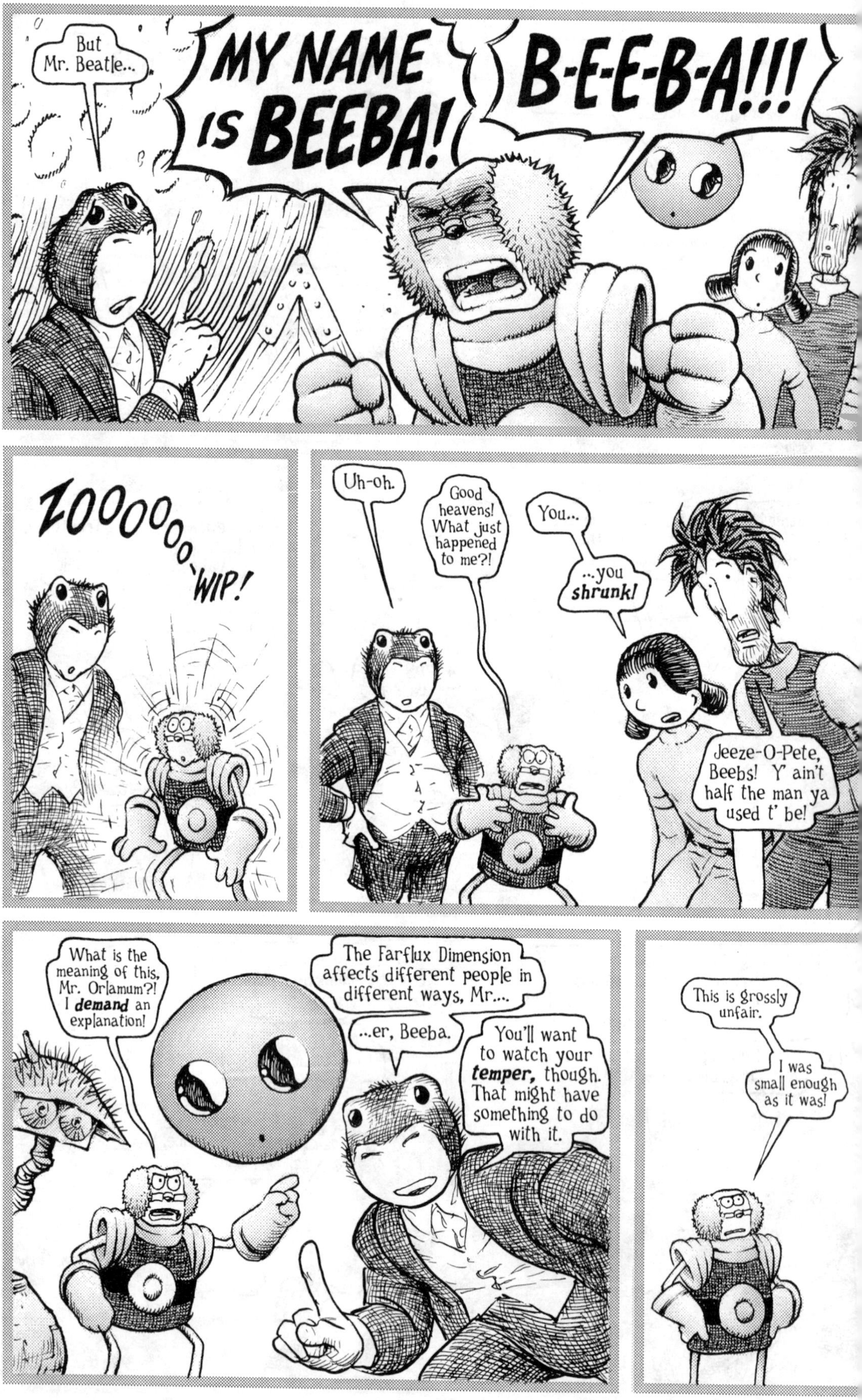
But Mr. Beatle...
MY NAME IS BEEBA!
B-E-E-B-A!!!
ZOOOOOO-WIP!
Uh-oh.
Good heavens! What just happened to me?!
You...
...you shrunk!
Jeeze-O-Pete, Beebs! Y' ain't half the man ya used t' be!
What is the meaning of this, Mr. Orlamum?! I demand an explanation!
The Farflux Dimension affects different people in different ways, Mr....
...er, Beeba.
You'll want to watch your temper, though. That might have something to do with it.
This is grossly unfair.
I was small enough as it was!

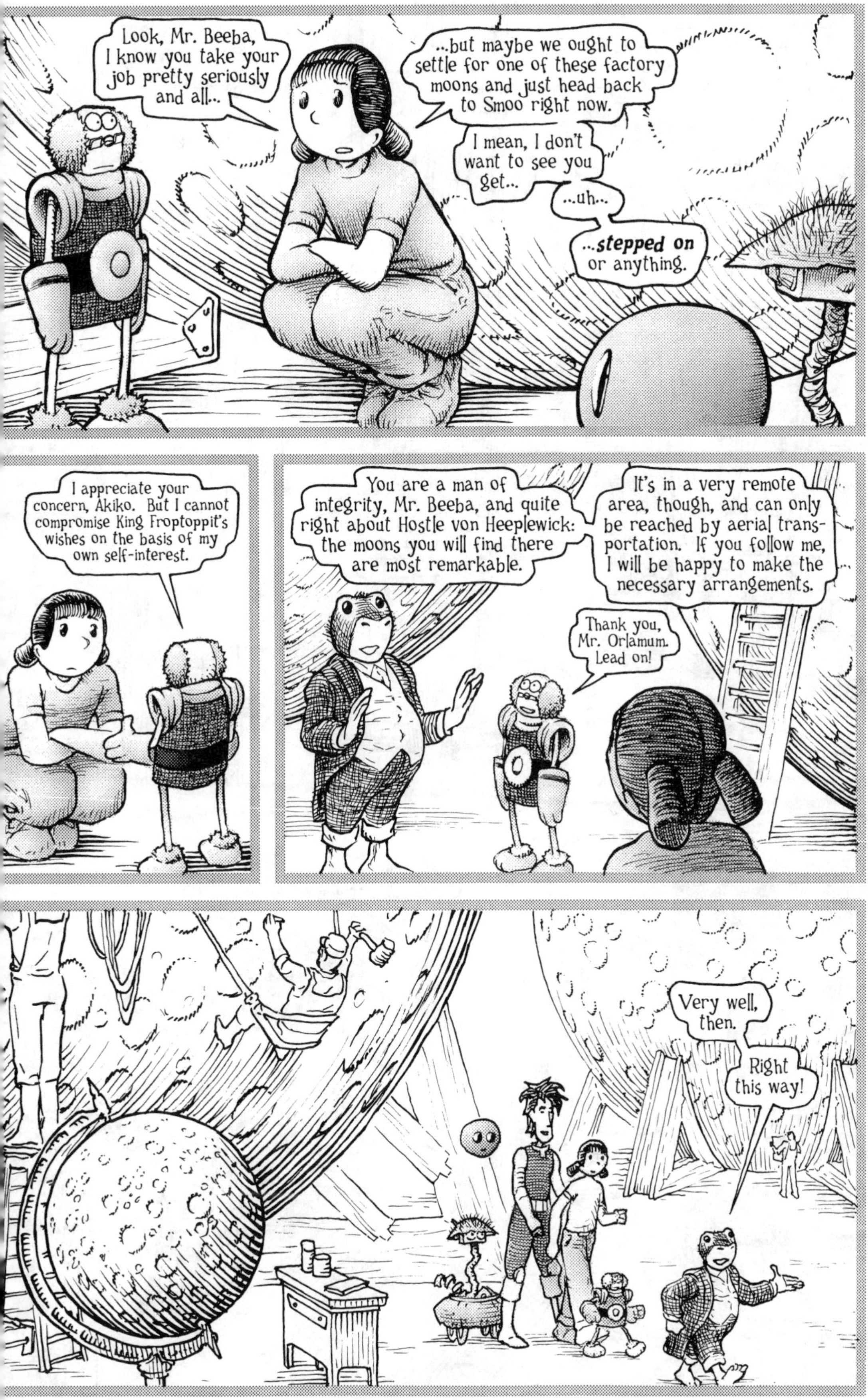
Look, Mr. Beeba, I know you take your job pretty seriously and all...
...but maybe we ought to settle for one of these factory moons and just head back to Smoo right now.
I mean, I don't want to see you get...
...uh...
...stepped on or anything.
I appreciate your concern, Akiko. But I cannot compromise King Froptoppit's wishes on the basis of my own self-interest.
You are a man of integrity, Mr. Beeba, and quite right about Hostle von Heeplewick: the moons you will find there are most remarkable.
It's in a very remote area, though, and can only be reached by aerial transportation. If you follow me, I will be happy to make the necessary arrangements.
Thank you, Mr. Orlamum. Lead on!
Very well, then.
Right this way!

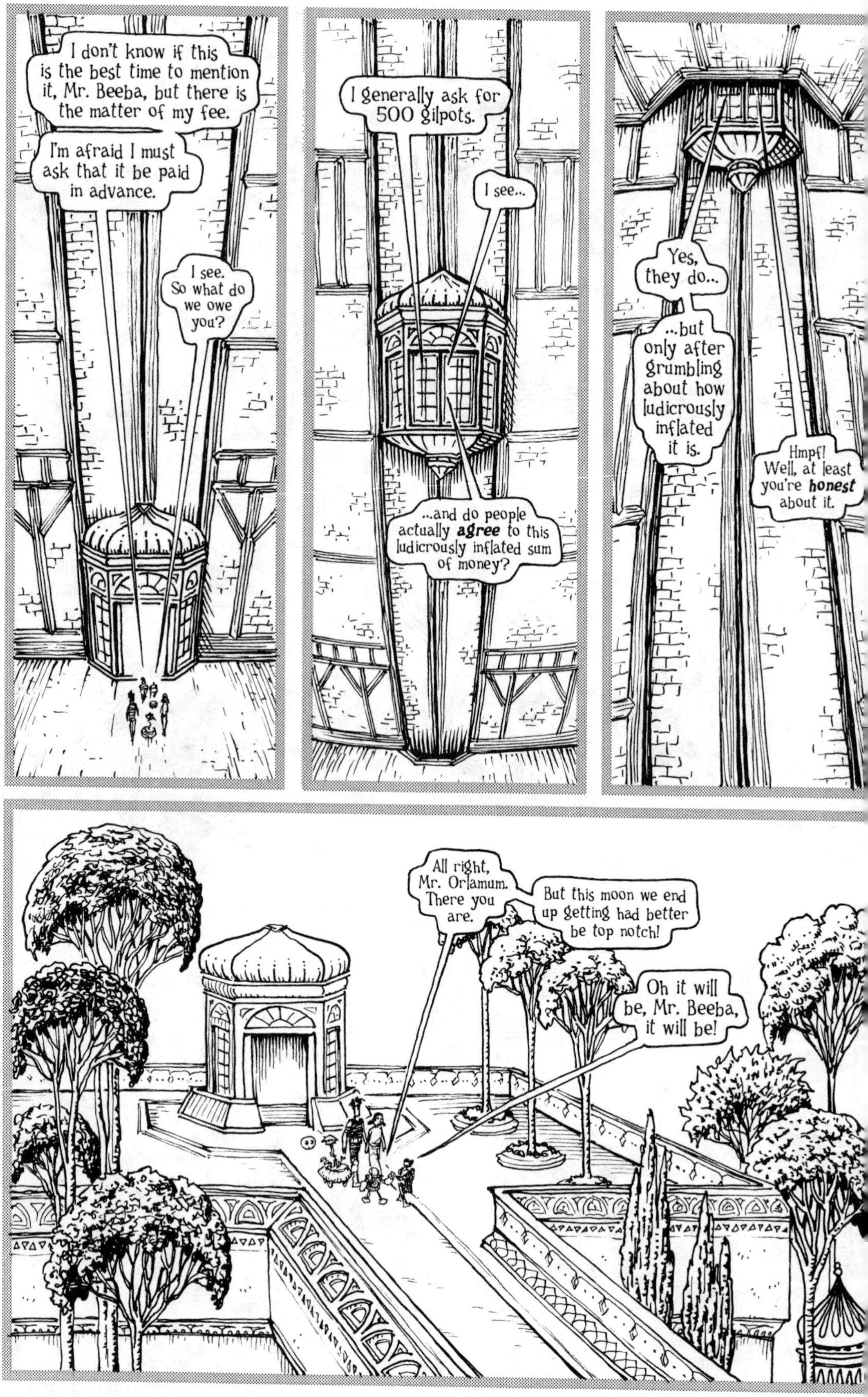
I don't know if this is the best time to mention it, Mr. Beeba, but there is the matter of my fee.
I'm afraid I must ask that it be paid in advance.
I see. So what do we owe you?
I generally ask for 500 gilpots.
I see...
...and do people actually **agree** to this ludicrously inflated sum of money?
Yes, they do...
...but only after grumbling about how ludicrously inflated it is.
Hmpf! Well, at least you're **honest** about it.
All right, Mr. Orlamum. There you are.
But this moon we end up getting had better be top notch!
Oh it will be, Mr. Beeba, it will be!

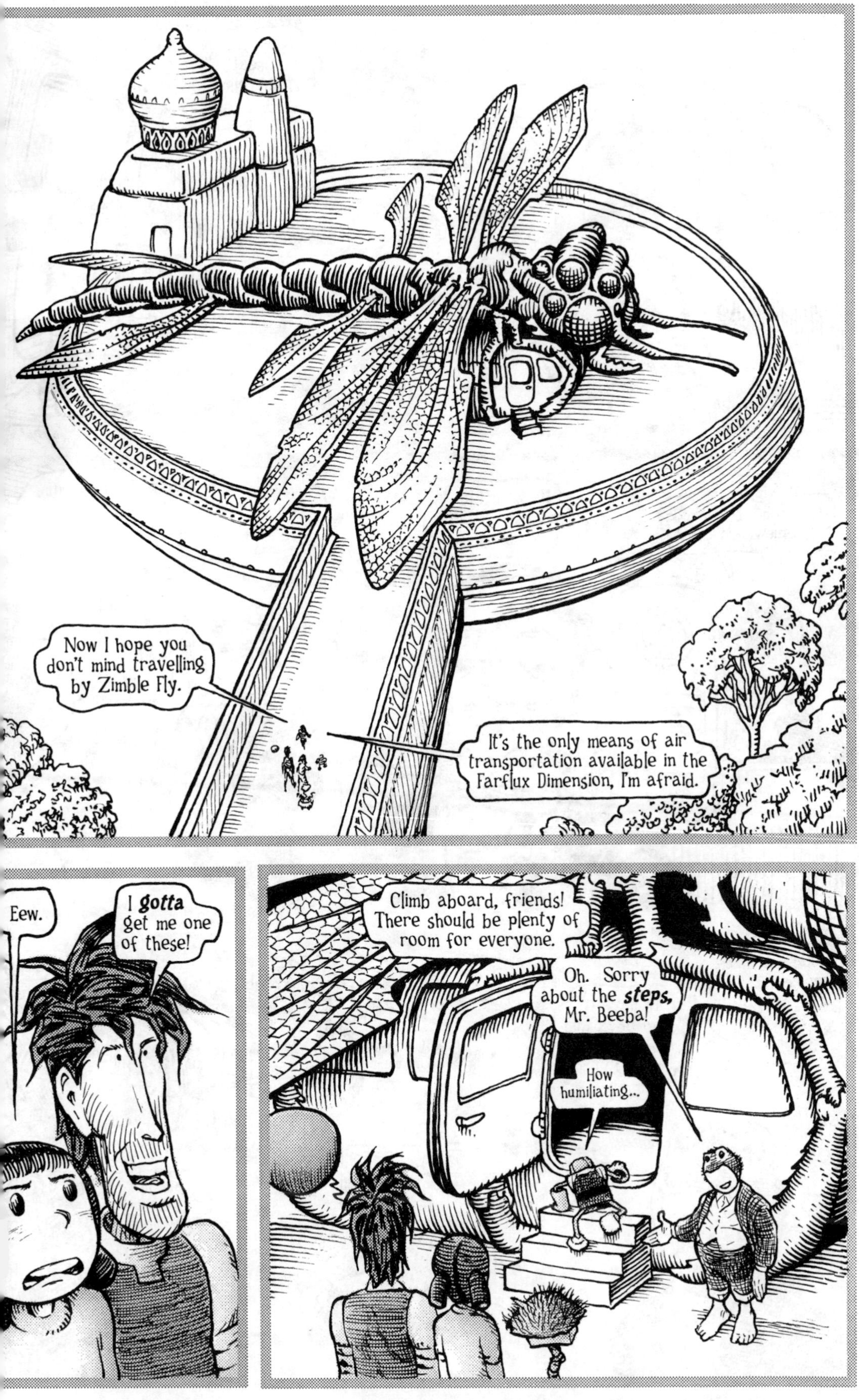

Now I hope you don't mind travelling by Zimble Fly.
It's the only means of air transportation available in the Farflux Dimension, I'm afraid.
Eew.
I **gotta** get me one of these!
Climb aboard, friends! There should be plenty of room for everyone.
Oh. Sorry about the **steps,** Mr. Beeba!
How humiliating...

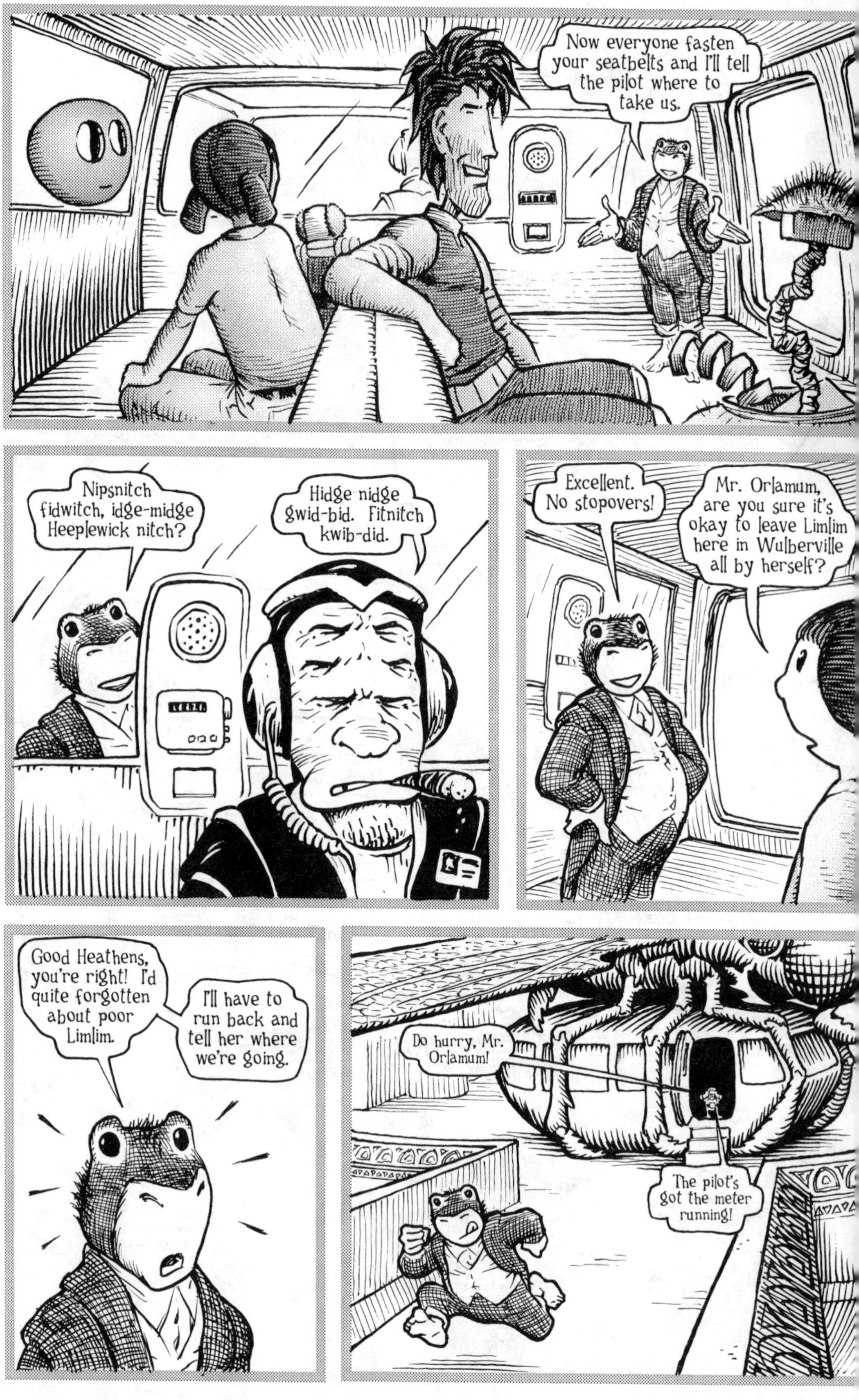

Now everyone fasten your seatbelts and I'll tell the pilot where to take us.
Nipsnitch fidwitch, idge-midge Heeplewick nitch?
Hidge nidge gwid-bid. Fitnitch kwib-did.
Excellent. No stopovers!
Mr. Orlamum, are you sure it's okay to leave Limlim here in Wulberville all by herself?
Good Heathens, you're right! I'd quite forgotten about poor Limlim.
I'll have to run back and tell her where we're going.
Do hurry, Mr. Orlamum!
The pilot's got the meter running!

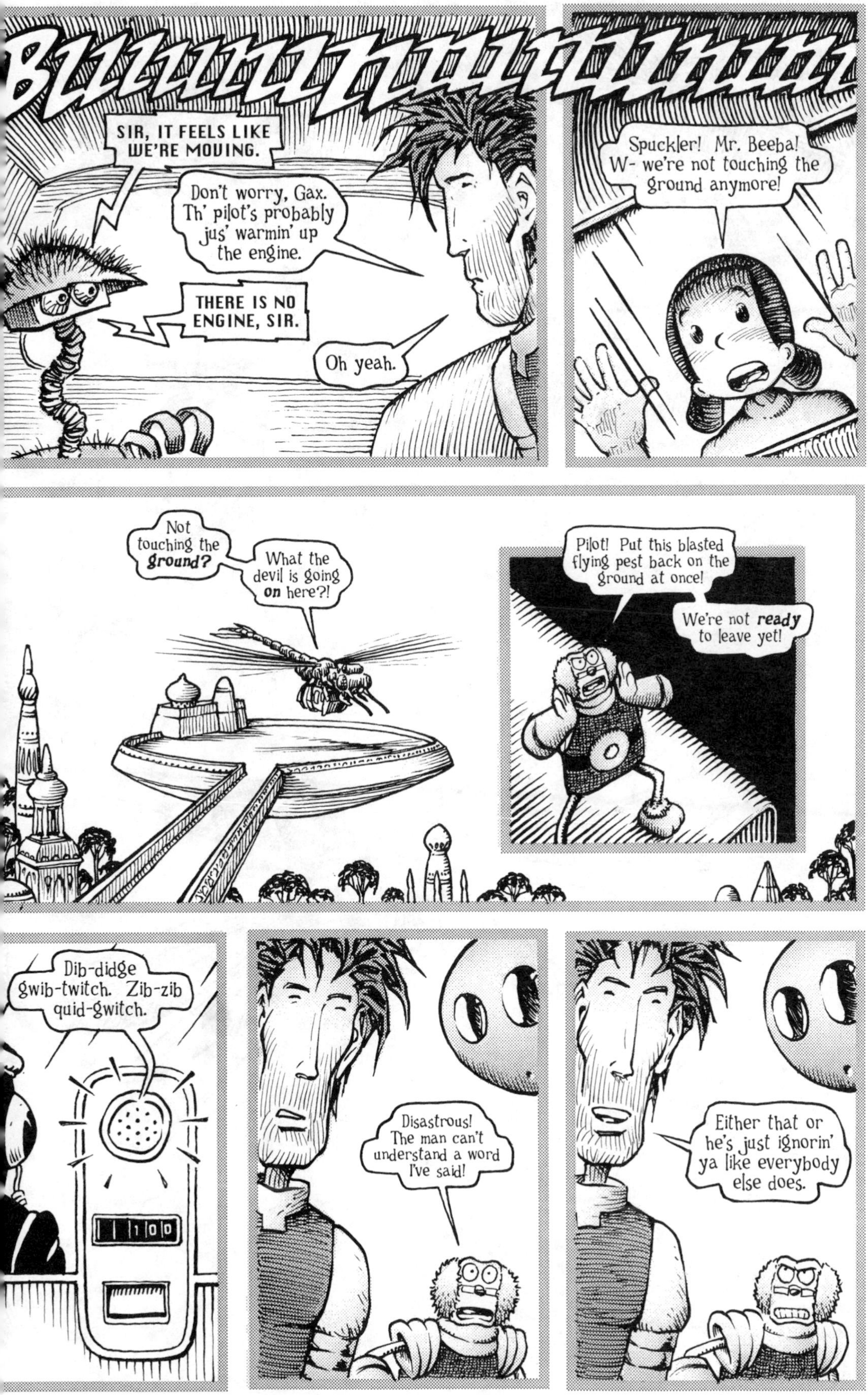

Bzzzzzzhmmmmmm
SIR, IT FEELS LIKE WE'RE MOVING.
Don't worry, Gax. Th' pilot's probably jus' warmin' up the engine.
THERE IS NO ENGINE, SIR.
Oh yeah.
Spuckler! Mr. Beeba! W- we're not touching the ground anymore!
Not touching the ground?
What the devil is going on here?!
Pilot! Put this blasted flying pest back on the ground at once!
We're not ready to leave yet!
Dib-didge gwib-twitch. Zib-zib quid-gwitch.
Disastrous! The man can't understand a word I've said!
Either that or he's just ignorin' ya like everybody else does.

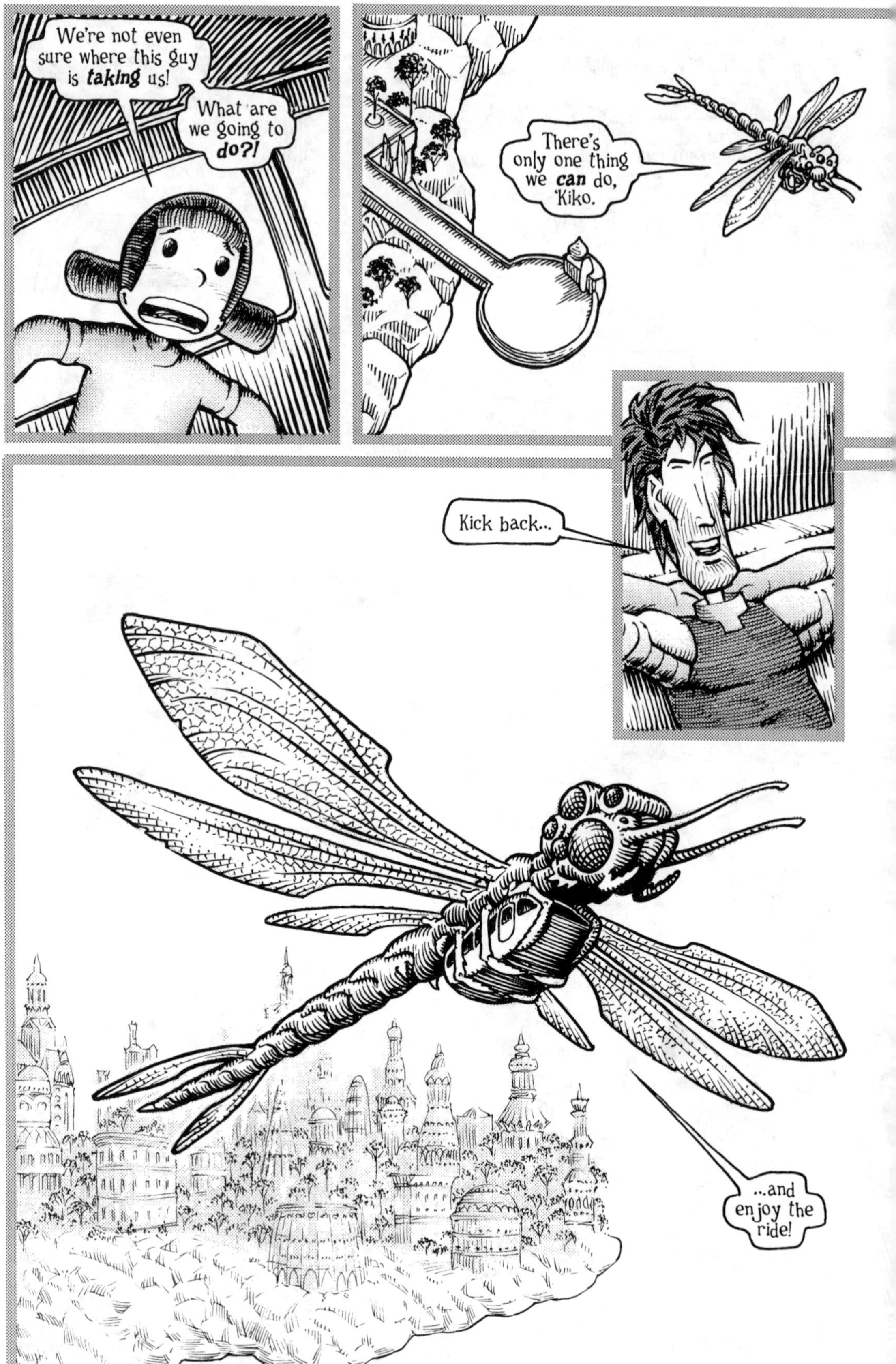

We're not even sure where this guy is *taking* us!
What are we going to ***do?!***
There's only one thing we **can** do, 'Kiko.
Kick back...
...and enjoy the ride!

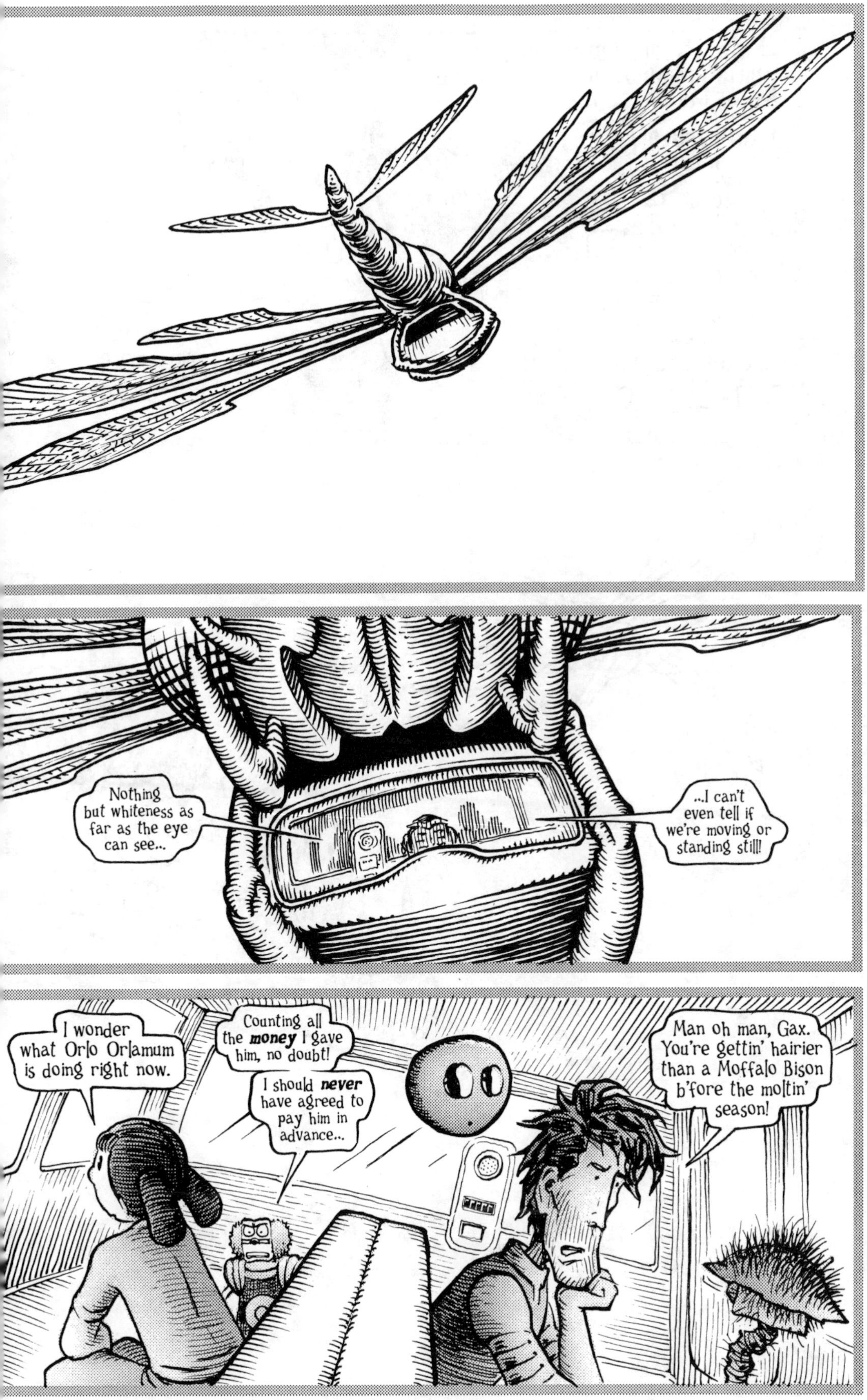
Nothing but whiteness as far as the eye can see...
...I can't even tell if we're moving or standing still!
I wonder what Orlo Orlamum is doing right now.
Counting all the **money** I gave him, no doubt!
I should **never** have agreed to pay him in advance...
Man oh man, Gax. You're gettin' hairier than a Moffalo Bison b'fore the moltin' season!

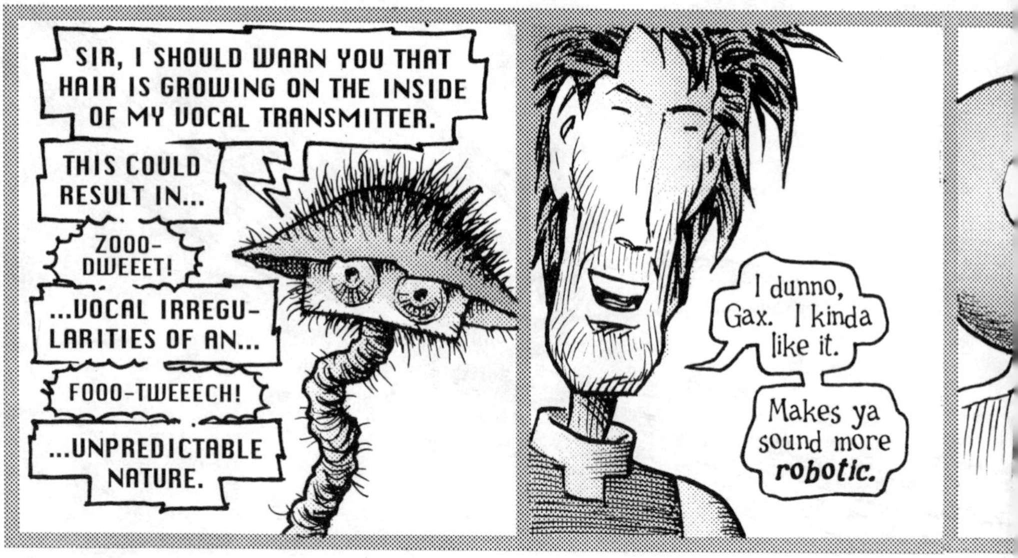
SIR, I SHOULD WARN YOU THAT HAIR IS GROWING ON THE INSIDE OF MY VOCAL TRANSMITTER.
THIS COULD RESULT IN...
ZOOO-DWEEET!
...VOCAL IRREGU-LARITIES OF AN...
FOOO-TWEEECH!
...UNPREDICTABLE NATURE.
I dunno, Gax. I kinda like it.
Makes ya sound more **robotic.**

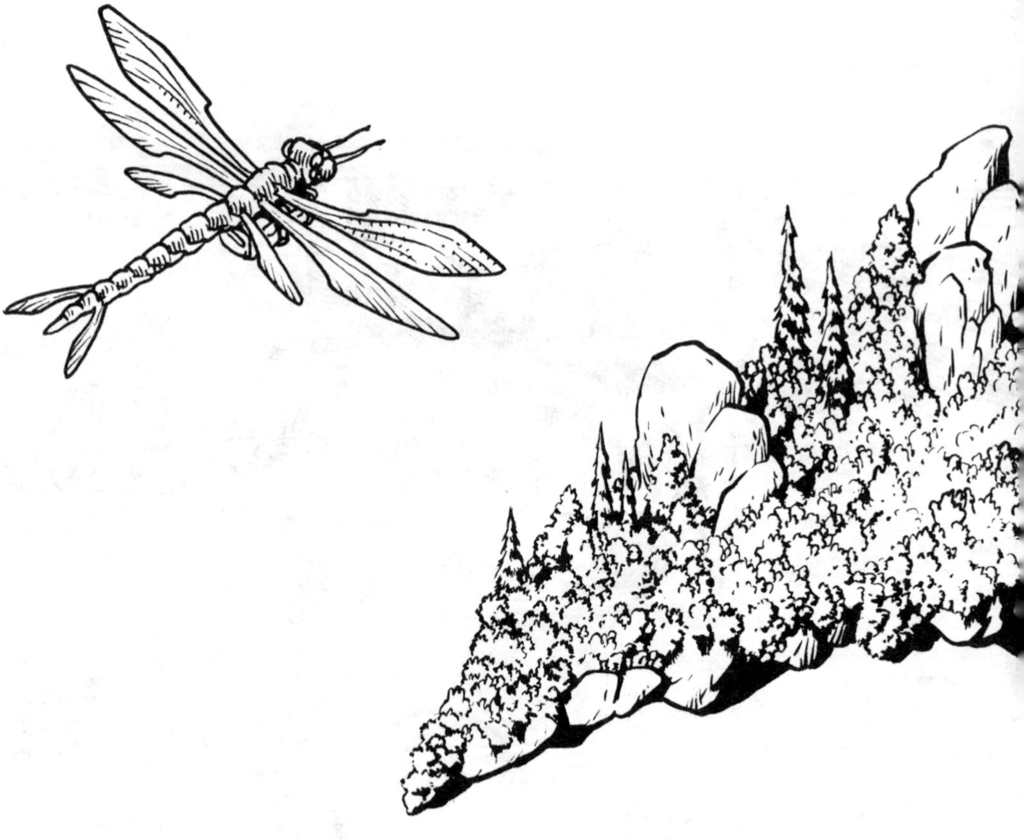

MoonshOpping

part three

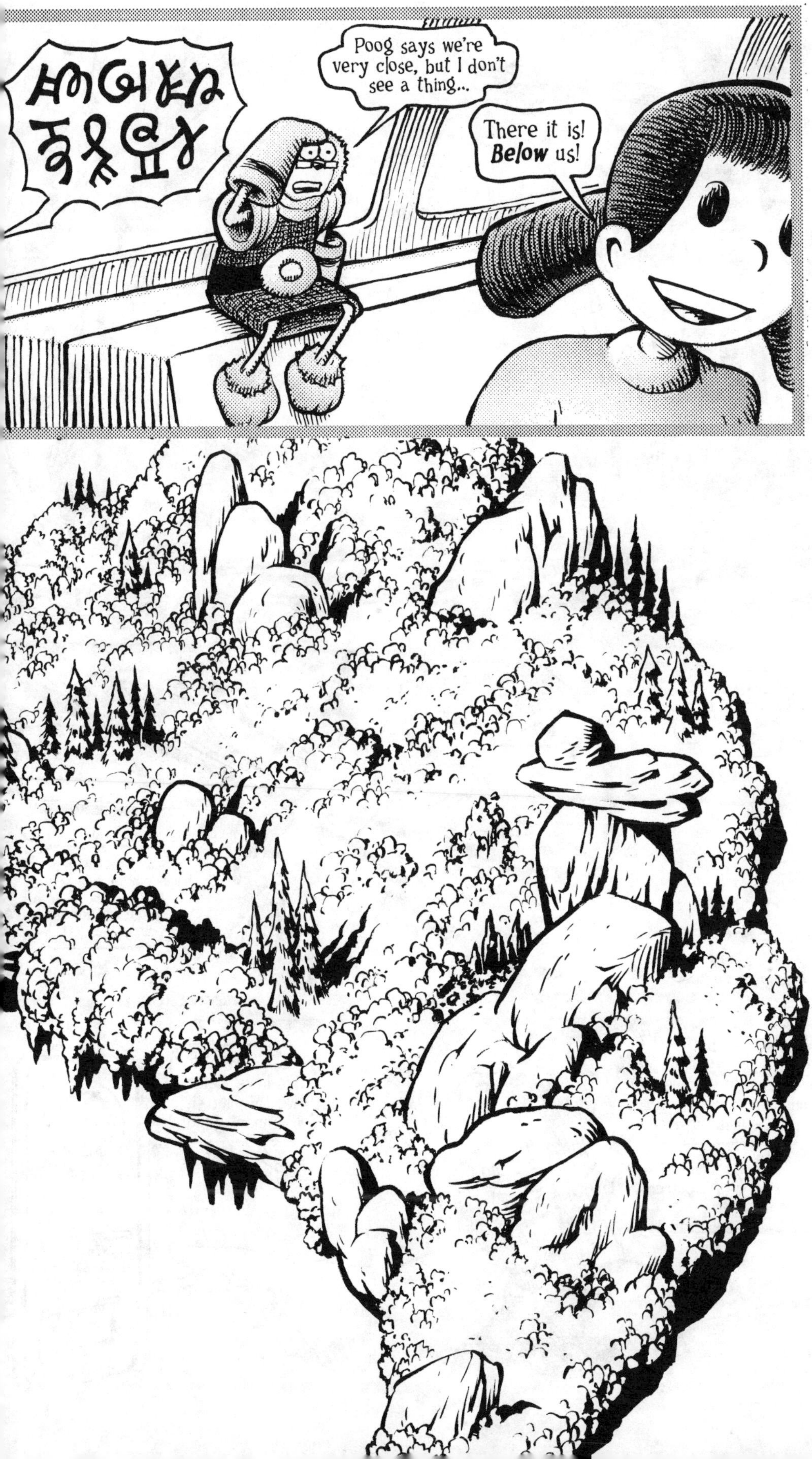
Poog says we're very close, but I don't see a thing...
There it is! *Below* us!

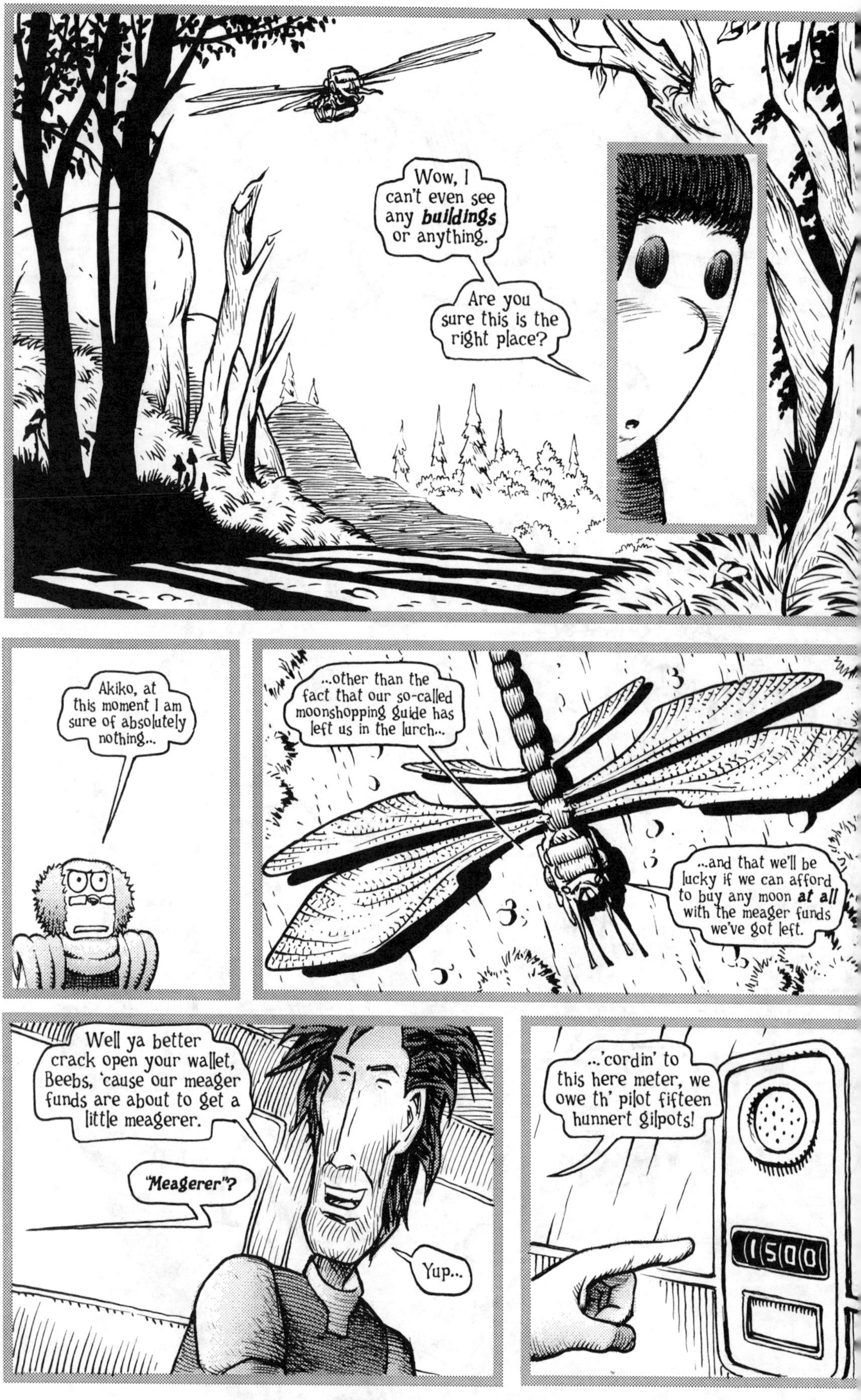
Wow, I can't even see any **buildings** or anything.
Are you sure this is the right place?
Akiko, at this moment I am sure of absolutely nothing...
...other than the fact that our so-called moonshopping guide has left us in the lurch...
...and that we'll be lucky if we can afford to buy any moon **at all** with the meager funds we've got left.
Well ya better crack open your wallet, Beebs, 'cause our meager funds are about to get a little meagerer.
"Meagerer"?
Yup...
...'cordin' to this here meter, we owe th' pilot fifteen hunnert gilpots!
1500

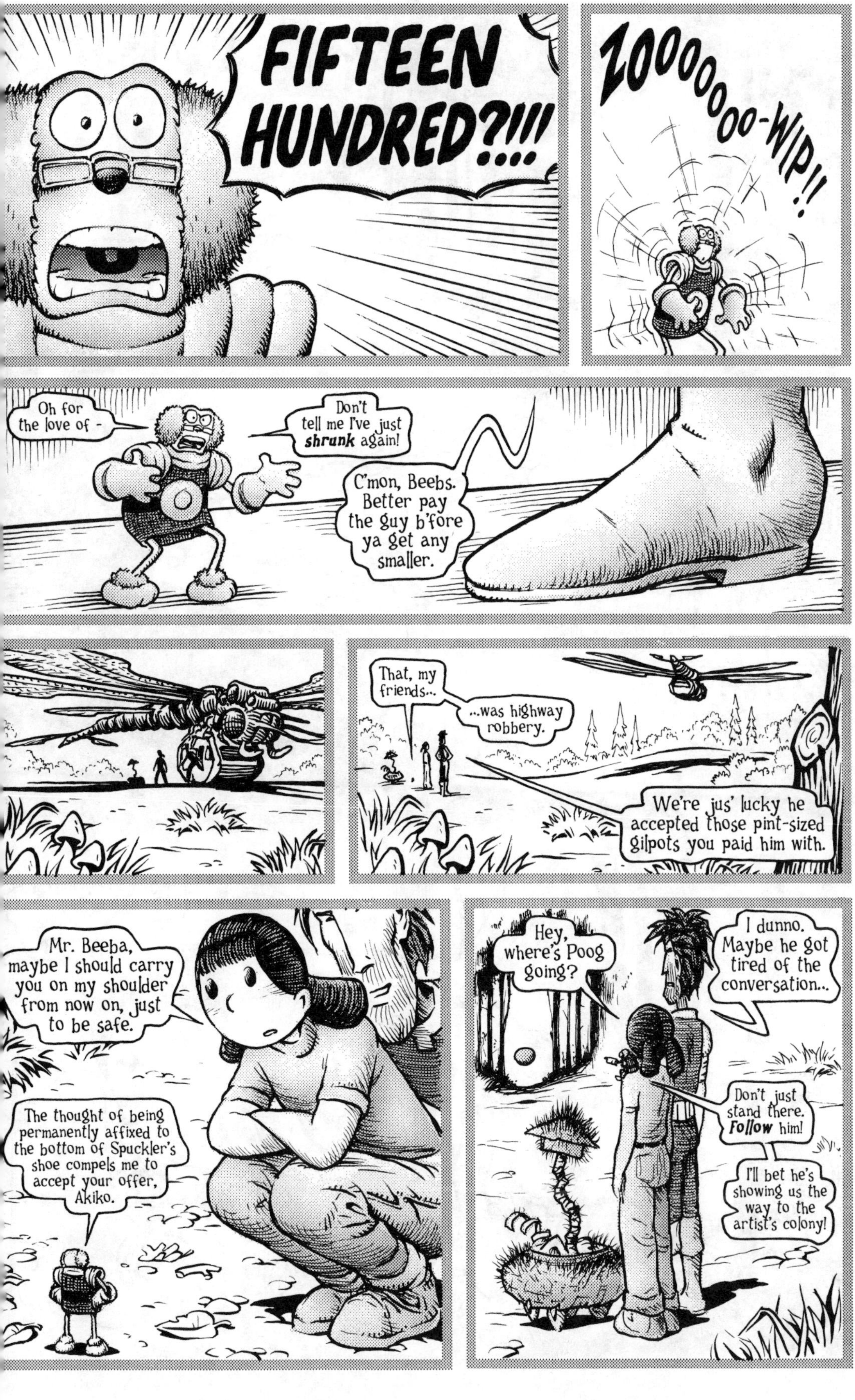
FIFTEEN HUNDRED?!!...
ZOOOOOOOO-WIP!!
Oh for the love of -
Don't tell me I've just **shrunk** again!
C'mon, Beebs. Better pay the guy b'fore ya get any smaller.
That, my friends...
...was highway robbery.
We're jus' lucky he accepted those pint-sized gilpots you paid him with.
Mr. Beeba, maybe I should carry you on my shoulder from now on, just to be safe.
The thought of being permanently affixed to the bottom of Spuckler's shoe compels me to accept your offer, Akiko.
Hey, where's Poog going?
I dunno. Maybe he got tired of the conversation...
Don't just stand there. **Follow** him!
I'll bet he's showing us the way to the artist's colony!

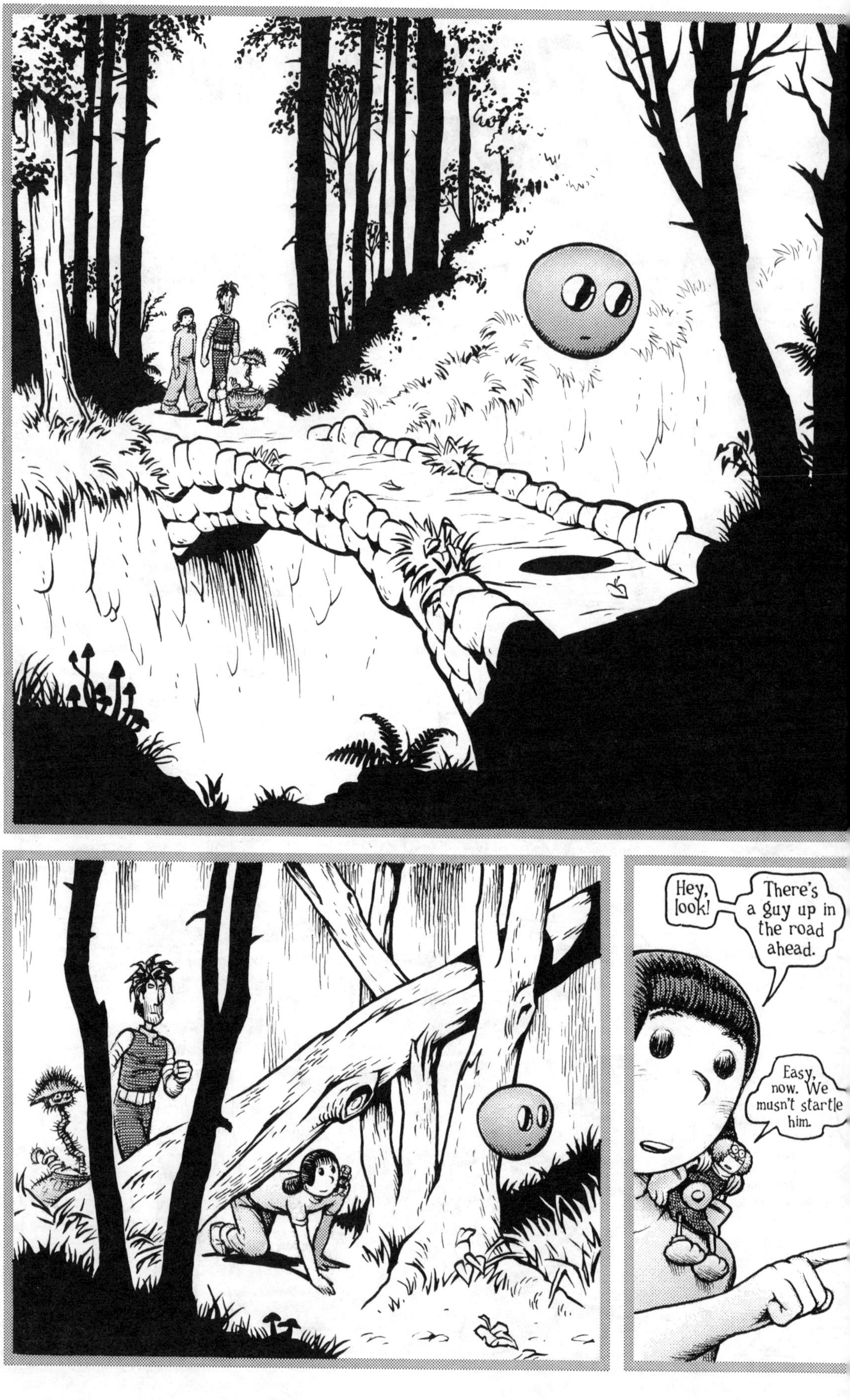

Hey, look!
There's a guy up in the road ahead.
Easy, now. We musn't startle him.

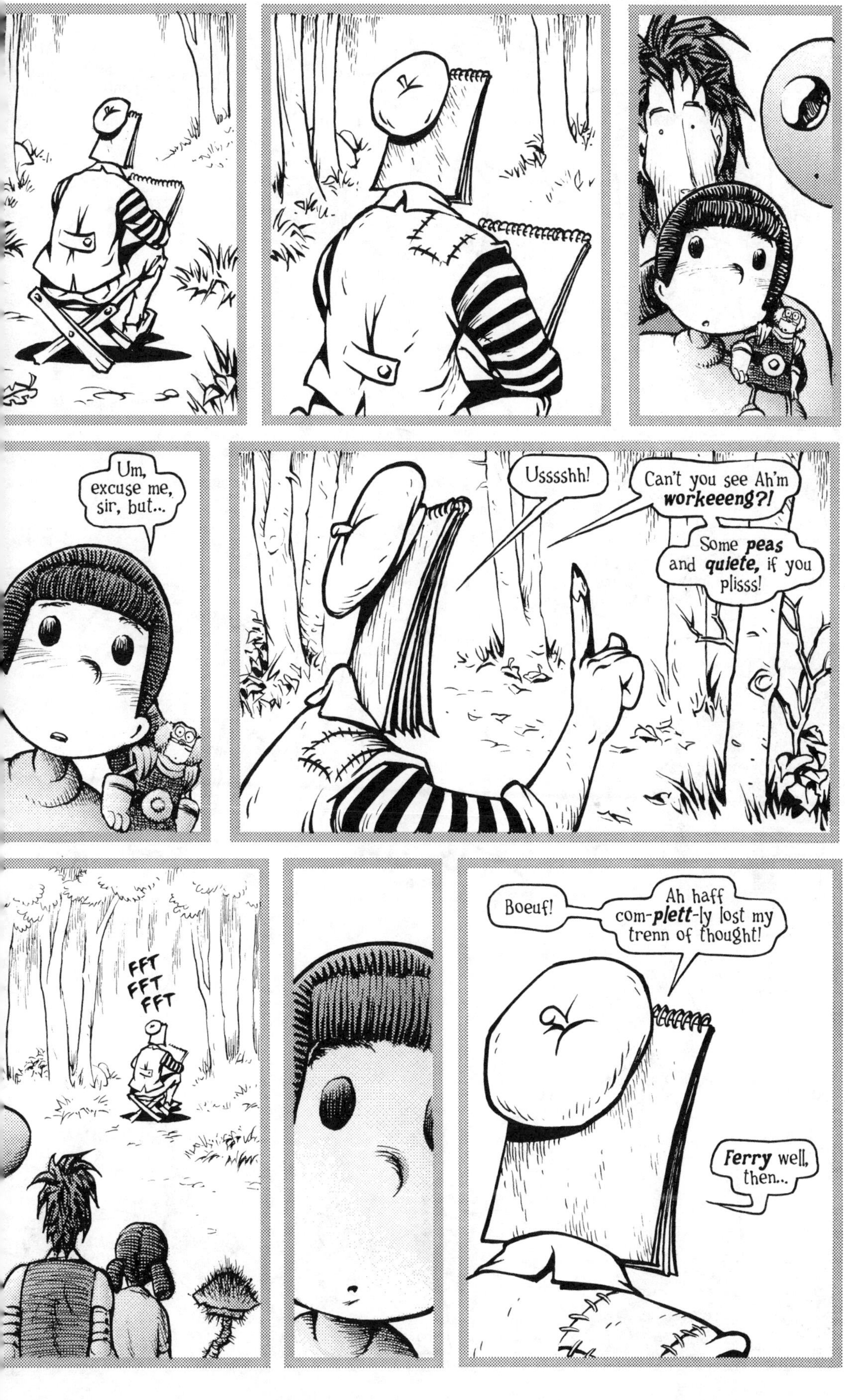
Um, excuse me, sir, but...
Usssshh!
Can't you see Ah'm **workeeeng?!**
Some **peas** and **quiete,** if you plisss!
FFT FFT FFT
Boeuf!
Ah haff com-**plett**-ly lost my trenn of thought!
Ferry well, then...

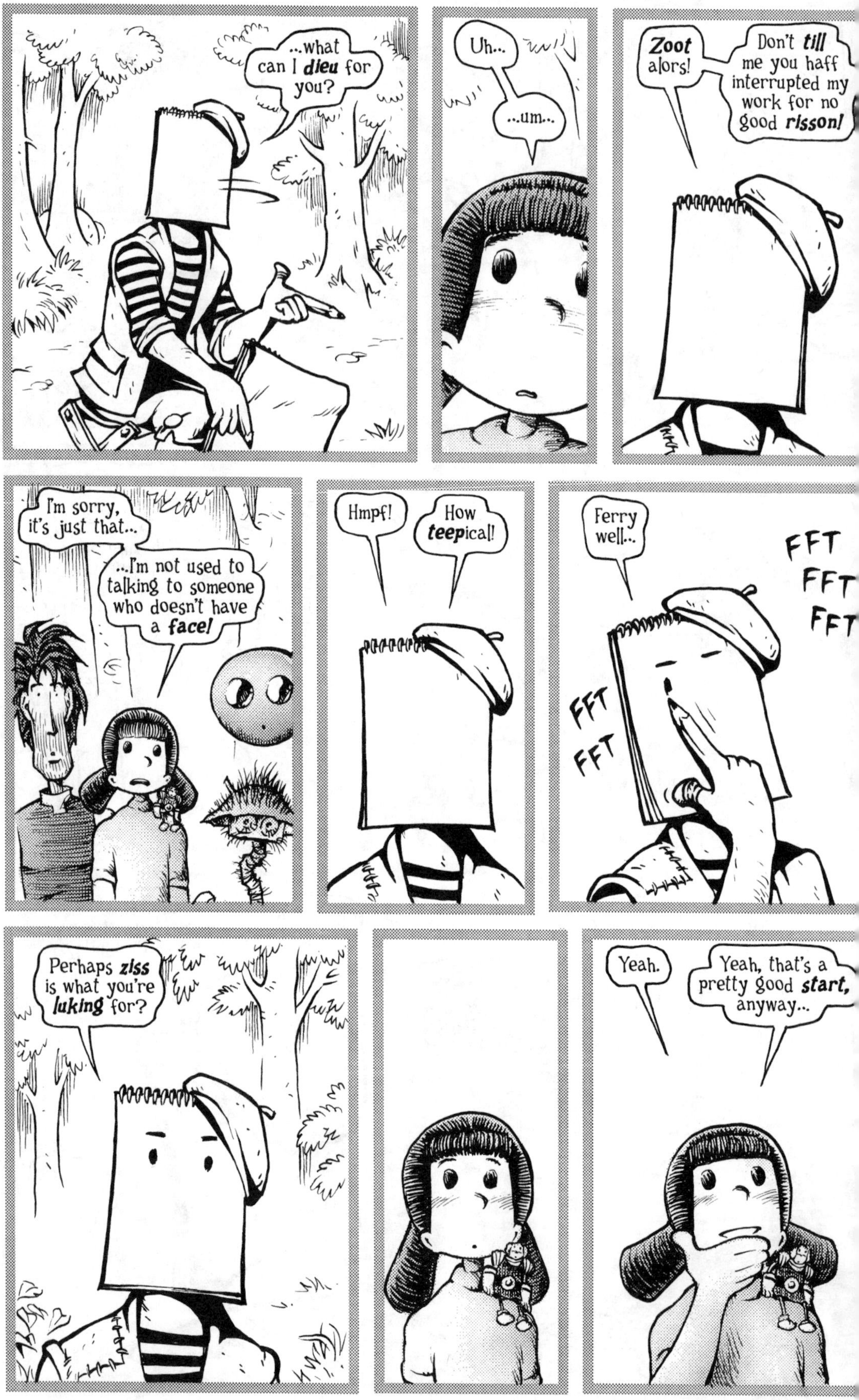
...what can I **dieu** for you?
Uh...
...um...
Zoot alors!
Don't **till** me you haff interrupted my work for no good **risson!**
I'm sorry, it's just that...
...I'm not used to talking to someone who doesn't have a **face!**
Hmpf!
How **teep**ical!
Ferry well...
FFT FFT FFT
FFT FFT
Perhaps **ziss** is what you're **luking** for?
Yeah.
Yeah, that's a pretty good **start,** anyway...

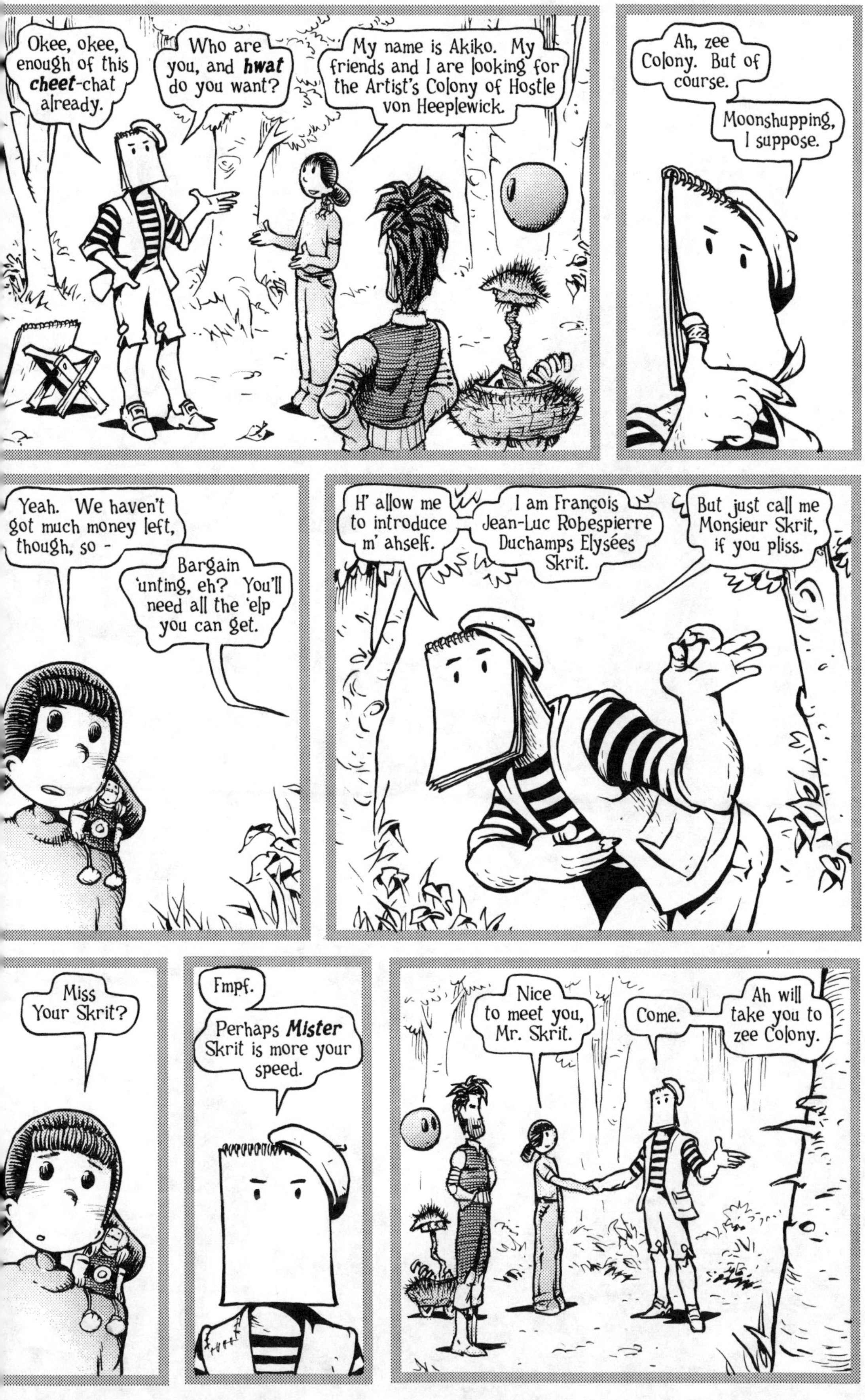
Okee, okee, enough of this **cheet**-chat already.
Who are you, and ***hwat*** do you want?
My name is Akiko. My friends and I are looking for the Artist's Colony of Hostle von Heeplewick.
Ah, zee Colony. But of course.
Moonshupping, I suppose.
Yeah. We haven't got much money left, though, so -
Bargain 'unting, eh? You'll need all the 'elp you can get.
H' allow me to introduce m' ahself.
I am François Jean-Luc Robespierre Duchamps Elysées Skrit.
But just call me Monsieur Skrit, if you pliss.
Miss Your Skrit?
Fmpf.
Perhaps ***Mister*** Skrit is more your speed.
Nice to meet you, Mr. Skrit.
Come.
Ah will take you to zee Colony.

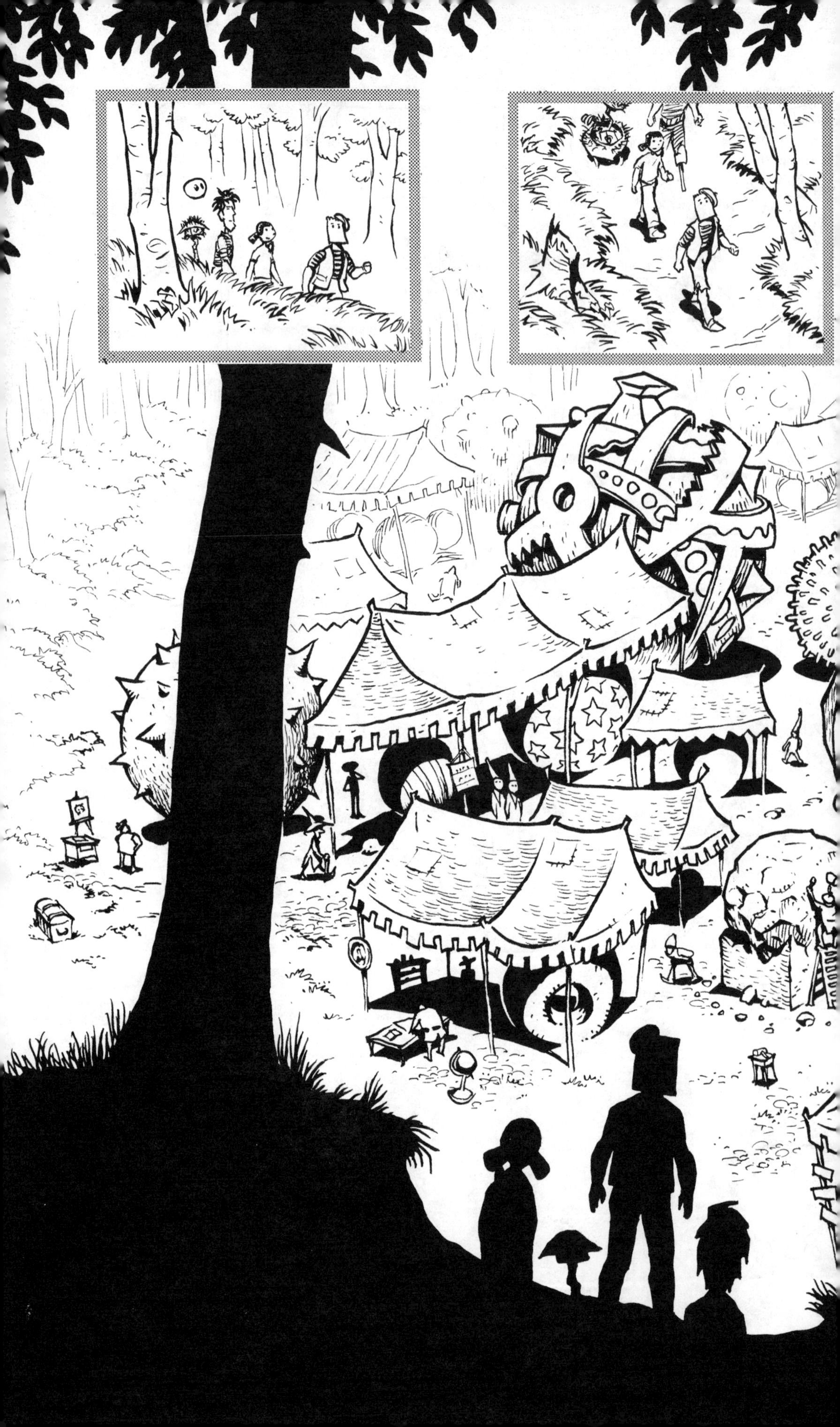

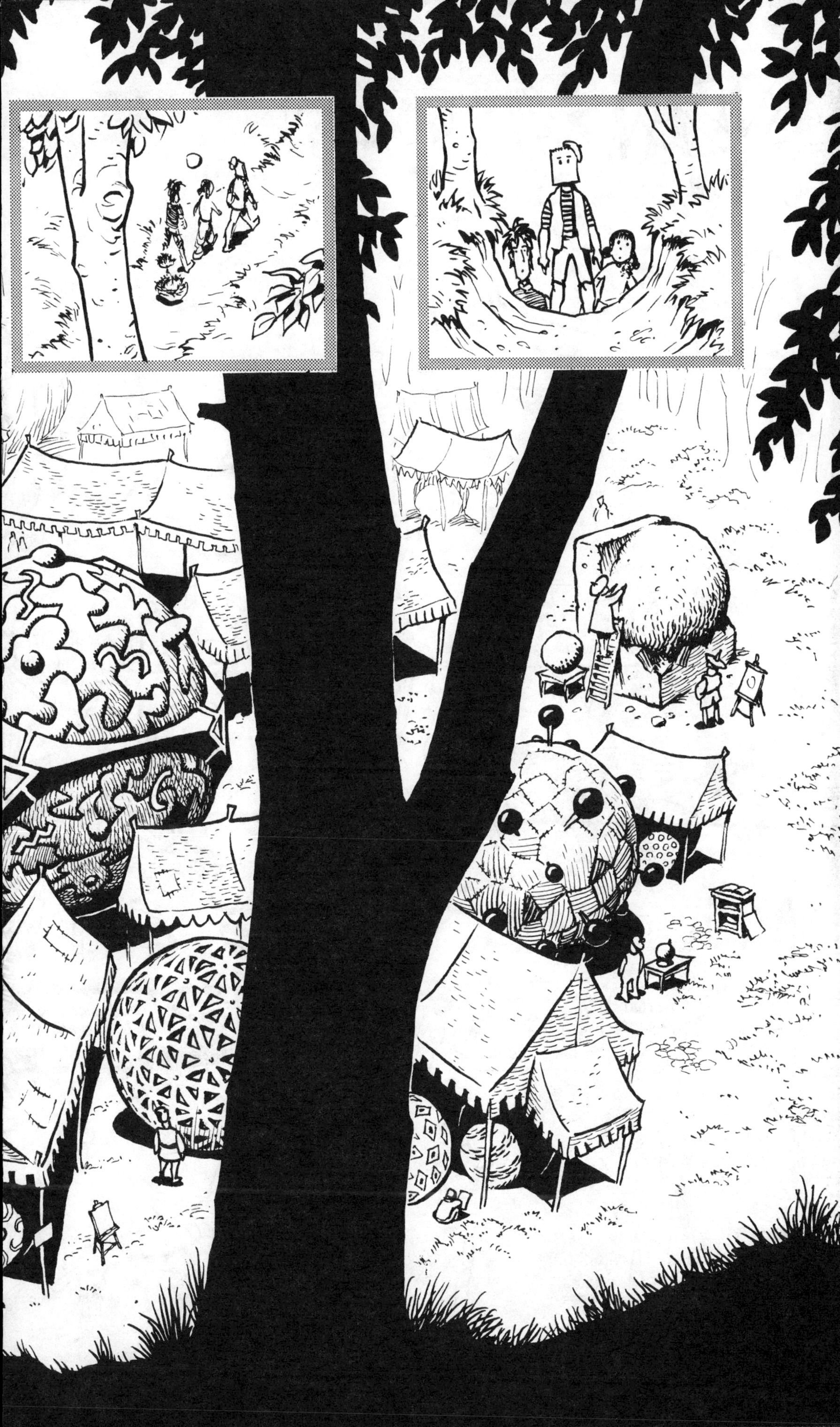

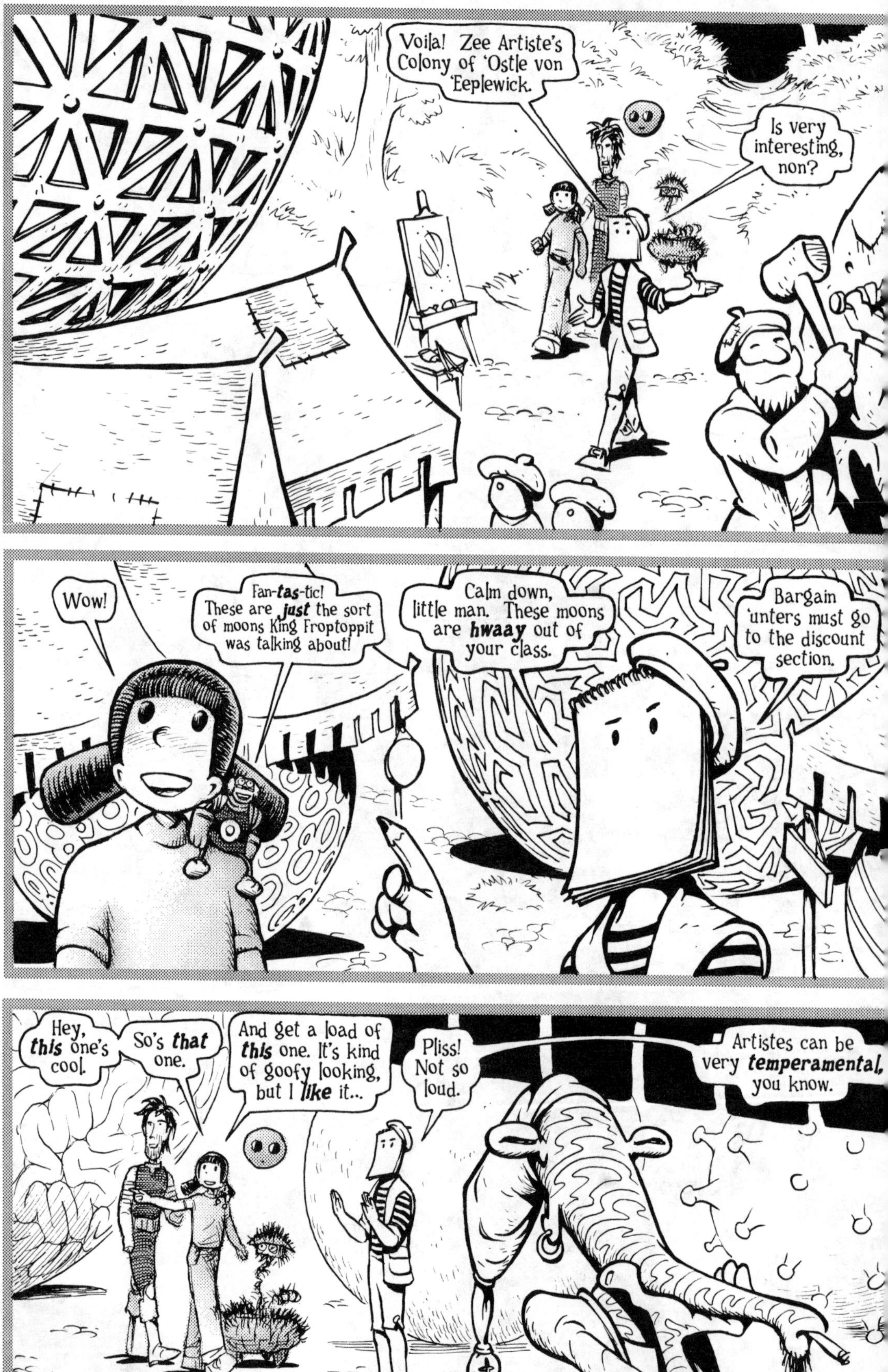

Voila! Zee Artiste's Colony of 'Ostle von 'Eeplewick.
Is very interesting, non?
Wow!
Fan-tas-tic! These are just the sort of moons King Froptoppit was talking about!
Calm down, little man. These moons are hwaay out of your class.
Bargain 'unters must go to the discount section.
Hey, this one's cool.
So's that one.
And get a load of this one. It's kind of goofy looking, but I like it...
Pliss! Not so loud.
Artistes can be very temperamental, you know.

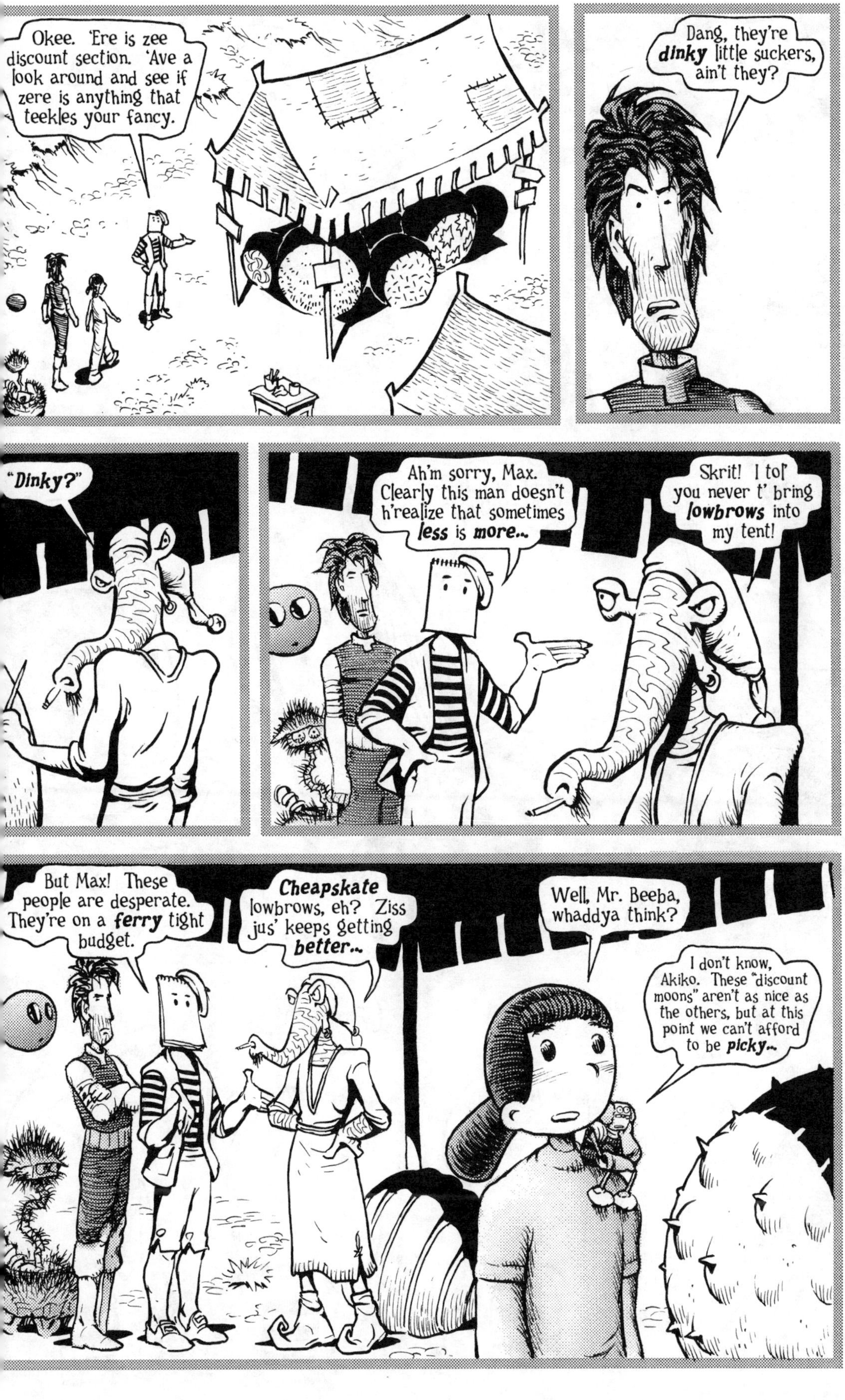
Okee. 'Ere is zee discount section. 'Ave a look around and see if zere is anything that teekles your fancy.
Dang, they're **dinky** little suckers, ain't they?
"**Dinky?**"
Ah'm sorry, Max. Clearly this man doesn't h'realize that sometimes **less** is **more..**
Skrit! I tol' you never t' bring **lowbrows** into my tent!
But Max! These people are desperate. They're on a **ferry** tight budget.
Cheapskate lowbrows, eh? Ziss jus' keeps getting **better..**
Well, Mr. Beeba, whaddya think?
I don't know, Akiko. These "discount moons" aren't as nice as the others, but at this point we can't afford to be **picky..**

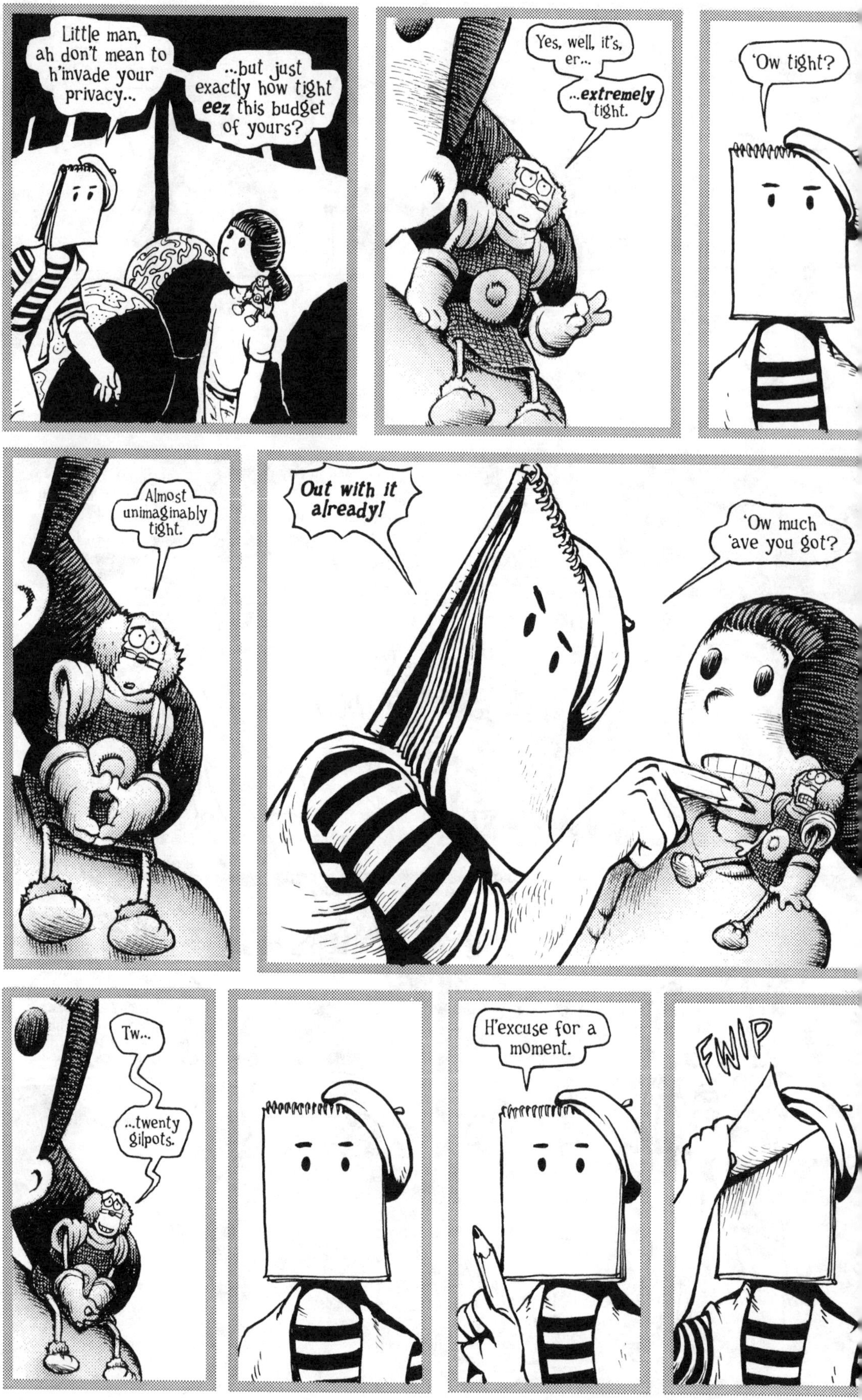
Little man, ah don't mean to h'invade your privacy...
...but just exactly how tight eez this budget of yours?
Yes, well, it's, er...
...extremely tight.
'Ow tight?
Almost unimaginably tight.
Out with it already!
'Ow much 'ave you got?
Tw...
...twenty gilpots.
H'excuse for a moment.
FWIP

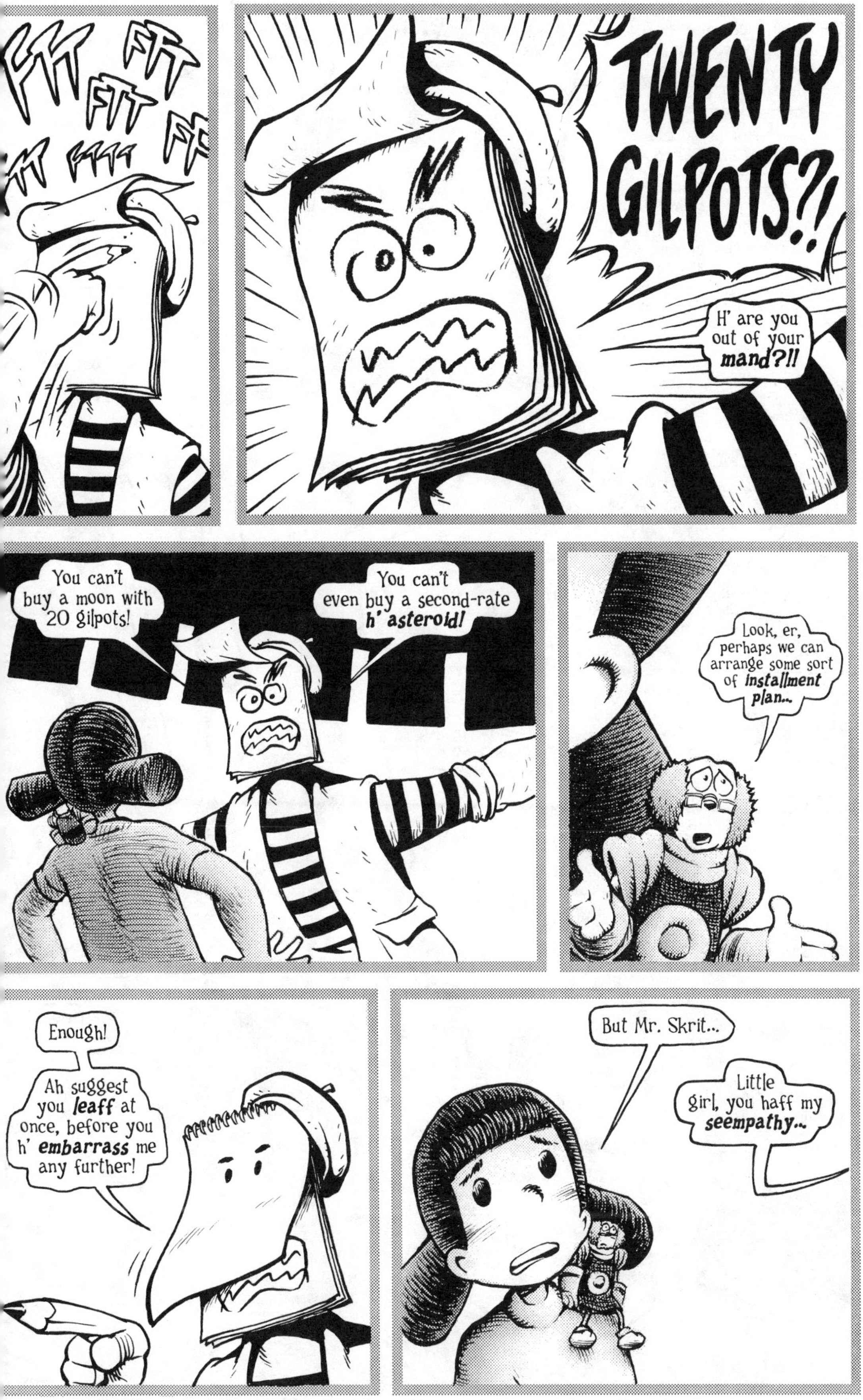
FFT FFT FFT FF FT FFFF FF
TWENTY GILPOTS?!
H' are you out of your mand?!!
You can't buy a moon with 20 gilpots!
You can't even buy a second-rate h' asteroid!
Look, er, perhaps we can arrange some sort of installment plan...
Enough!
Ah suggest you leaff at once, before you h' embarrass me any further!
But Mr. Skrit...
Little girl, you haff my seempathy...

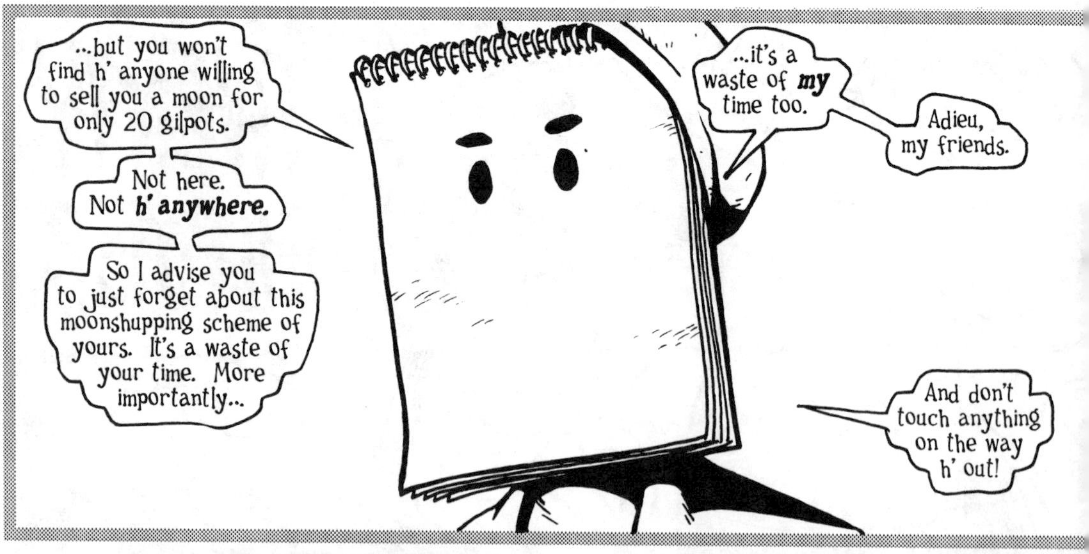
...but you won't find h' anyone willing to sell you a moon for only 20 gilpots.
Not here. Not **h' anywhere.**
So I advise you to just forget about this moonshupping scheme of yours. It's a waste of your time. More importantly...
...it's a waste of **my** time too.
Adieu, my friends.
And don't touch anything on the way h' out!

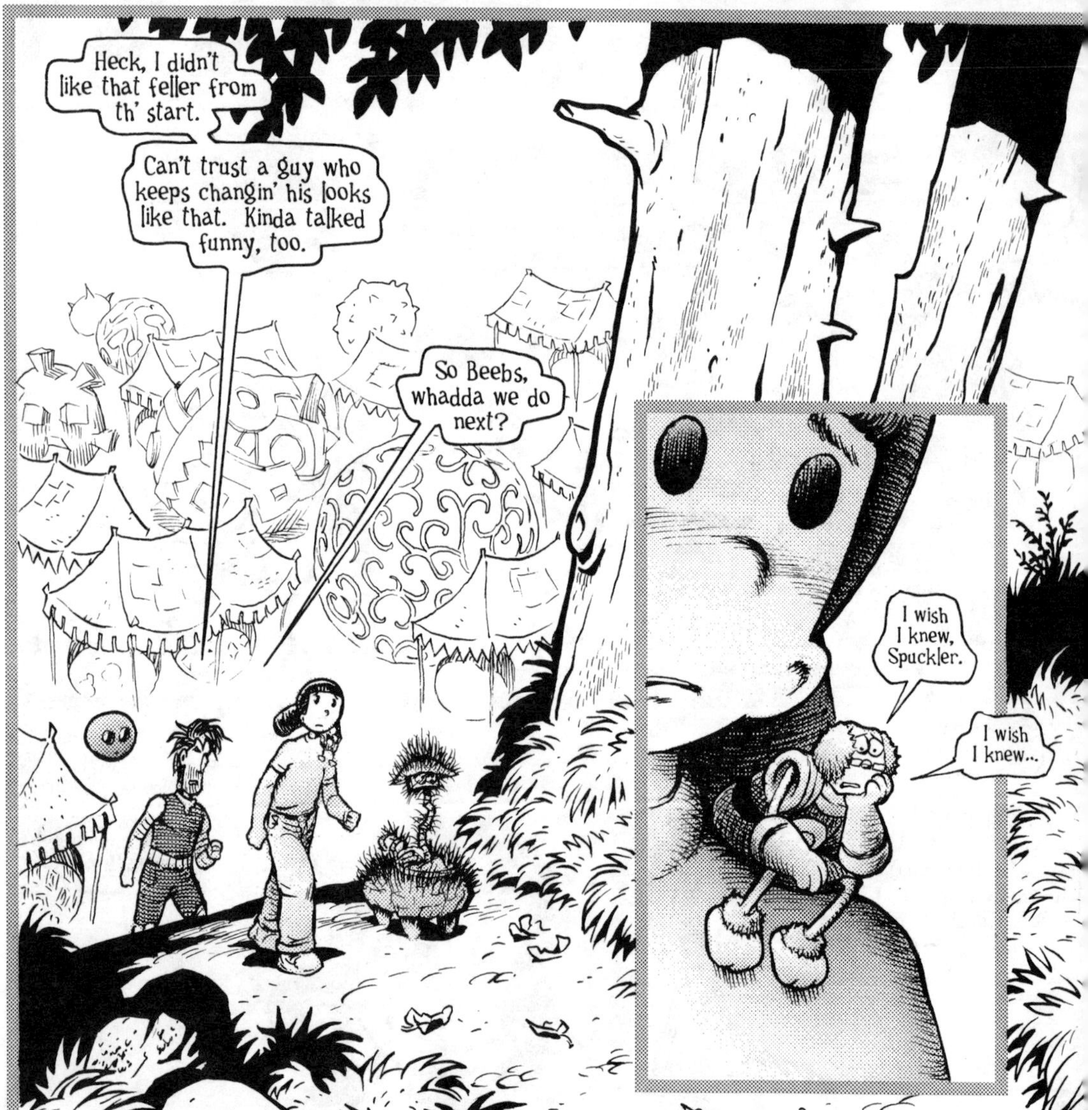
Heck, I didn't like that feller from th' start.
Can't trust a guy who keeps changin' his looks like that. Kinda talked funny, too.
So Beebs, whadda we do next?
I wish I knew, Spuckler.
I wish I knew...

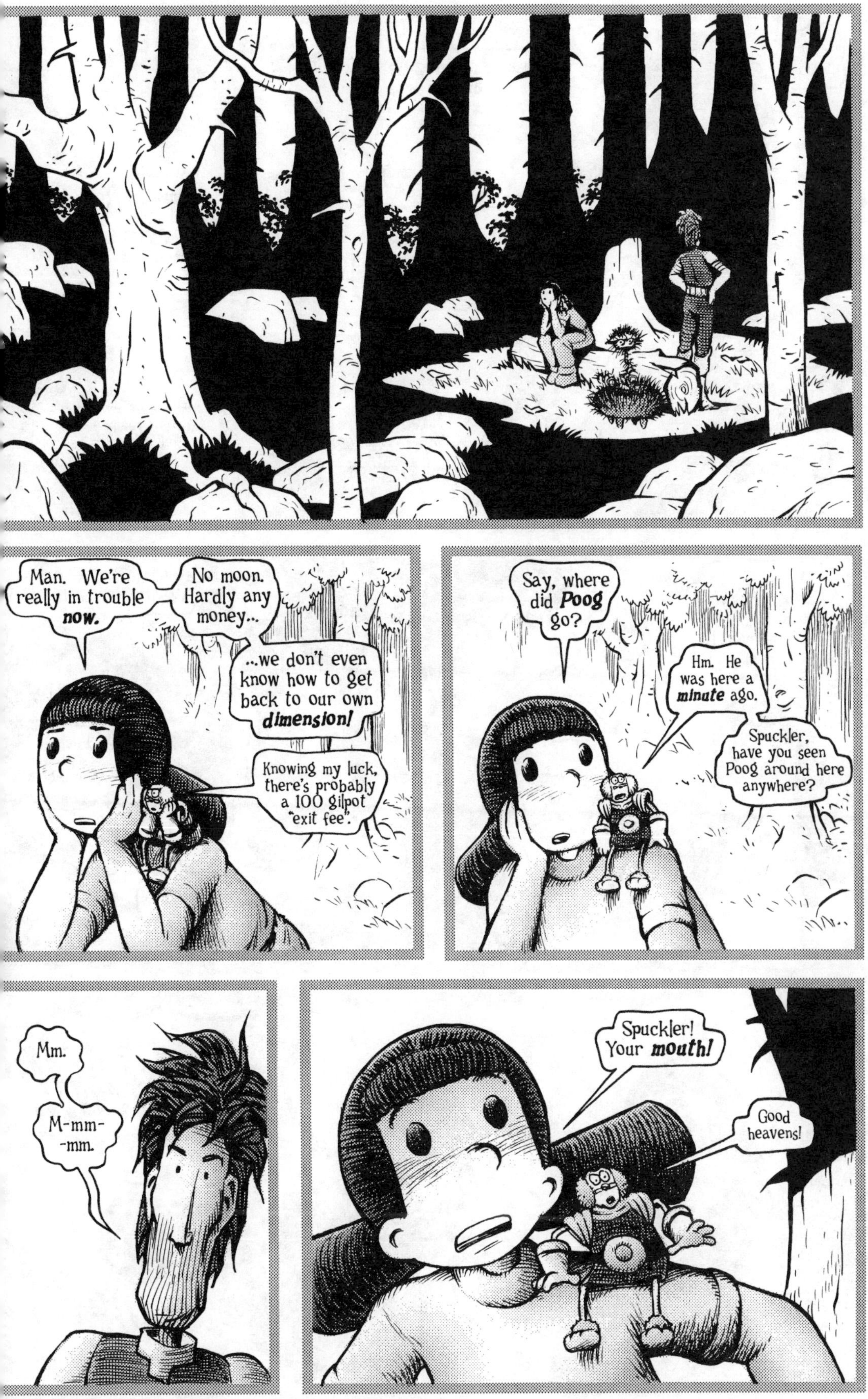

Man. We're really in trouble **now.**
No moon. Hardly any money...
...we don't even know how to get back to our own **dimension!**
Knowing my luck, there's probably a 100 gilpot "exit fee".
Say, where did **Poog** go?
Hm. He was here a **minute** ago.
Spuckler, have you seen Poog around here anywhere?
Mm.
M-mm- -mm.
Spuckler! Your **mouth!**
Good heavens!

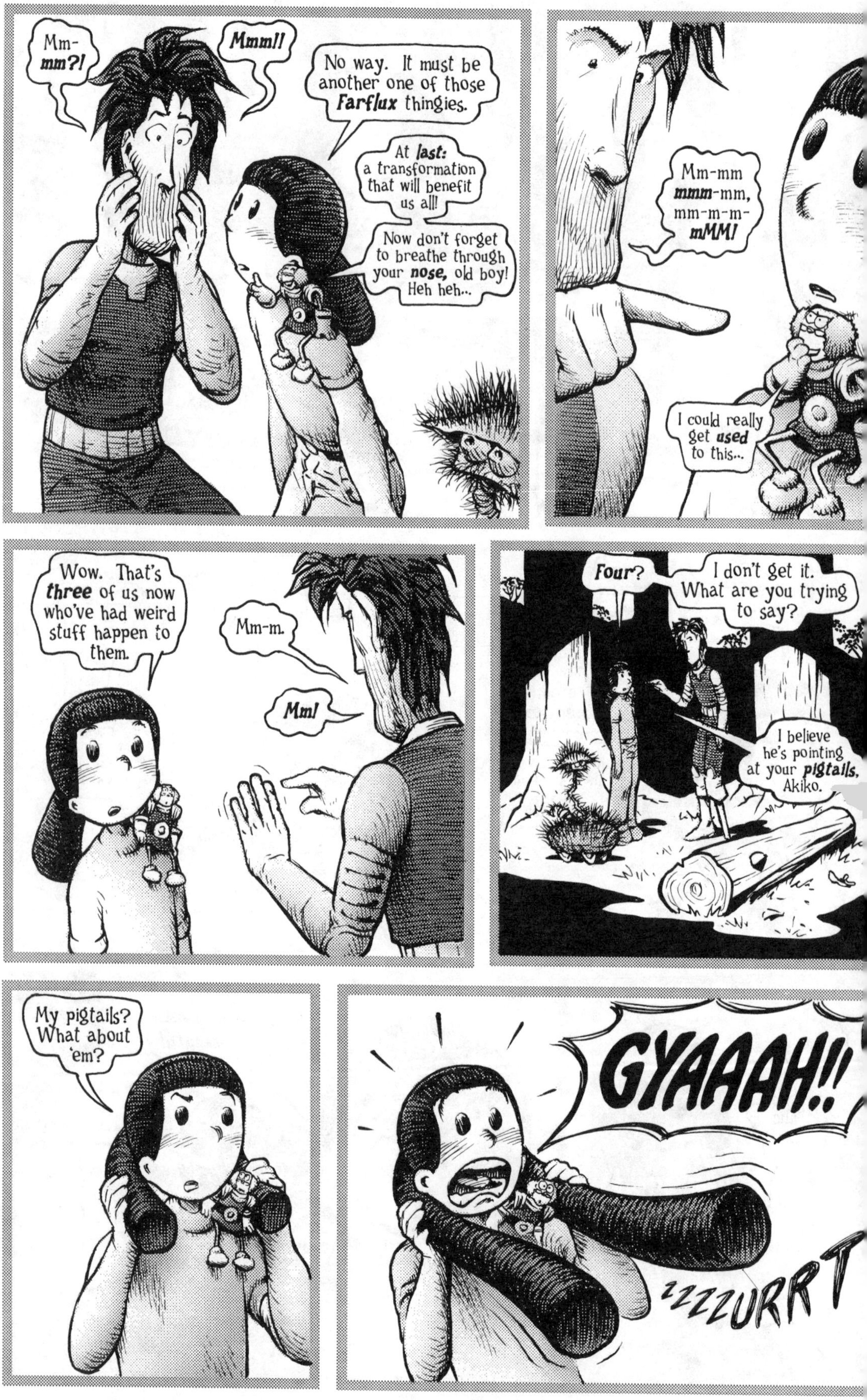

Mm-
mm?!
Mmm!!
No way. It must be another one of those **Farflux** thingies.
At **last:** a transformation that will benefit us all!
Now don't forget to breathe through your **nose,** old boy! Heh heh...
Mm-mm **mmm**-mm, mm-m-m-**mMM!**
I could really get **used** to this...
Wow. That's **three** of us now who've had weird stuff happen to them.
Mm-m.
Mm!
Four?
I don't get it. What are you trying to say?
I believe he's pointing at your **pigtails,** Akiko.
My pigtails? What about 'em?
GYAAAH!!
ZZZZURRRT

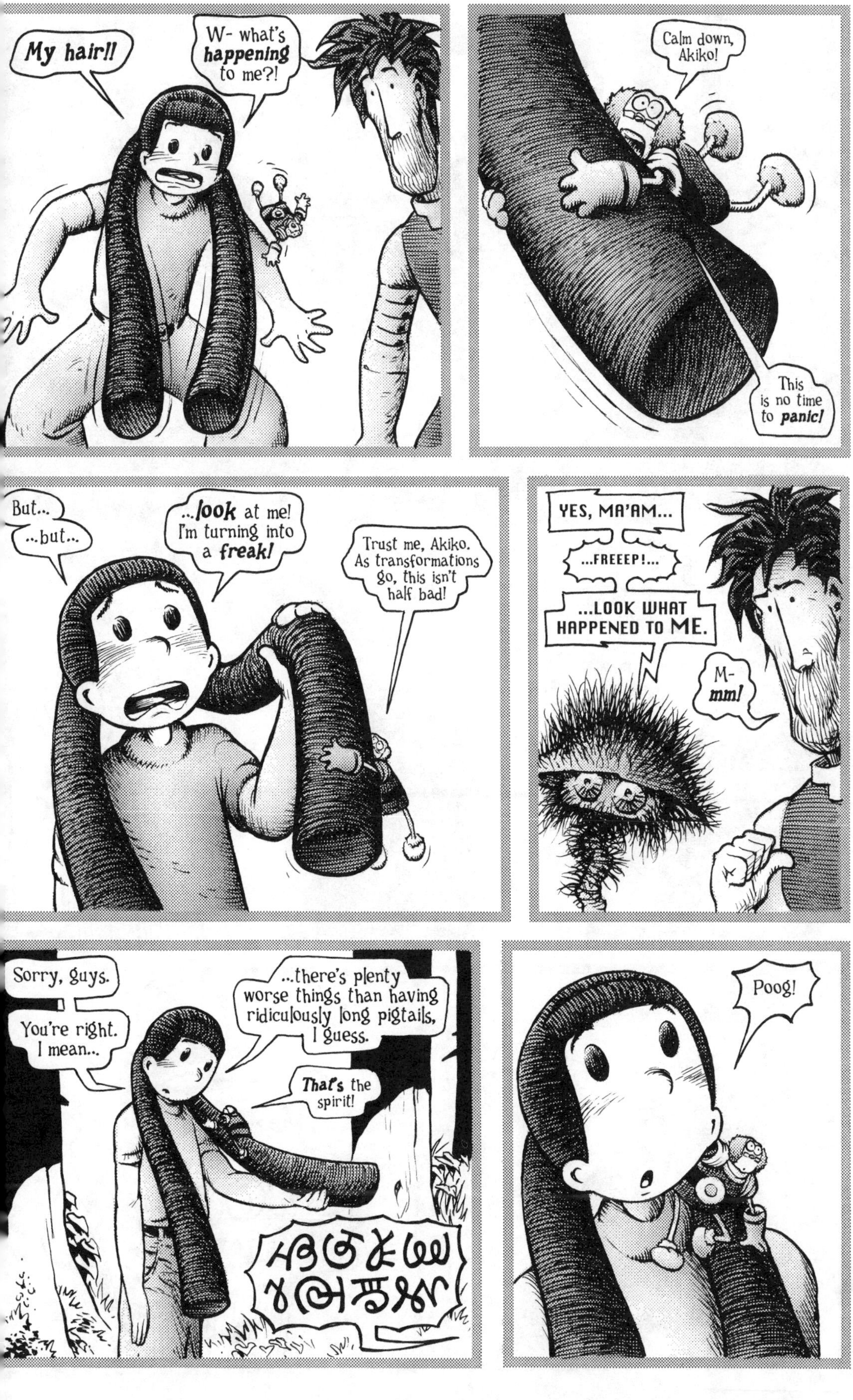
My hair!!
W- what's happening to me?!
Calm down, Akiko!
This is no time to panic!
But... ...but...
...look at me! I'm turning into a freak!
Trust me, Akiko. As transformations go, this isn't half bad!
YES, MA'AM...
...FREEEP!...
...LOOK WHAT HAPPENED TO ME.
M-mm!
Sorry, guys.
You're right. I mean...
...there's plenty worse things than having ridiculously long pigtails, I guess.
That's the spirit!
Poog!

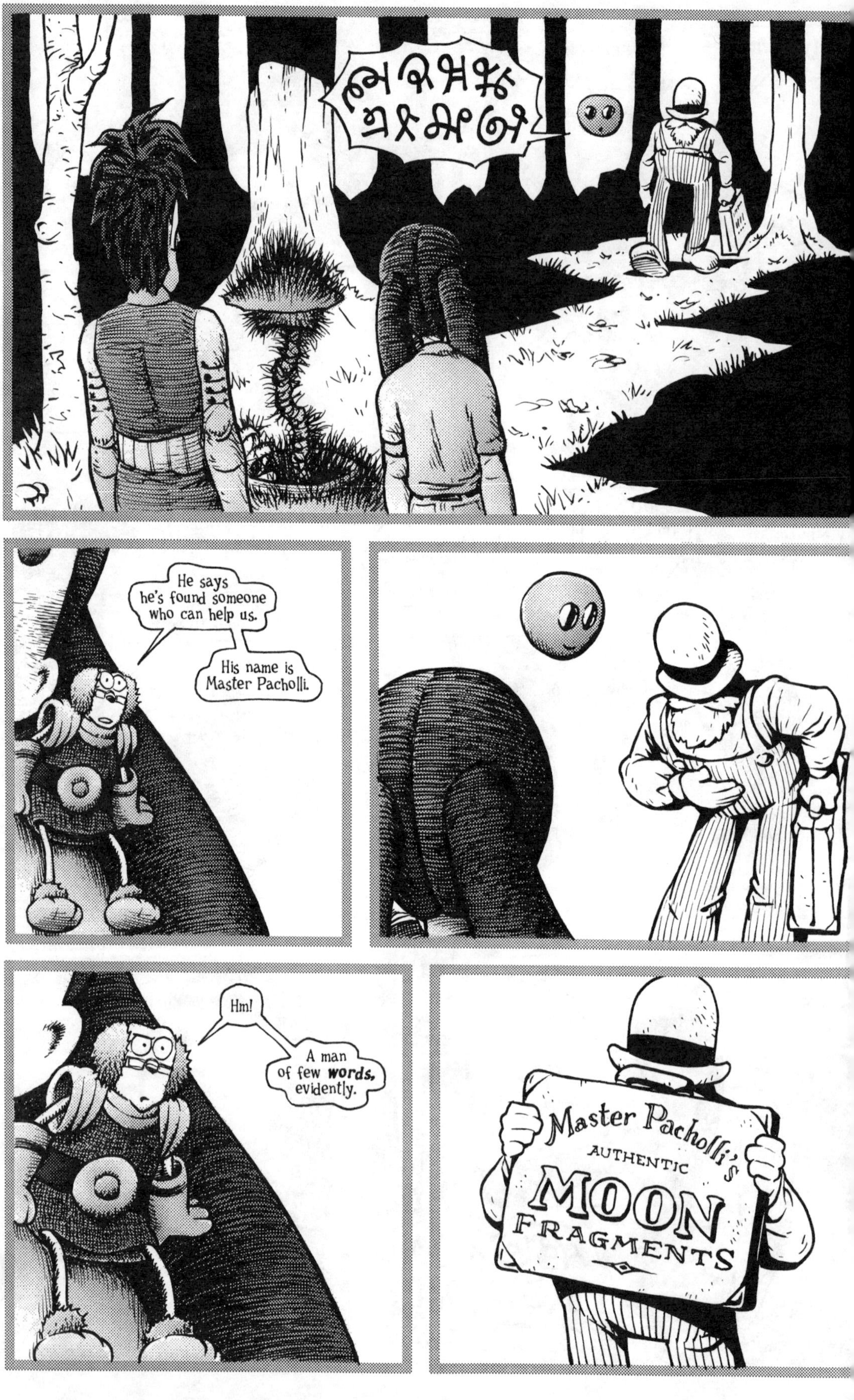
He says he's found someone who can help us.
His name is Master Pacholli.
Hm!
A man of few **words,** evidently.
Master Pacholli's
AUTHENTIC
MOON
FRAGMENTS

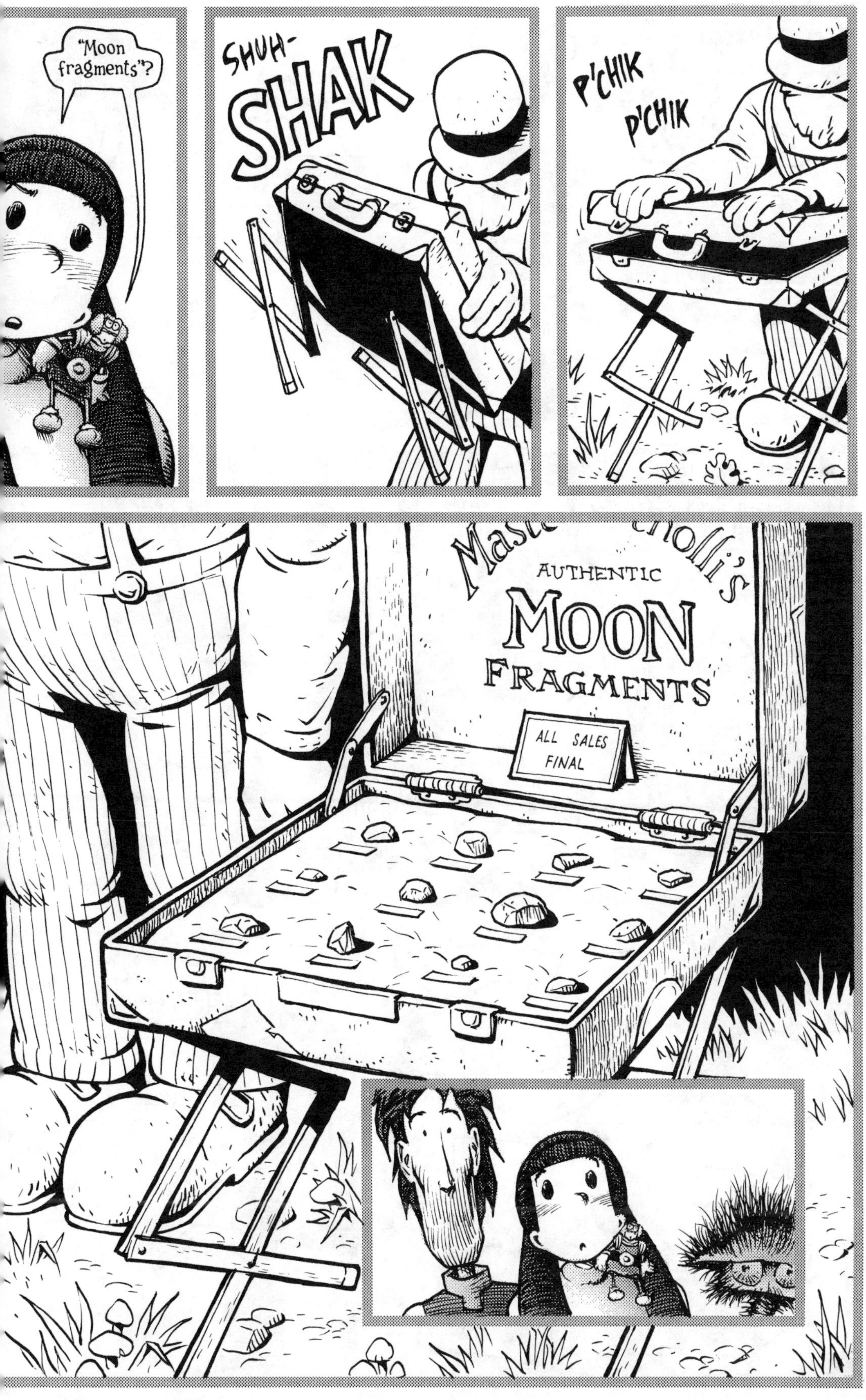
"Moon fragments"?
SHUH-SHAK
P'CHIK P'CHIK
AUTHENTIC
MOON
FRAGMENTS
ALL SALES FINAL

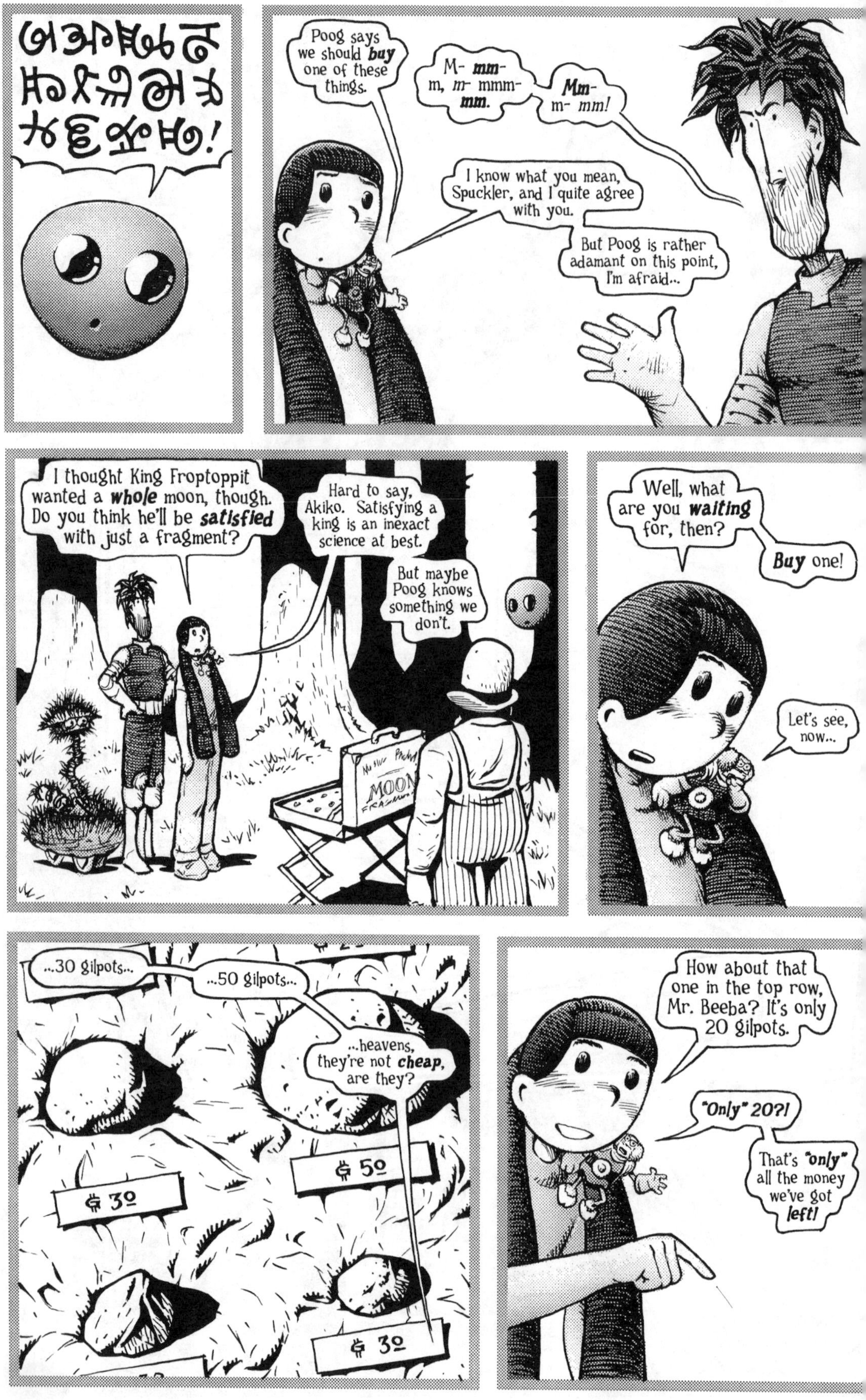
Poog says we should **buy** one of these things.
M- **mm**- m, *m*- mmm- **mm.**
Mm- m- *mm!*
I know what you mean, Spuckler, and I quite agree with you.
But Poog is rather adamant on this point, I'm afraid...
I thought King Froptoppit wanted a ***whole*** moon, though. Do you think he'll be ***satisfied*** with just a fragment?
Hard to say, Akiko. Satisfying a king is an inexact science at best.
But maybe Poog knows something we don't.
MOON
Well, what are you ***waiting*** for, then?
Buy one!
Let's see, now...
...30 gilpots...
...50 gilpots...
...heavens, they're not ***cheap***, are they?
₲ 30
₲ 50
₲ 30
How about that one in the top row, Mr. Beeba? It's only 20 gilpots.
"Only" 20?!
That's ***"only"*** all the money we've got ***left!***

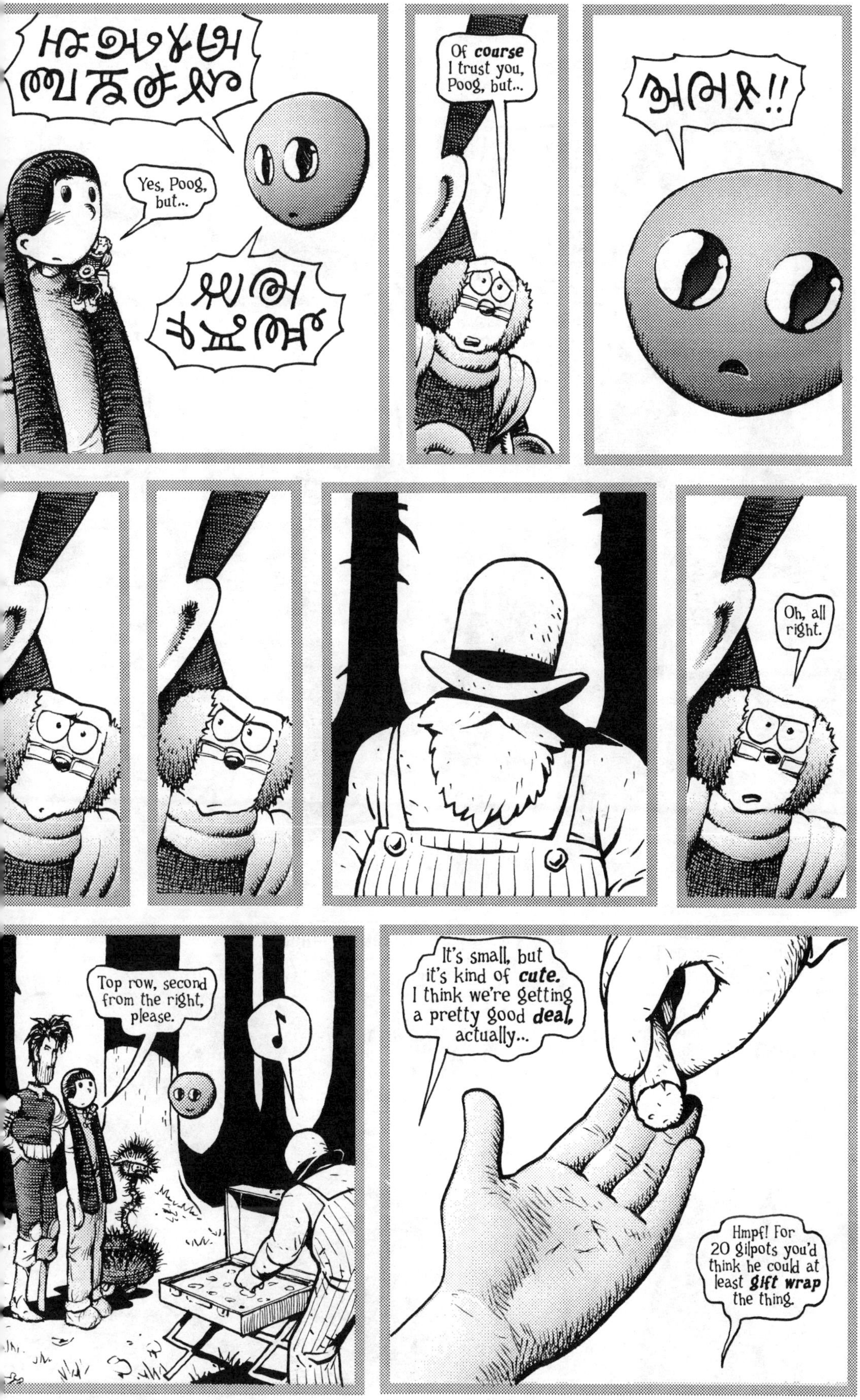
Yes, Poog, but...
Of course I trust you, Poog, but...
Oh, all right.
Top row, second from the right, please.
♪
It's small, but it's kind of cute. I think we're getting a pretty good deal, actually...
Hmpf! For 20 gilpots you'd think he could at least gift wrap the thing.

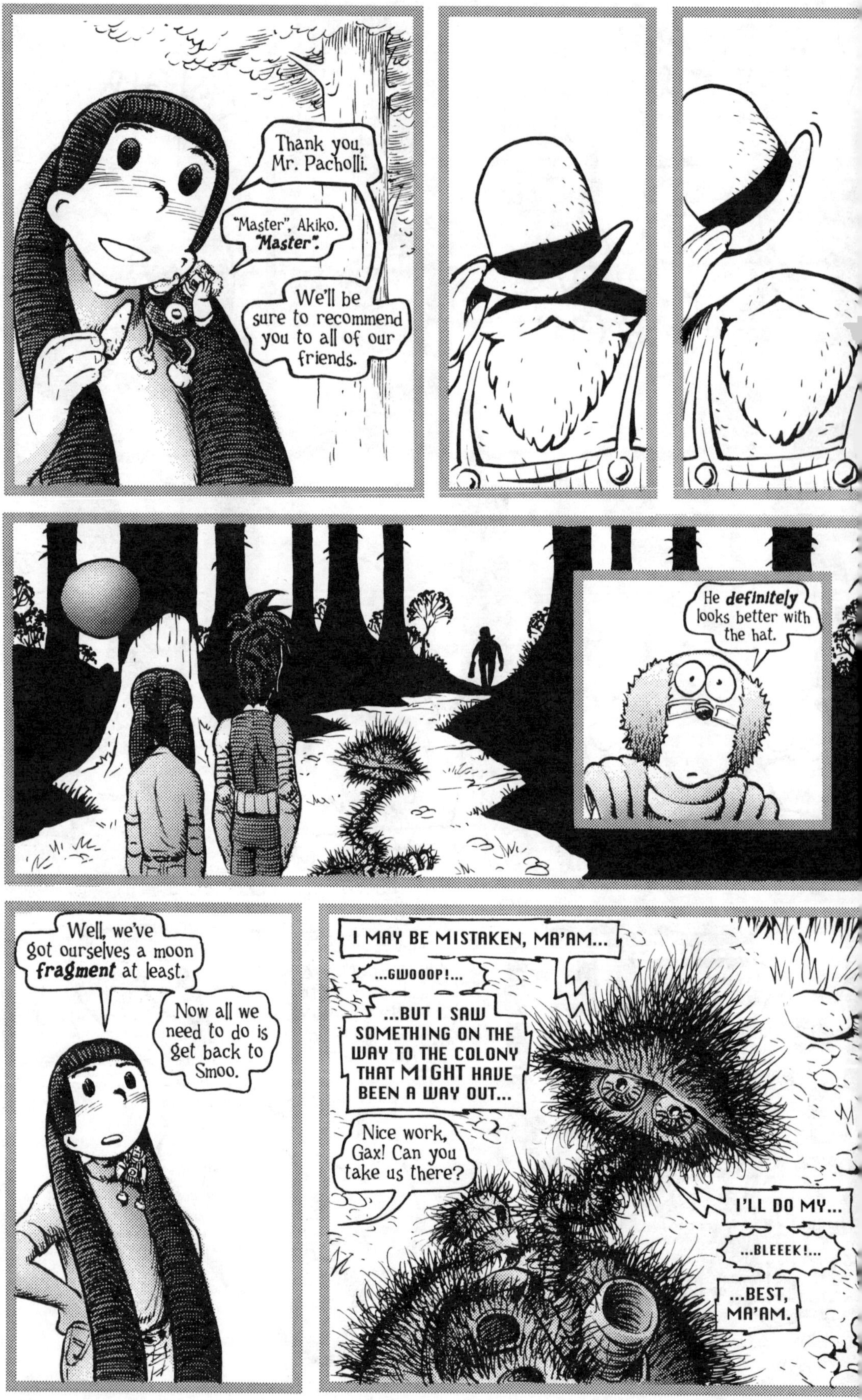
Thank you, Mr. Pacholli.
"Master", Akiko. "Master".
We'll be sure to recommend you to all of our friends.
He definitely looks better with the hat.
Well, we've got ourselves a moon fragment at least.
Now all we need to do is get back to Smoo.
I MAY BE MISTAKEN, MA'AM...
...GWOOOP!...
...BUT I SAW SOMETHING ON THE WAY TO THE COLONY THAT MIGHT HAVE BEEN A WAY OUT...
Nice work, Gax! Can you take us there?
I'LL DO MY...
...BLEEEK!...
...BEST, MA'AM.

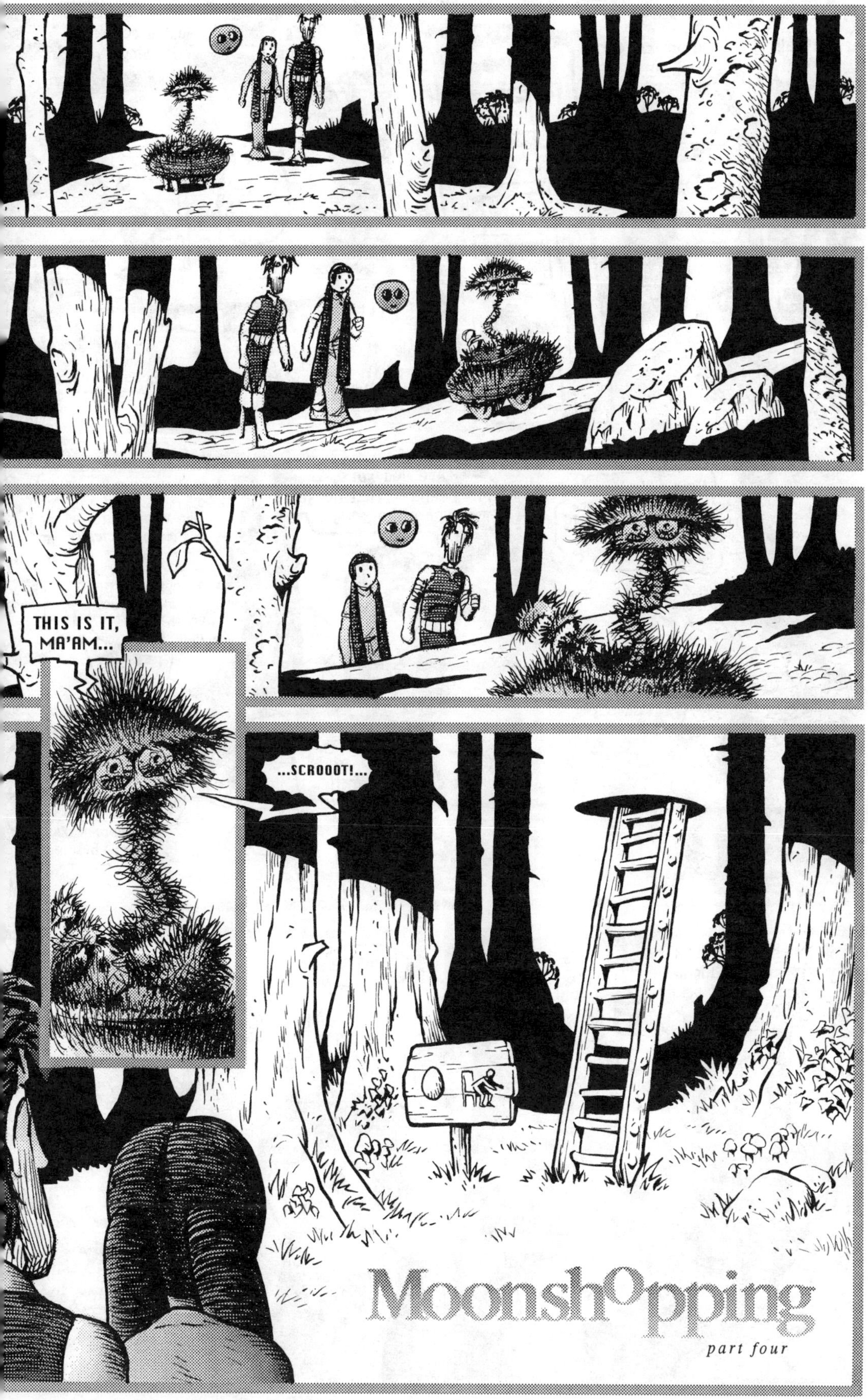
THIS IS IT, MA'AM...
...SCROOOT!...
Moonshopping
part four

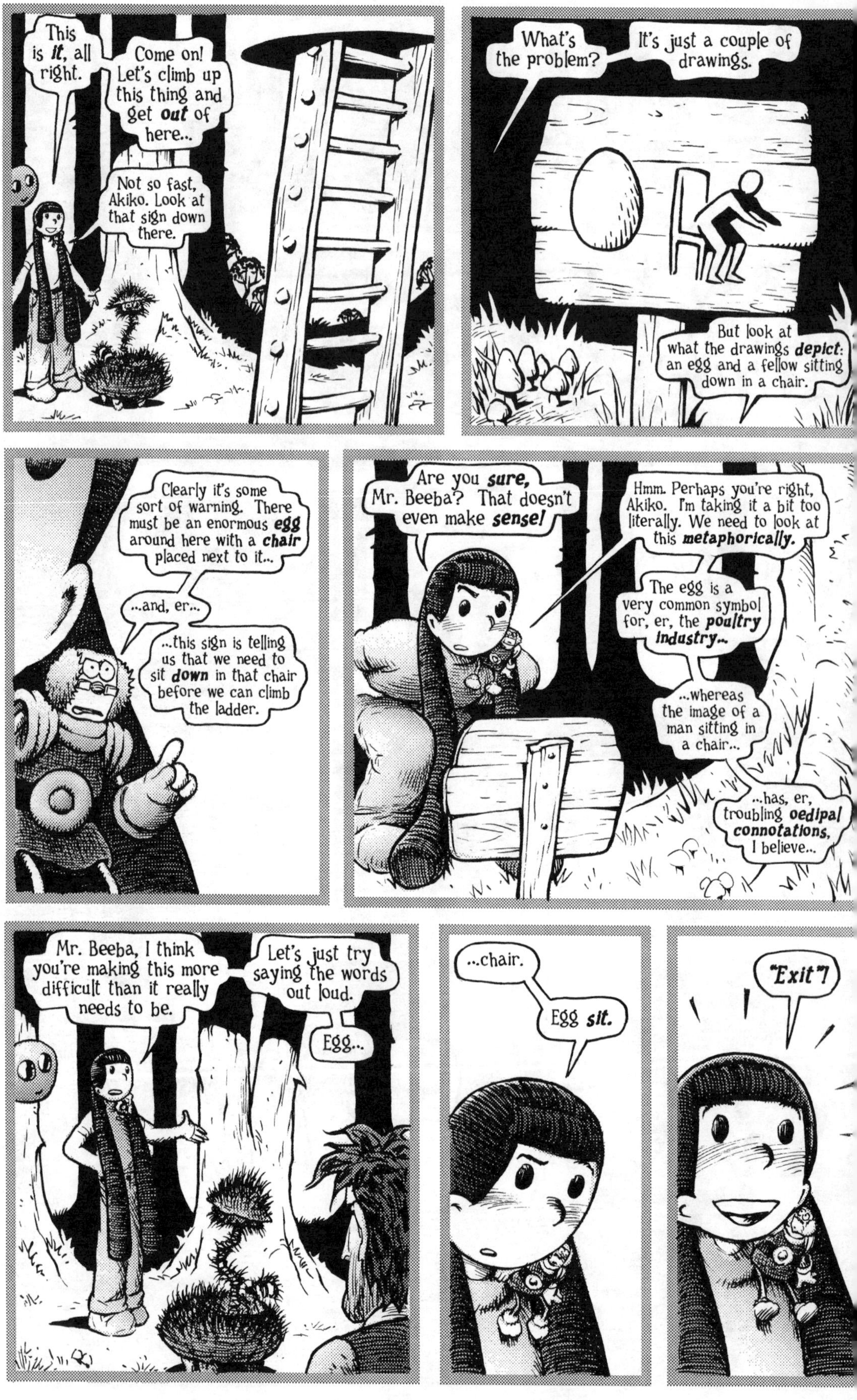
This is *it*, all right.
Come on! Let's climb up this thing and get *out* of here...
Not so fast, Akiko. Look at that sign down there.
What's the problem?
It's just a couple of drawings.
But look at what the drawings *depict*: an egg and a fellow sitting down in a chair.
Clearly it's some sort of warning. There must be an enormous *egg* around here with a *chair* placed next to it...
...and, er...
...this sign is telling us that we need to sit *down* in that chair before we can climb the ladder.
Are you *sure*, Mr. Beeba? That doesn't even make *sense!*
Hmm. Perhaps you're right, Akiko. I'm taking it a bit too literally. We need to look at this *metaphorically.*
The egg is a very common symbol for, er, the *poultry industry...*
...whereas the image of a man sitting in a chair...
...has, er, troubling *oedipal connotations*, I believe...
Mr. Beeba, I think you're making this more difficult than it really needs to be.
Let's just try saying the words out loud.
Egg...
...chair.
Egg *sit.*
"Exit"!

Very clever, Akiko!

Thanks, Mr. B!

Who'd have guessed that a familiarity with **bad puns** could prove so useful?

All right, enough goofing around!

Time to say, "Goodbye, Farflux Dimension..."

...and, "Hello...

...uh... ..."pitch black tunnel."

Don't worry, Akiko. It won't be dark for long...

Are you sure? I can't see a **thing!**

Well, neither can I. Just keep climbing!

Whoah! It's getting harder to keep my **footing**...

I SHOULD THINK SO, MA'AM. YOU'RE STEPPING ON....

...ZREEEEEP!...

...MY HELMET.

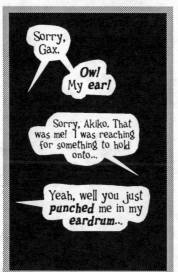

Sorry, Gax.

Ow! My **ear!**

Sorry, Akiko. That was me! I was reaching for something to hold onto...

Yeah, well you just **punched** me in my **eardrum**..

I **said** I was **sorry**, Akiko. There's no need to get **snippy**...

Mm- m-mmm- mm-mm!

I'M SORRY, SIR. I CAN'T MAKE OUT A WORD YOU'RE SAYING...

ᛰᛉᛏᛃ!

Can everyone just **shut up for a minute?!**

All right. I think I'm at the top of the ladder.

What do I do now?

Reach around above your head. There **should** be a door.

I don't feel any...

...Wait a minute! There's some sort of *covering* up here.

If I can just *lift* it...

GR-GRUTT

Okay! It's *moving!*

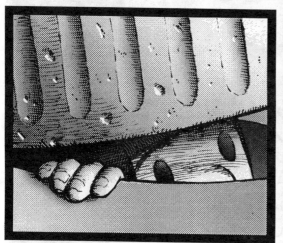

GRUTT
GRUTT
GRUTT

No way!

We're right back where we started!

Never in my life has it been so delightful to see *gray asphalt...*

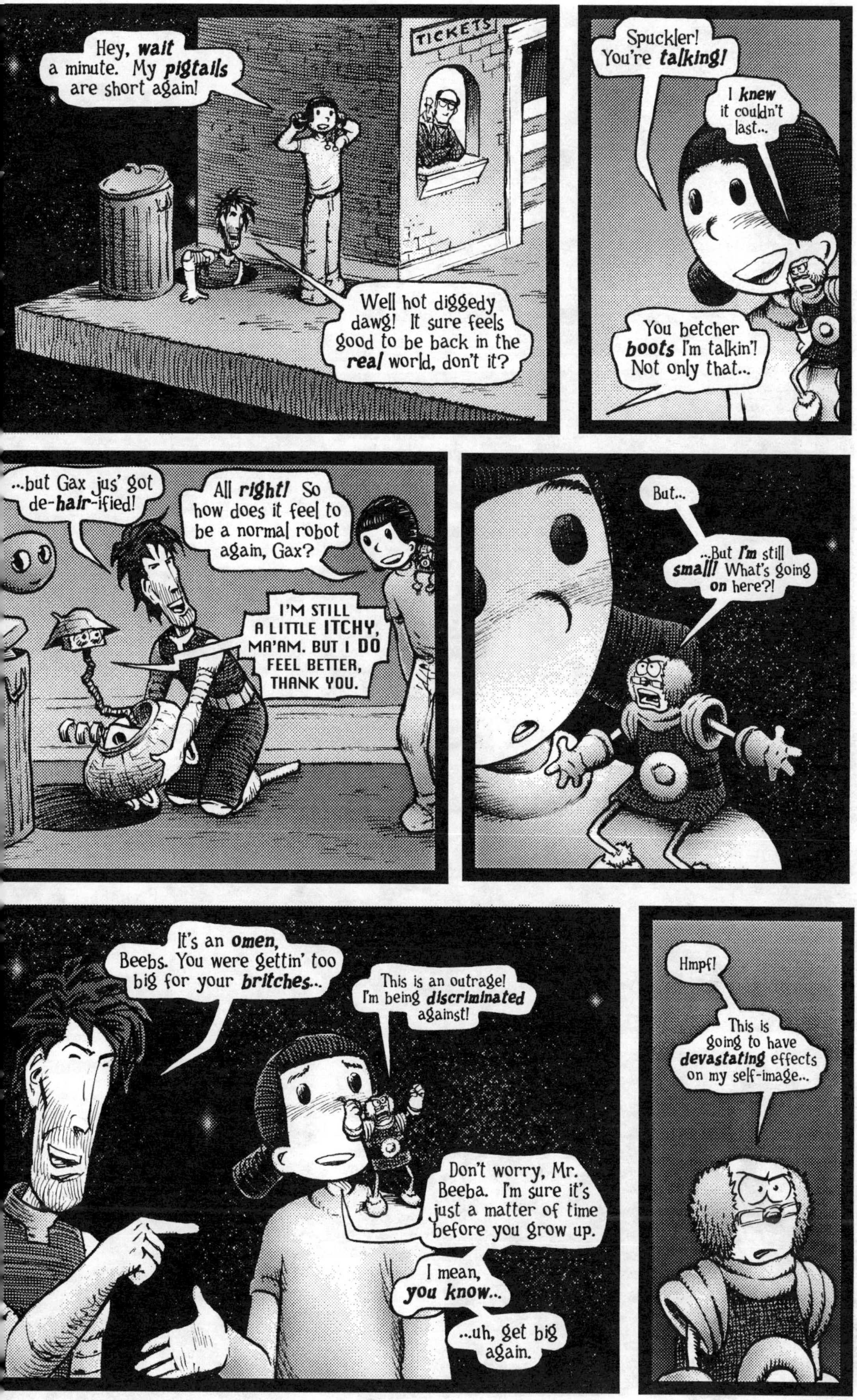
Hey, wait a minute. My pigtails are short again!
TICKETS
Well hot diggedy dawg! It sure feels good to be back in the real world, don't it?
Spuckler! You're talking!
I knew it couldn't last..
You betcher boots I'm talkin'! Not only that..
..but Gax jus' got de-hair-ified!
All right! So how does it feel to be a normal robot again, Gax?
I'M STILL A LITTLE ITCHY, MA'AM. BUT I DO FEEL BETTER, THANK YOU.
But..
..But I'm still small! What's going on here?!
It's an omen, Beebs. You were gettin' too big for your britches..
This is an outrage! I'm being discriminated against!
Don't worry, Mr. Beeba. I'm sure it's just a matter of time before you grow up.
I mean, you know..
..uh, get big again.
Hmpf!
This is going to have devastating effects on my self-image..

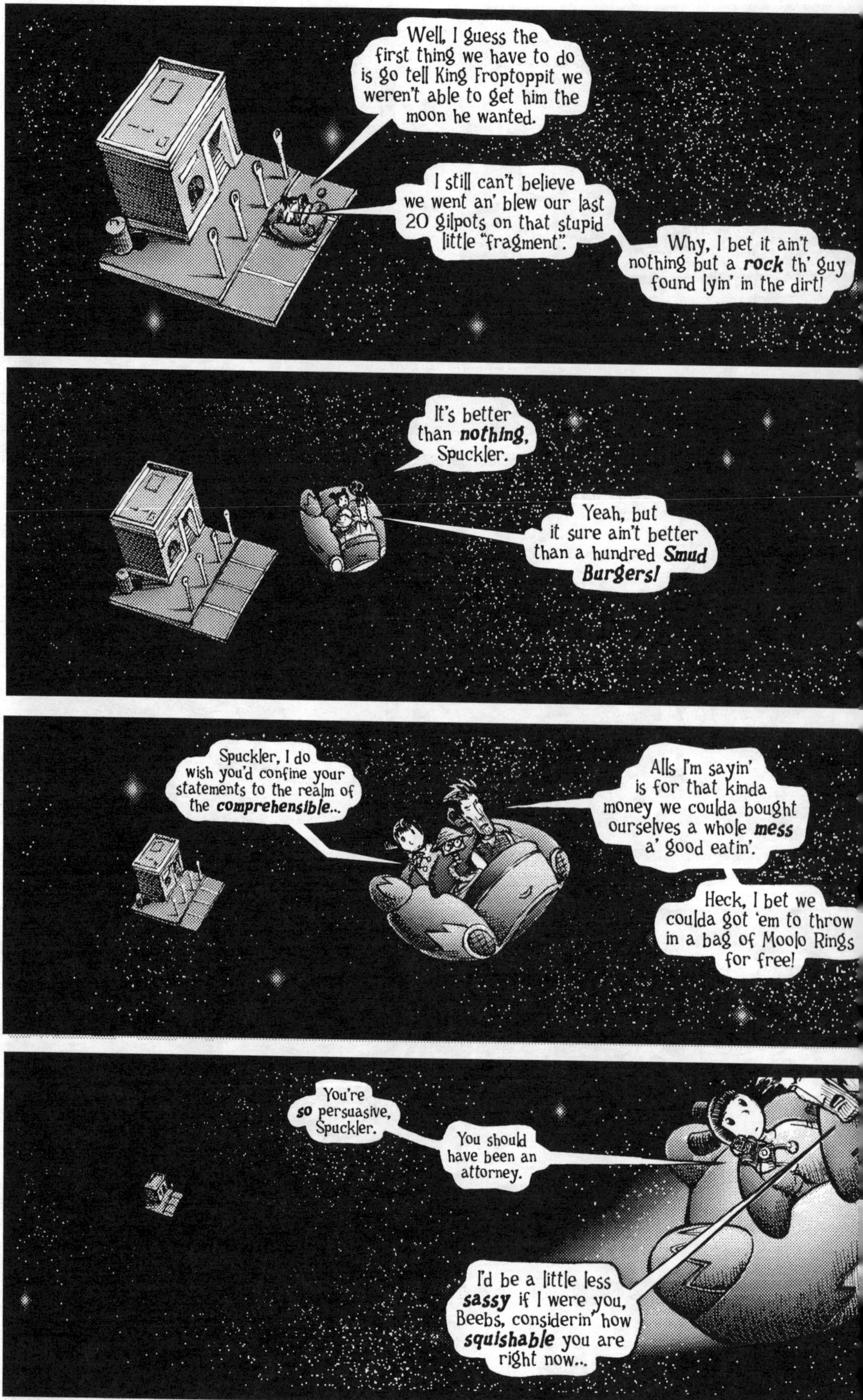
Well, I guess the first thing we have to do is go tell King Froptoppit we weren't able to get him the moon he wanted.
I still can't believe we went an' blew our last 20 gilpots on that stupid little "fragment".
Why, I bet it ain't nothing but a rock th' guy found lyin' in the dirt!
It's better than nothing, Spuckler.
Yeah, but it sure ain't better than a hundred Smud Burgers!
Spuckler, I do wish you'd confine your statements to the realm of the comprehensible...
Alls I'm sayin' is for that kinda money we coulda bought ourselves a whole mess a' good eatin'.
Heck, I bet we coulda got 'em to throw in a bag of Moolo Rings for free!
You're so persuasive, Spuckler.
You should have been an attorney.
I'd be a little less sassy if I were you, Beebs, considerin' how squishable you are right now...

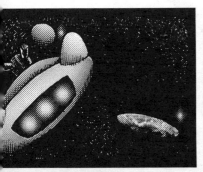

Poog says to stop right here for a moment.

Here? In th' middle of nowhere?!

Akiko, he wants you to take the moon fragment out of your pocket...

...and place it on the palm of your hand.

What's wrong? Does he think I *broke* it or something?

Just do as he says, Akiko.

See, Poog? I didn't break it.

Okay, I might have *scratched* it a little, but...

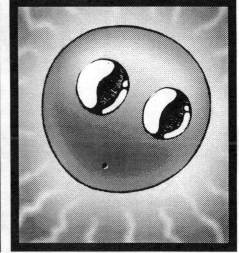

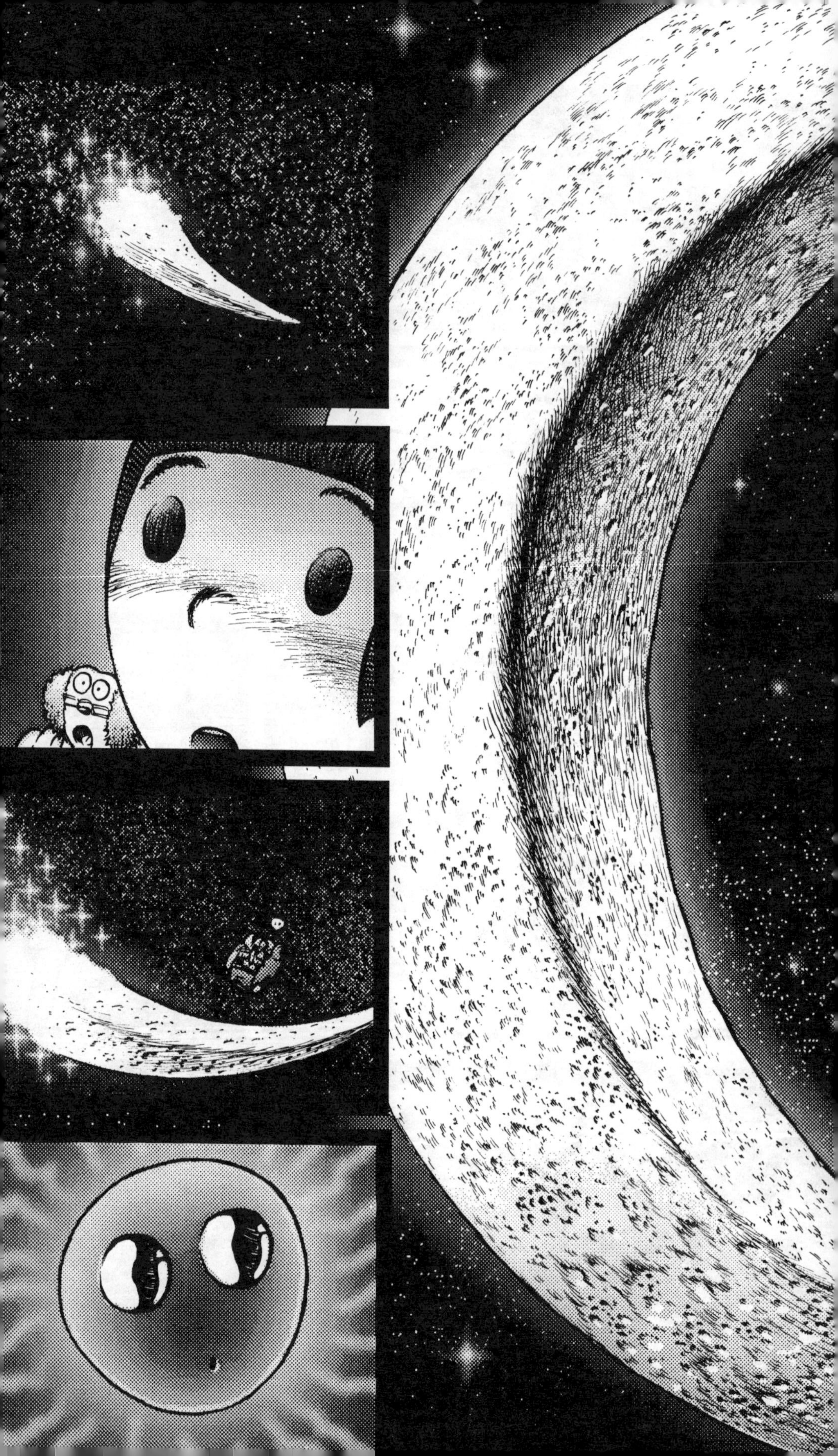

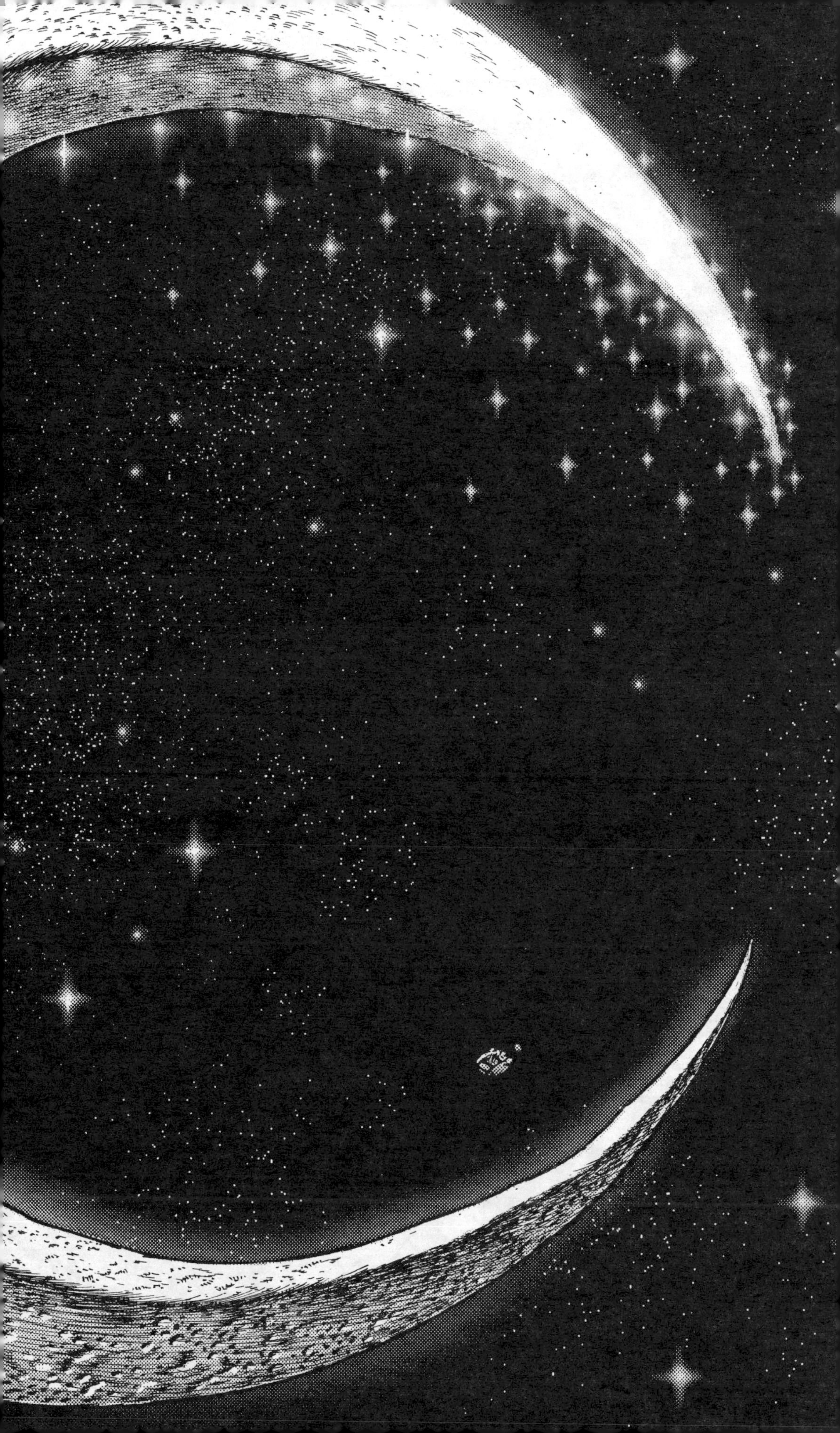

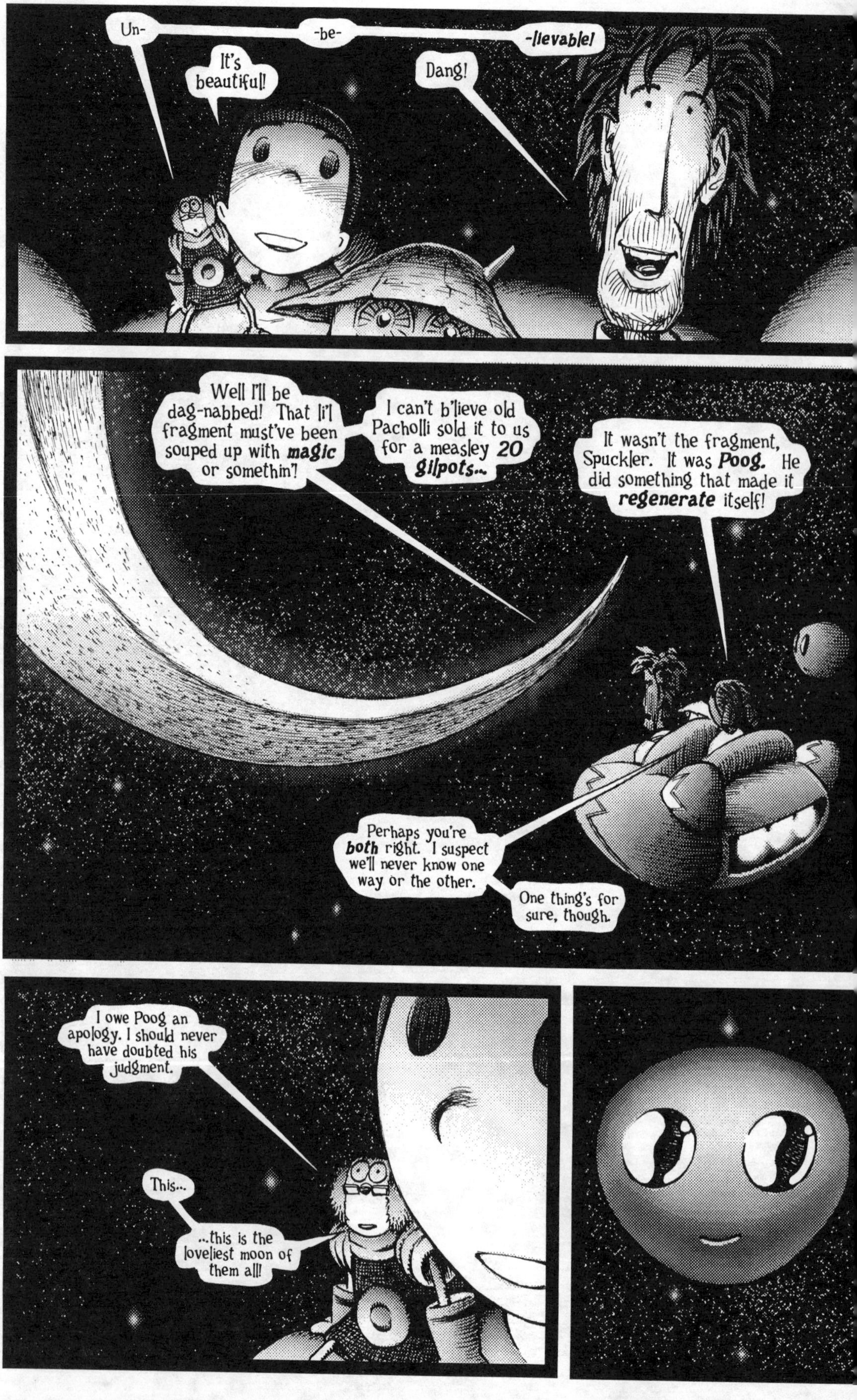

Un- -be- -lievable!
It's beautiful!
Dang!
Well I'll be dag-nabbed! That li'l fragment must've been souped up with **magic** or somethin'!
I can't b'lieve old Pacholli sold it to us for a measley **20 gilpots**..
It wasn't the fragment, Spuckler. It was **Poog.** He did something that made it **regenerate** itself!
Perhaps you're **both** right. I suspect we'll never know one way or the other.
One thing's for sure, though.
I owe Poog an apology. I should never have doubted his judgment.
This..
..this is the loveliest moon of them all!

epilogue

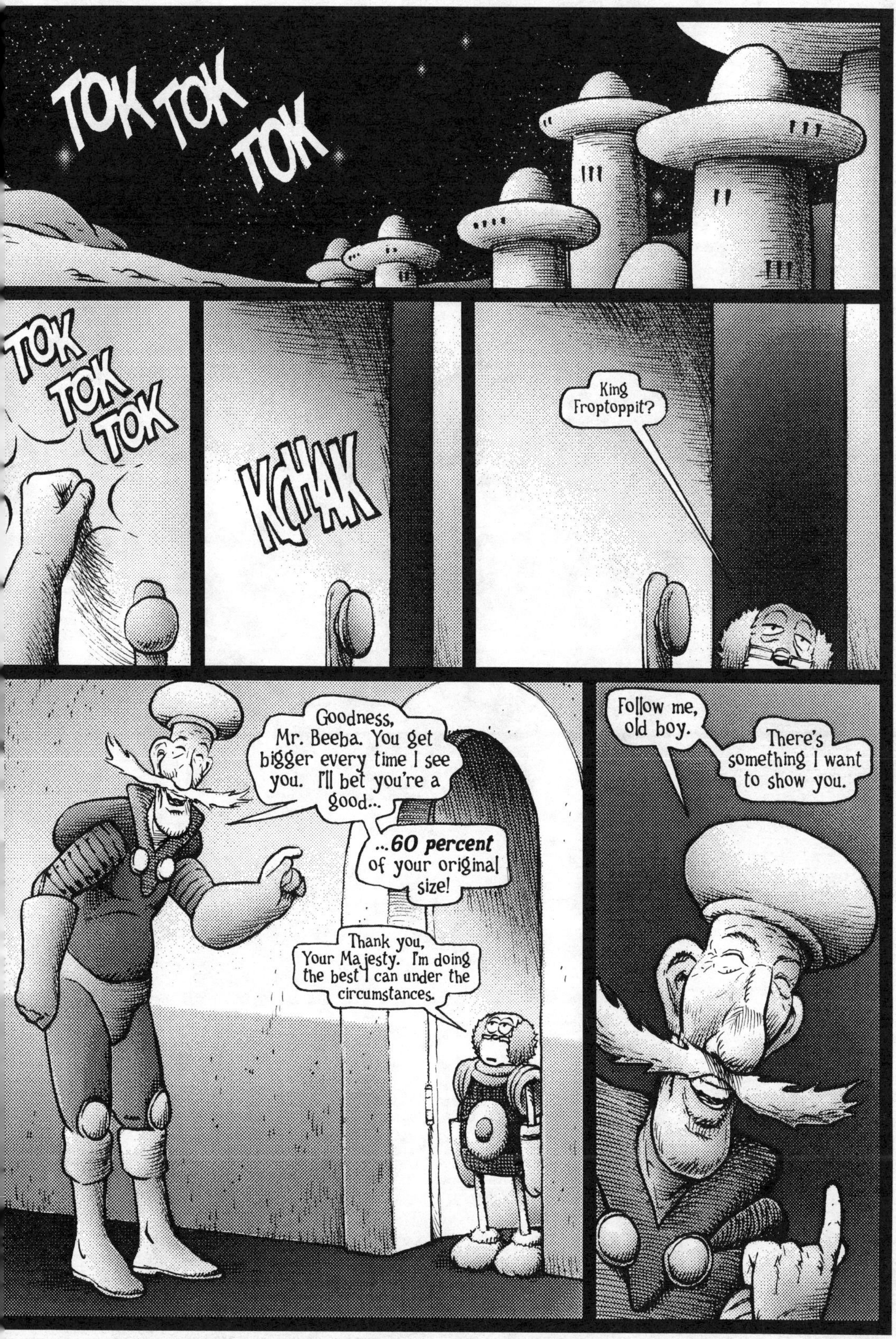
TOK TOK TOK
TOK TOK TOK
KCHAK
King Froptoppit?
Goodness, Mr. Beeba. You get bigger every time I see you. I'll bet you're a good...
...60 percent of your original size!
Thank you, Your Majesty. I'm doing the best I can under the circumstances.
Follow me, old boy.
There's something I want to show you.

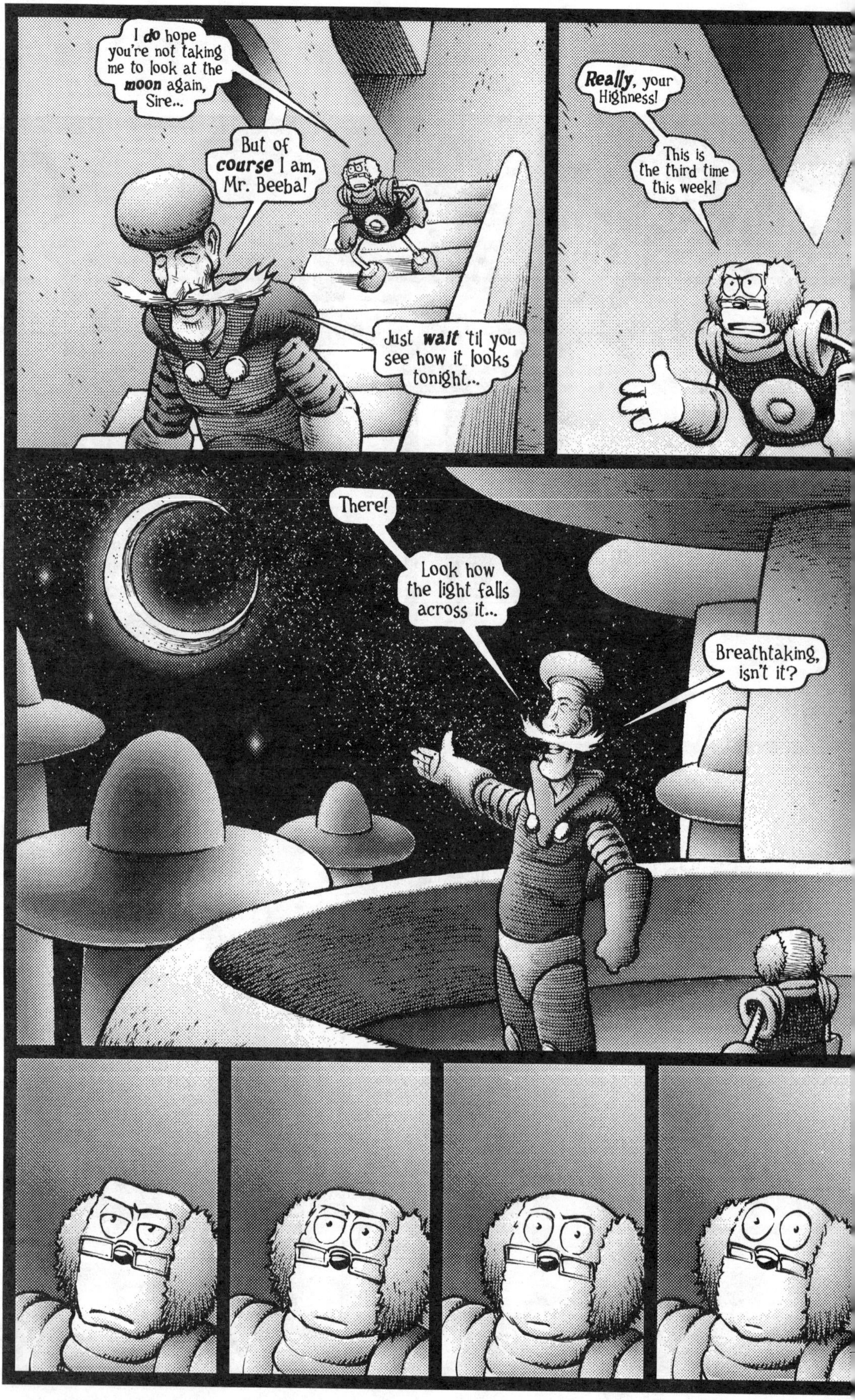

I **do** hope you're not taking me to look at the **moon** again, Sire...
But of **course** I am, Mr. Beeba!
Just **wait** 'til you see how it looks tonight...
Really, your Highness!
This is the third time this week!
There!
Look how the light falls across it...
Breathtaking, isn't it?

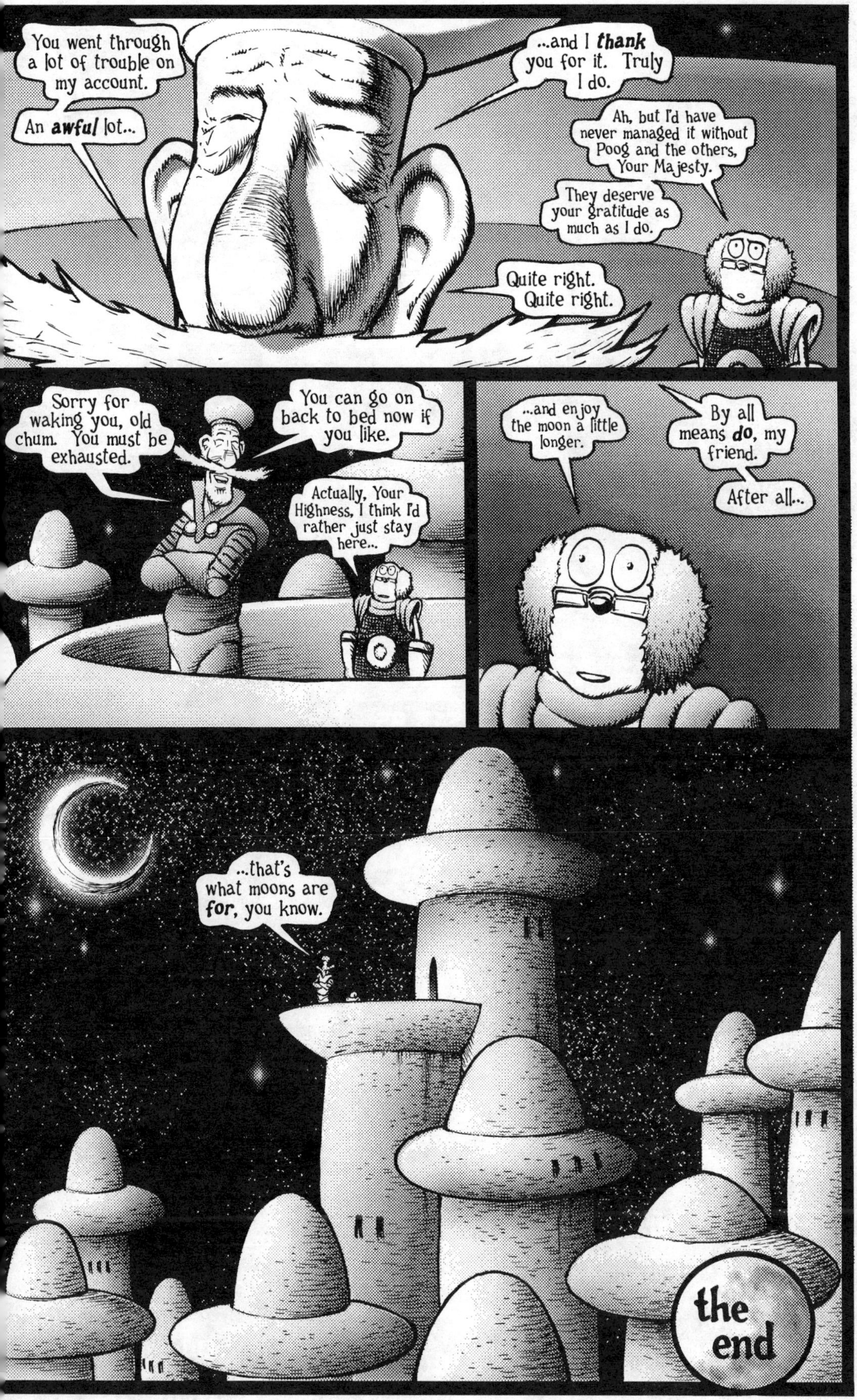
You went through a lot of trouble on my account.
An **awful** lot...
...and I **thank** you for it. Truly I do.
Ah, but I'd have never managed it without Poog and the others, Your Majesty.
They deserve your gratitude as much as I do.
Quite right. Quite right.
Sorry for waking you, old chum. You must be exhausted.
You can go on back to bed now if you like.
Actually, Your Highness, I think I'd rather just stay here...
...and enjoy the moon a little longer.
By all means **do**, my friend.
After all...
...that's what moons are **for**, you know.
the end

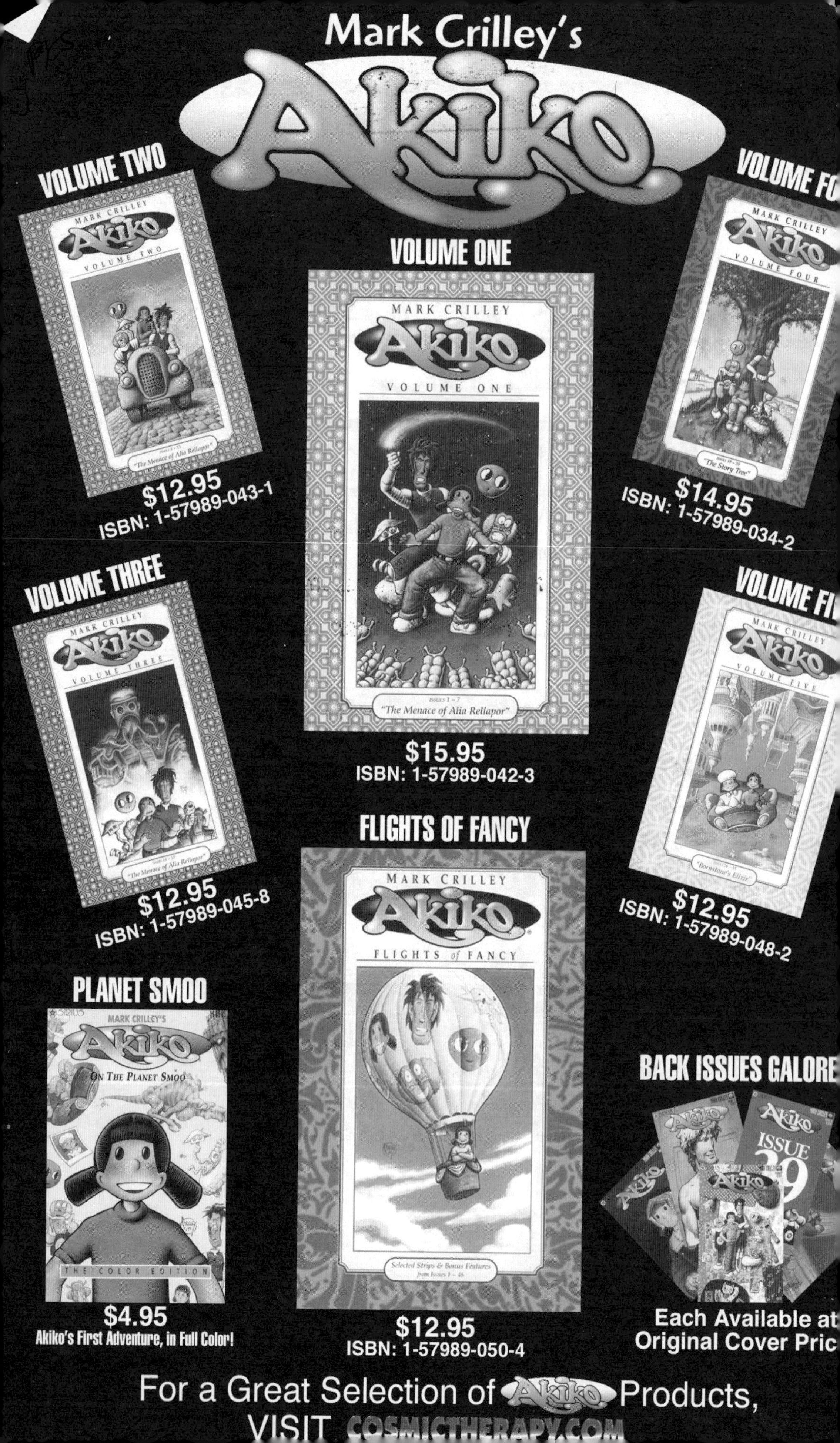
Mark Crilley's
Akiko
VOLUME TWO
$12.95
ISBN: 1-57989-043-1
VOLUME ONE
$15.95
ISBN: 1-57989-042-3
VOLUME FO
$14.95
ISBN: 1-57989-034-2
VOLUME THREE
$12.95
ISBN: 1-57989-045-8
VOLUME FI
$12.95
ISBN: 1-57989-048-2
FLIGHTS OF FANCY
$12.95
ISBN: 1-57989-050-4
PLANET SMOO
$4.95
Akiko's First Adventure, in Full Color!
BACK ISSUES GALORE
Each Available at
Original Cover Pric
For a Great Selection of Akiko Products,
VISIT COSMICTHERAPY.COM